No Better Boy
Listening to Paddy Canny

In memory of
Paddy Canny
(1919–2008)
Legendary East Clare Fiddler

No Better Boy

Listening to Paddy Canny

Helen O'Shea

THE LILLIPUT PRESS

First published 2023 by
THE LILLIPUT PRESS
62–63 Sitric Road, Arbour Hill
Dublin 7, Ireland
www.lilliputpress.ie

ISBN 9781843518655

A CIP record for this title is available from the British Library.

10 9 8 7 6 5 4 3 2 1

The Lilliput Press gratefully acknowledges the financial support of the Arts Council/An Chomhairle Ealaíon

Designed and typeset by David Spratt
Cover photo: Paddy Canny, 1956 (Peter Conway)
Printed in Poland by Drukarnia Skleniarz

Every effort has been made to identify and contact the owners and copyright holders of photographs reproduced here. The author welcomes information that would enable her to identify and contact them.

Contents

Introduction	vii
Carnegie Hall, 1956	1
Back to the Bog	2
Roots	4
A Farmer's Son	7
A Priest's Housekeeper	10
The Music of War	13
'The Scariff Martyrs'	17
Born in a Time of War	19
Mother	21
'Twas My Father Gave Me the Music	23
Paddy Gets Away	26
No Better Boy	28
Like a Wave in the Ocean	32
Double Act	36
Jack Gets Away	39
The Bee and the Boo	42
Part and Parcel	44
Dancing Out of the House	46
Ballynahinch	49
The Threshing Mill	53
Rooney	56
His Master's Voice	59
Under the Bridge	62
Gone	65
Kathy the Governor's American Wake	66
Goodbye, Johnny Dear	68
Spring	71
Plans	72
The Cuckoo	74
Getting a Band Together	77
Mr Reid	80
Paddy on the Wireless	84
Are You Anything to Pat Canny?	88
Mrs Crotty	90
The Coleman Cup	92
Off to Jamaica	94
New York House Session	96
Friends and Rivals	101
Kiltannon	104
Movies of Happiness	108
Nothing so Beautiful	109
London, 1958	114
All-Ireland Champions	117
Double Wedding	121
Ciarán at Maghera	123
Bowing Out	127
Lonesome	131
Tommie	134
The Bill and Joe Show	138
The Elusive Fiddler	142
The Accident	145
The Two of Us Now	147
Homecoming	148
Musical Friends	150
A Night in Kelly's	152
A Living Legend	156
Gradam	160
The Death has Occurred ...	164
The Other Paddy Canny	165
Time Line	167
Glossary	168
Sources	170
Acknowledgments	176
Index of Names	179

Transcriptions

'The Britches'   25
'Sandy's Reel'   31
'Ballinasloe Fair'   35
'O'Malley's'   41
'The Primrose Lass'   45
'Paddy Fahey's'   51
'The Mills are Grinding'   57
'Ballinasloe Fair'   61
'The Great Big Roaming Ass'   64
'Goodbye, Johnny Dear'   70
'Murray's Fancy'   75
'Garrett Barry's'   86
'Paddy Kelly's'   98

'The Caves of Kiltannon'   107
'The Cuckoo'   113
'Rolling in the Barrel' and
    'In the Tap Room'   119
'Trim the Velvet'   125
'Sergeant Early's Dream'   130
'The Bunch of Keys'   137
'The Flax in Bloom'   141
'Lena Madden's'   155
'The Old Blackthorn'   159
'Banish Misfortune' and
    'The Pipe on the Hob'   163

Introduction

N*o Better Boy* tells stories based on the life of the renowned Irish fiddle player Paddy Canny, who lived in north-east County Clare, Ireland, between 1919 and 2008. The book opens with his solo performance in 1956 at New York's Carnegie Hall—an extraordinary achievement for a boy raised on a marginal farm without electricity or motor vehicles or radio and where the magic of the gramophone was accessible only through the good grace of neighbours. Paddy remained a farmer throughout a long life that saw major political, economic and social changes as well as transformations in the settings in which he played music and the meanings that music had for listeners.

Music articulates the musician's inner experience where words fail to do so. At the same time, it embodies cultural values, as when it is repurposed to represent the nation. This book attempts to convey both the experiences that informed Paddy Canny's journey and the circumstances that informed his listeners' understanding of it. Throughout, there is an emphasis on sound and listening, not only because they are essential to the musician's art, but also because, during Paddy's lifetime, the way people listened to music and its role in their lives changed radically.

With very few written records of Paddy Canny's life, the stories told here are distilled from other stories: those Paddy told to several generations of radio interviewers, stories told by his family and friends, stories from folklore and stories told by historians. Included in this material are accounts of Paddy's personal life, including his illness and a rift in the extended family. I am particularly grateful to those who offered these insights, knowing that they might be published, as it is in learning of Paddy's personal difficulties that the reader might come to understand him, not as a musical myth, but as a man who suffered, as we all do.

I listened to Paddy Canny's music, tracking down rare recordings in archives in Ireland and the USA and others made at informal gatherings or by musicians who visited Paddy. In order to understand and transcribe Paddy's distinctive style of playing, I spent many hours listening to slowed-down recordings. It was this forensic listening that revealed to me the immense complexity and artistry of his music.

As an oral historian working in rural Australia in the 1990s and later in researching *The Making of Irish Traditional Music* (2008), I came to understand memory as a creative process in interplay with an individual's self-identity and values. Many well-polished stories about Paddy Canny contained common themes: the poor boy who succeeds in the world; the musician who enchants his listeners; and

> Music articulates the musician's inner experience where words fail to do so. At the same time, it embodies cultural values, as when it is repurposed to represent the nation.

the recluse who avoids visitors and obligations. I have listened carefully for accuracy and consistency, but also for emotional undercurrents, such as adulation or resentment, in order to avoid foundering on the rock of scepticism or being sucked into the whirlpool of sentimentality, my own included.

I also researched the soundscape of Paddy's life and times. In the 1920s, northeast Clare was rich in the sounds of nature, of farm and domestic work, of fairy lore and religious practice, and the recreational sounds of music, singing, storytelling and dancing. On a small farm of poor land in the Sliabh Aughty mountains, which spread north into Galway and spill south towards the fertile grazing land around Tulla, Pat Canny taught his sons Jack, Mickie and Paddy their music. This acoustic territory reverberated with voices from neighbouring districts raised in outrage at unjust land distribution and fervent speeches at election rallies and recruitment drives for a nationalist militia. There were the sounds of British military action and the secretive voices of a guerilla force relying on local people for information and, later, voices opposing the compromise of the peace settlement, which excluded six Northern counties from Ireland's newly independent state.

There were stories heard *sotto voce* in private gatherings: about men who had betrayed their neighbours, accusations of dishonest dealings, family disputes, gossip about children born out of wedlock and outcasts sent to industrial schools or mental hospitals, and warnings about houses haunted by tuberculosis. Other stories came from far away: letters from America, news from workers returning from England, newspapers reporting national and international events, magazine revelations of movie stars' scandals and dance crazes and the latest fashions.

Changes in this soundscape affected the way people listened to music and how they valued what they heard. From the 1920s, gramophones sent from America embodied emigrants' success, while New York Irish music recordings presented local players with new performance standards and the remote, but now imaginable, possibility of achieving the virtuosity or even the career of a recording artist. Radio was another innovation, which, like the gramophone, represented the fantasy of a prosperous, cosmopolitan life, while at the same time transmitting nationalist ideology, in which music also performed a role.

From beyond the everyday world, the sound of fiddling was heard emerging from haunted houses and fairy forts. Fear of the fairies, who might abduct children or sicken a cow, or cause all manner of mischief, was assuaged by an assortment of rituals. While the priests railed against these superstitions, it was to Biddy Early (1798–1874) that an earlier generation took their troubles. A *cailleach feasa* or wise woman, raised by a herbalist mother in a remote valley above Feakle, she was renowned for her clairvoyance and her ability to diagnose and heal the misfortunes and illnesses of those 'touched' by the fairies, despite opposition from the Church.

Brian Merriman's was another, more distant, voice against which the forces of religion and propriety shouted back. Like Biddy Early's, his life's work was rejected, reinterpreted and finally celebrated in the late twentieth century. Merriman (*c.*1749–1805) grew up in the picturesque country overlooking Lough Graney, near Killanena. His famous long poem, *Cúirt an Mheán Oíche* (*The Midnight*

This soundscape changed in ways that affected the way people listened to music and how they valued what they hear. From the 1920s, gramophones sent from America embodied emigrants' success, while New York Irish music recordings presented local players with new performance standards and the remote, but now imaginable, possibility of achieving the virtuosity or even the career of a recording artist.

Court) begins with a description of Lough Graney in the elevated language of the classical *aisling* or dream-vision poem and a parody even before he switches to a salty vernacular and the beautiful maiden of convention turns up as a twenty-foot harridan armed with a big stick. Dragged to the Queen of the Fairies' court, the poet witnesses a woman's case against all young unmarried Irishmen. Replete with vivid descriptions of promiscuity, impotence, infidelity and squalor, Merriman's satirical humour also skewers clerical celibacy. When the Fairy Queen rules that all young men must marry or be flogged, a horde of women set upon the poet, who wakes from his dream.

In his own time, when Irish was spoken universally, Merriman's masterpiece was widely acclaimed and recited at weddings and wakes. *The Midnight Court*, with its denunciation of corrupt Anglo-Irish landlords and their English laws and of the repression of sexuality, was an anti-establishment riposte across time to the early twentieth century in rural Ireland, where late marriage was customary, women were relegated to powerless drudgery and the society was in thrall to a powerful and punitive Church. Frank O'Connor's 1945 translation of Merriman's poem was banned for obscenity and, even in 1968, armed men had to guard a commemorative plaque before its unveiling by a government minister.

There is a common misperception that Irish traditional music has enjoyed a continuity of performance and popularity for many centuries. Even since the mid-nineteenth century, there have been two major ruptures, resulting in radical shifts in the class of people playing, their repertoire and the music's social meaning. In the early nineteenth century, itinerant musicians played for outdoor dancing at fairs and celebrations. After the Great Famine of the 1840s had wiped out most of those artisan musicians, there was a shift in rural Ireland to domestic music making and a great flowering of music among the new generation of tenant farmers. This was the point at which dancing became a popular domestic recreation. In Paddy Canny's district of Glendree, set dancing—quadrille sets adapted from the ballroom and accompanied by Irish tunes and rhythms—arrived in 1880. It was only after this that the district became renowned as a centre of fiddle playing, due to the success of one teacher, Paddy McNamara, known as Blind Paddy Mac, and his pupils, who included Paddy Canny's father Pat.

Another rupture came in the late 1930s, a time of hardship and gathering disillusion in rural Ireland. The promise of the independent Irish state had been eroded by an economic war with Britain, which saw the export market for Irish agricultural products virtually disappear, with a consequent increase in rural poverty and emigration. A moral panic involving the alleged immorality of so-called 'jazz' music and unsupervised modern dancing saw the conservative de Valera government, the Catholic Church and the nativist Gaelic League join forces to support the 1935 Public Dance Halls Act, which outlawed unlicensed dances. Together with a confluence of social changes, including mass emigration, the relocation of small farms, clerical opposition, and alternative entertainments, this legislation brought to an end the house dances where Paddy Canny had played as a teenager and which had been at the centre of local social life.

By 1940, most musicians in the rural townlands of north-east Clare had put away their instruments, with only a handful of more ambitious fiddle players continuing to develop their music. Some, including Paddy Canny and his friend PJoe Hayes, formed a dance band to compete at music festivals and play for dances in the new parish halls. Paddy was the only one of his cohort chosen to give solo recitals on the radio and soon became known to a national community of listeners. In the 1950s, a revival of traditional music began, influenced by two key phenomena in which Paddy Canny and some other local musicians participated: the formation of Comhaltas Ceoltóirí Éireann, the national traditional musicians' organisation, with its annual *fleadh cheoil* (music festival), where Paddy won the national fiddle competition; and the state radio station's broadcasts of traditional musicians recorded in country locations. Hearing local musicians on the radio boosted the status of traditional music, encouraging some of the musicians who, decades earlier, had put away their instruments, to play again at festivals and in pubs. Their status increased in the 1970s when urban revival musicians visited to listen to their 'authentic' style and the rising class of productive farmers came to regard traditional music as an appropriately patriotic accomplishment for their children to learn. The revival saw music that once had been exclusively a complement to dancing become a national emblem valued for its artistry.

Numerous generations have listened to Paddy Canny's music. Apart from his father's rudimentary lessons, Paddy was self-taught. For his contemporaries, his music was remarkable for its virtuosity and sophistication. At the same time, dancers were quick to point out that his music was better for listening than for dancing; music for the ears, not the feet. In the early years of the traditional music

There is a common perception that Irish traditional music has enjoyed a continuity of performance and popularity for many centuries. Since the mid-nineteenth century, there have been two major ruptures, resulting in radical shifts in the class of people playing, their repertoire and the music's social meaning.

revival, Paddy's advanced technical skills impressed the gatekeepers at competitions and radio stations, while audiences were drawn also to his music's haunting melancholy.

For more recent generations, Paddy's music has been a touchstone for an authentic, local style, despite his acknowledged influence by the great Sligo fiddlers, whose New York recordings he had imitated in his youth. Another influence was Dublin fiddle player Tommie Potts, with whom Paddy shared a preference for tunes in darker keys and a belief in the spiritual power of music. In addition to the hybridity and eclecticism that are fundamental to the musician's art, among Paddy's contemporaries an individual style was well regarded—indeed, expected—and a musician was easily recognisable from bowing choices, intonation, tempo, personal settings of tunes, or idiosyncrasies like 'singing' or groaning as they played.

Musicians love Paddy Canny's playing for its quiet comfort and beauty, a lyricism that on closer listening reveals intricate embellishments and melodic and rhythmic undercurrents beneath the surface simplicity and regularity of Irish dance music. Generations of listeners have recognised a lonesome voice in Paddy Canny's music, evident in the long sweep of his bow, in the way he articulates the moods of a tune through changes in volume and tempo—changes that break the rules of dance music—and in his flexible intonation, which draws from an older tonality. There is poetry in the flow of his music across the 'bar line' between an offbeat and the main beat, the way a poet continues a thought into the next line of verse, and in the caesuras when he breaks that flow with an emphatic silence. When, at the age of seventy-eight, Paddy finally released his only solo album, he was recognised as a master of Irish traditional music and a living legend.

When, at the age of seventy-eight, Paddy released a solo album into the now specialised traditional music market, he was recognised as a master of Irish traditional music and a living legend.

Carnegie Hall, 1956

It is the night of St Patrick in New York City. The MC's booming voice, the festive crowd's sudden roar, the thunder of clapping, subside into silence. A man steps to the microphone. The footlights shine his shoes and catch the satin lining of his new suit. Out beyond the loneliness of the stage, the auditorium's vast mouth opens towards him, strings of lights marking the tiers, layer upon dazzling layer.

The musician's eyes bend to the bow held feather-light by the heft of his farmer's arm, his left hand ready above the fingerboard. His jaw, holding the violin steady, remains relaxed, leaving a gap for the inward breath. When his bow urges the first note into life, then surges into the tune, the auditorium fades and the musician merges back into himself, into the home of his music as it expands full and rounded in the perfect acoustic of Carnegie Hall.

This concert hall, its white masonry embellished with gold, was once considered the most beautiful in the world. Since Tchaikovsky's opening concert in 1891, Carnegie Hall has hosted generations of A-listers, from Fritz Kreisler to Duke Ellington, Billie Holiday to Maria Callas and, since 1913, the sell-out St Patrick's Day Concert where, tonight, six thousand Irish-American eyes are fixed on Paddy Canny, All-Ireland Champion: Violin.

How did he get here? There's one answer in Jascha Heifetz's worn-out quip:

'Hey, mister, how do you get to Carnegie Hall?'
'Practise, practise, practise!'

But there was also the pull of the New York Irish, the immigrant cohort that grew to dominate the city's politics and populate its civic services and which comes together each year in the St Patrick's Day Parade, a tradition of nearly two hundred years. This very afternoon, the Lord Mayor of Dublin led 120,000 marchers along Fifth Avenue, swept clean of snow, a million and more cheering them on.

New York's competing schools of Irish dancing and music thrive in the Bronx, in Brooklyn and in Queens, Irish bands play in dancehalls and Irish musicians consort in downtown bars. Although recent arrivals, dancehall impresario Bill Fuller and his wife, the ebullient Carmel Quinn, have taken charge of the St Patrick's Day Concert. Between laughing at Carmel's stories and sighing at her sweet old songs, the audience gets to hear the cream of local talent. For decades, New York's celebrated Sligo fiddlers have taken the stage and, this year, their guest star is Paddy Canny.

Facing page: Paddy Canny plays on St Patrick's night, Carnegie Hall, 1956

Back to the Bog

Since childhood, Paddy has known all the teeming life of the bog, from the smallest lizards and frogs and the modest wagtails to the outspoken ducks and crows and the silent, commanding kestrel. He knows where to find the grouse, as fat as his mother's hens, and the snipe that skulk in the wettest spots. He is at home.

On a bright April morning, Paddy Canny and Dr Bill Loughane sail for home. A little too bright, perhaps, and that pipe band blasting out farewell cheer perhaps a little too loud, for they have only just emerged from their final night of music. Hundreds of Clare men and women had crowded into the Irish club in the Bronx to shake their hands and listen to them playing music from home with New York's finest fiddlers. And here they are again, Paddy Killoran, Larry Redican, Andy McGann and Lad O'Beirne, playing their hearts out on the dock—musicians who, until a month ago, Paddy Canny had known only as disembodied sounds emerging from gramophone records. Now they are friends. With them are Paddy O'Brien and Joe Cooley, two of the best accordion players ever to come out of Ireland and two of the best friends Paddy has. And might never see again. As the liner pulls out into the Hudson, people point to Paddy and Dr Bill, up on the deck with their fiddles out, playing the old favourites, 'The Salley Gardens' and 'Lord McDonald's', as they fade into the distance.

During the whole month away, Paddy pencilled a single entry in his pocket diary:

'Cars very fast in NY. Tired out.'

He had imagined that this city of eight million souls would guarantee him a comfortable anonymity. Now, he knew more people in New York than he did at home. The trip has been taxing for a man as private as Paddy, whose days are grounded in farm work, punctuated by nights out with the band or radio broadcasts in Dublin and a rare weekend at a fleadh. This was his first, terrifying trip in an aeroplane and his first time on an ocean liner. How far away was America!

New York had been hectic from the word go: the confusion of crowded city streets and the punishing pace, rushing from television studio to radio station to dancehall stage, and then the long nights at house parties and in bars. Of course, everyone wanted to know when Paddy would be moving over. It made sense, with things at home still going backwards, each day more than a thousand people leaving Ireland. But Paddy is not going backwards: he has a farm of good land. He is not comfortable in any city and will never have the gift of the gab that gets you places in America. On the tender chugging from the liner to the quay at Cobh—the *Titanic*'s last stop before the iceberg and the fateful step out of Ireland for millions of emigrants—Paddy and Dr Bill play together one more time and the trip is over. America is over.

The path to the Glendree Bog

At home in East Clare, Paddy goes straight to the bog. As he says, 'I'd like it quiet sometimes, to be left alone.' No better place for solitude than the Glendree Bog, wild and open, high above the slow industry of farming. He can stand on the top of his world and let the wind blow the last of the city from him. He can inspect the Cannys' wall of peat where, year after year, his father had cut slithers of turf, tossing them off the *sleán* for Jack and Mickie and himself to spread. In recent years, he and Mickie had loaded the asses with baskets of turf to sell to the County Council. On a misty day Paddy can see just his own two feet treading the same stony path where those asses had tested them every time, skittering away from the straight and narrow. On a clear day he can see across West Clare to the sea, even to the islands. A flash of sunlight might fall on the fields of Ballinruan and his uncle's house, where he first played for dancing. North, beyond Maghera Mountain, its flanks now dark with conifers, are the plains of South Galway, where musicians are thick on the ground. His gaze might fall then to the valley of Cloonnagro and back to the crook in the road and the Cannys' home place.

Higher up the bog, towards the dark eye of Lough Ea, jags of sandstone, dragged and dropped by an ancient glacier, are spotted with lichen, yellow and white. Between these outcrops the bog blankets the heights, its surface carpeted with purple moor-grass and deergrass and creeping tormentil and brightened in summer by snowy heads of bog cotton. This is common ground, rough grazing for cattle from nearby farms. Later in the year, drier sections of the bog will glow purple when the heather blooms, its bell-flowers rustling in the relentless wind. Since childhood, Paddy has known all the teeming life of the bog, from the smallest lizards and frogs and the modest wagtails to the outspoken ducks and crows and the silent, commanding kestrel. He knows where to find the grouse, as fat as his mother's hens, and the snipe that skulk in the wettest spots. He is at home.

Roots

This is how today's residents like to identify their district: as *Glean Draoi*, glen of the druid, a spiritual place. Others have suggested *Gleann Dríth*, glen of the wren, the little brown *dreolín*, the trickster whose cunning won him the title King of All Birds.

Time has worn Maghera, the highest point in the Sliabh Aughty mountains, to just four hundred metres of sandstone rock. Until the early seventeenth century, the hills and valleys below Sliabh Aughty's bogs were covered in deciduous woodland, especially oak, which gave its name, 'Derry'—from doire, oak-wood— to many of the area's townlands. 'Glendree' may have the same derivation: *Gleann Daireach*, a wooded valley. Or it may have been named for an earlier time, when Druids retreated into forests to perform their rituals. This is how today's residents like to identify their district: as *Glean Draoi*, glen of the druid, a spiritual place. Others have suggested *Gleann Dríth*, glen of the wren, the little brown *dreolín*, the trickster whose cunning won him the title King of All Birds.

Until recent times, this wild country was considered too poor and precipitous for cultivation. A lonely place, remote from roads and houses, where human presence was marked only by the tracks of people crossing the mountains and the bare boulders where Mass was held in the times when Catholic priests were outlaws. Throughout the eighteenth century, as Ireland's population swelled, the magnificent oak forests were cleared and the land settled by Catholic families evicted from other parts of Ireland. The area highest up the mountain remained wilderness, leased by gentry for seasonal hunting and fishing. Glendree's ownership changed hands among estate owners—McGrath to O'Callaghan to Moloney—until, at the end of the century, it was sold to Joseph Peacock, a Dublin entrepreneur who undertook an ambitious reclamation project.

By this time, even the higher slopes of Glendree had been denuded of woodland, to build British ships and make French wine barrels, and later to burn in charcoal furnaces as fuel for the region's ironworks. Peacock's workforce rooted out stones and built them into walls dividing his estate into ten-acre farms. They cleared the heather and improved the soil with tons of lime, brought up the mountain track in the same horse carts that had carried limestone rocks down to the kilns outside Tulla. Peacock reclaimed seventy ten-acre farms and built a house on each of them. Like any property developer, his next step was to sell.

In Dublin, Sir Robert Kane bought Peacock's estate off the map, paying four thousand pounds for two and a half thousand acres of bogland and poor, mountainy country on which tenants would struggle to pay rent. Kane was acclaimed as one of the great minds and progressive spirits of his age, a brilliant chemist and educator whose passion for applied science was evident in his survey of Ireland's potentially profitable natural resources. His brilliance did not extend, however, to

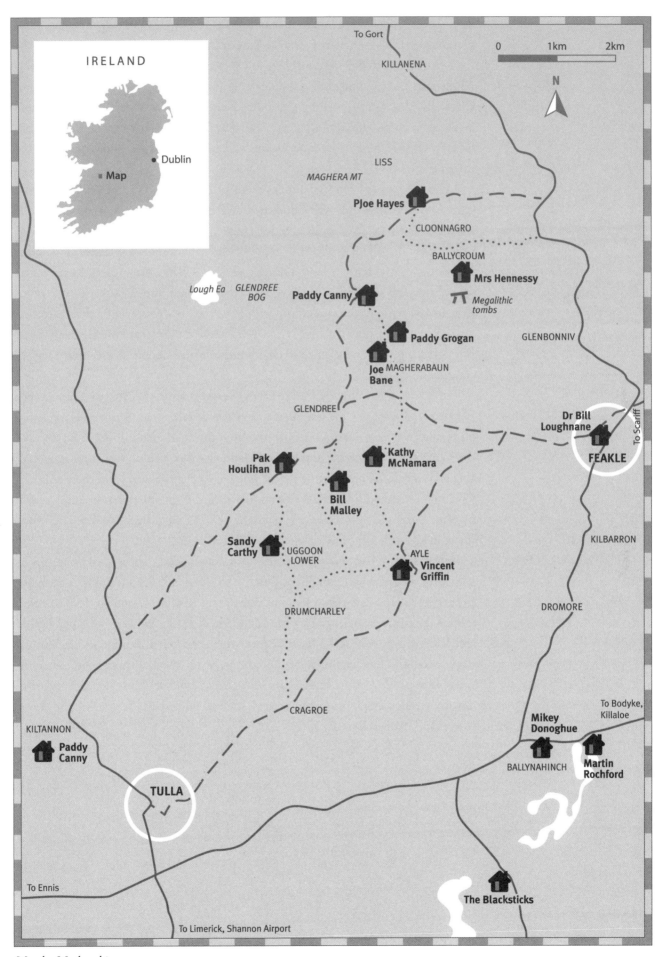

IRELAND

Dublin

Map

To Gort

KILLANENA

0   1km   2km

N

LISS

MAGHERA MT

PJoe Hayes

CLOONNAGRO

BALLYCROUM

Mrs Hennessy

Lough Ea   GLENDREE BOG

Paddy Canny

Megalithic tombs

GLENBONNIV

Paddy Grogan

Joe Bane   MAGHERABAUN

GLENDREE

Dr Bill Loughnane

FEAKLE

To Scariff

Pak Houlihan

Kathy McNamara

Bill Malley

Sandy Carthy   UGGOON LOWER

KILBARRON

AYLE

Vincent Griffin

DRUMCHARLEY

DROMORE

CRAGROE

To Bodyke, Killaloe

Mikey Donoghue

KILTANNON

Paddy Canny

Martin Rochford

BALLYNAHINCH

TULLA

To Ennis

To Limerick, Shannon Airport

The Blacksticks

Map by Markmaking

land speculation. While much of East Clare is renowned for its rich pastures and picturesque lakes—excellent grazing country—the Glendree estate was remote from markets, with large areas of bog and rock and infertile land. Once he inspected his purchase, an appalled Kane declared himself broke. So he raised the rent. Ironically, his lawyer son Robert Romney Kane, who inherited the estate, became an assistant commissioner under the 1881 Land Law Act, the first of the Acts that oversaw the breaking up of large estates and gave tenants the opportunity to buy their farms.

Some call Upper Glendree hungry country. Its acid soils can be coaxed to grow crops—even grass—only when doctored with lime. A patchwork of different soils and rock and bog, it is unsuitable for extensive grazing. By 1840, the townland was already densely populated because of the inheritance law requiring Catholic tenants to divide their land among their sons. While attempting to raise rent money by cultivating crops and livestock, these tenant farmers subsisted on potatoes. In 1845, blight devastated the Irish potato crop, a catastrophe that stretched across seven years, during which time *An Gorta Mór*, the Great Hunger, dealt death through starvation and disease to over a million Irish people. Twice that number emigrated.

In the years that followed, Paddy Canny's great-grandfather Patrick leased a very poor farm of land at Curraun, on the very top of Glendree. A *corrán* is a reaping hook, and it is true that, seen from the bog, the roads around the farm do take the shape of a long handle and curved blade. But two fields away, there is a small ring fort, a circular embankment that once protected a family and their animals. Its name—Keeraun Fort or *Lios Caoráin*—means fort of the bog. It could be five hundred years old or a thousand; it might be older than that. No one knew. But they did know that the fairies lived there now.

Patrick Canny had moved around, from Newmarket, where there were problems with drinking and gambling, then on to Barefield, outside Ennis, and again to Liss, in Killanena Parish. His sons Johnny and Michael leased land at Curraun, joining the frontier society of Upper Glendree. With land in each of Tulla, Feakle and Killanena parishes, the farm of forty-two acres felt like a kingdom. Within a few years, the brothers divided the land between them, although neither farm was able to produce more than a bare subsistence. Michael Canny's property looks down the valley to Cloonnagro. Johnny's is the farm shaped like a sickle and this is where Pat Canny is born in 1867.

A Farmer's Son

It is late October and young Pat Canny is glad to see the back of the farming year. The hay is saved and will feed the animals through the winter, the turf they have brought down from the bog will keep the family warm and cook their dinners, the spuds dug and buried again in their rick will feed them until the summer.

Pat's parents are happy—relieved, more like it—to be well prepared for winter. Pat remembers the time when he was twelve years old, the fear in his parents' faces when they heard rumours of blighted potato crops and cholera that was wiping out poultry on farms just across the mountain. They were lucky that year, but will never take their food for granted, not after the horror that each had survived.

After the devastation of the Famine, the new generation of tenant farmers built solid stone houses with an extra room beside the kitchen—the main living area—and a sleeping loft above. Children not needed on the farm have to make a living elsewhere: marry into another farm, find work in the town, join a religious order. Most emigrate. Before he can marry and take over the farm, the chosen son might become almost an old man himself, waiting for his father to relinquish his authority. It is a matter of survival, for the family and the farm.

In the year 1880, the Land League makes its first appearance in Clare when a branch is set up in Feakle, three miles down the mountain from Glendree. This marks the beginning of the Land War, a period of violent struggles against landlords who will evict tenants unable to pay their rents, but will not lease them enough land to make money on. Landlords are threatened or worse, their cattle driven from their fields or maimed where they stand, their pastures ploughed up and walls broken down. But grazing cattle is more profitable than rents, and so the evictions continue.

In Glendree, the land is too poor to fatten cattle and evictions are few. In 1880, the news that most excites the district's youngsters is that the celebrated dancer, Callaghan of Flagmount, has brought home a new kind of dancing that is done indoors, rather than at the fairground to a piper's tune. Once stately quadrilles performed in the ballroom, over time these 'set dances' have been invigorated by Irish steps and the drive of Irish music. Now everyone is dancing the sets. And the beauty of it is that, if your kitchen is too small for four couples, you can dance the half-set with only two. But mostly they dance in houses with big kitchens and where there are no young children underfoot. To hold their own in a night of dancing, the youth of the district quickly master the South Galway Set from Gort as well as the Caledonian and the good old Plain Set, the Clare Set. The dances are tricky

The dances are tricky enough, with a tangle of different ways the couples move in and out and round about, but once you have it, that set is yours for life.

There is something magical in the power of music. Little wonder that in the old stories, music and dancing are signposts to the treacherous fairy realm.

enough, with a tangle of different ways the couples move in and out and round about, but once you have it, that set is yours for life. And in a district like Glendree, where every family knows every other, there is never a shortage of youngsters to dance.

In January, matches are made and fathers walk the land of future sons-in-law, wary of being duped by borrowed cattle and, after St Brigid's Day, provisions are bought for wedding breakfasts more extravagant than any father would wish. Barns are cleaned out for dancing and a piper or a fiddler engaged, for a wedding would be a poor thing without singing and dancing and music.

There is something magical in the power of music. Little wonder that in the old stories, music and dancing are signposts to the treacherous fairy realm. There was that harvest time when the neighbours came, as they did every year, to share the work of spreading and turning the new-mown hay and raking it into windrows. While the work party—the *meitheal*—was resting for a bite to eat, Johnny Canny sang. Sitting sideways on his stool, one hand beneath his chin, Johnny gave them song after song, his voice clear and pure as spring water, casting a spell that lasted the whole afternoon. No one went back to work and everyone remembered that day.

In the coldest, rainiest months of winter, with harvest dances long gone and weddings still to come, the young men of Glendree crave recreations. Dancing in-doors promises to brighten the long evenings and many houses now have spacious kitchens with flagstone floors perfect for dancing. But dances are no good without music. If there is no concertina or melodeon in the house, the dancers might have to jig the music themselves. Until recently, playing music was a profession for dis-abled men or dancing masters or Travellers who would combine it with other work of the road, like horse trading and tin-smithing. Now, farming people are getting musical instruments and learning to play them. Pat Canny gets it into his head that he and his friends should learn to play their own music. Seriously. On the fiddle.

A few of the Glendree lads get their hands on fiddles and for a while go for les-sons with Ben Cooley. But Ben is in Scariff, ten miles away. Then Pat has a better idea: they will bring a teacher to Glendree and set up their own school for fiddle playing. There is a blind fiddler in Cooleen Bridge, not far outside Feakle, Paddy McNamara, who has a good name. They will fetch him and keep him at Canny's for the winter. Johnny Canny is all for it, having music in the house night and day. Then in the month of February, when the farming year begins again, Paddy Mac's pupils will make a collection for his fee and put him into the horse cart and land him home. And next October they will collect him again.

Pat Canny and his friend Tommy McNamara join the class, along with Mick Donoghue and his boy Mikey. Pat Moloney comes up from Magherabaun, Michael Tuohy from Feakle and Paddy Hayes from Maghera. Liz Brody might come down from Flagmount. At the beginning, Paddy Mac shows them where to find the notes on their fiddles and goes on to teach them half a tune a night. As he plays the tune, he will call out the names of the notes. If they are not quick at matching their playing to the master's noting, they can always copy where he puts down his fingers. The arrangement goes on for five winters, by which time the class has all the reels and jigs and hornpipes and polkas and flings they will need to play for the different figures of the sets.

Pat Canny has had the best chance to learn. In the morning, he would take up the fiddle and play through his tunes until old Paddy Mac shouted down from the loft: 'You have it!' or else 'You have to go back on that again!' Pat has a good ear for music and has learned all of Paddy Mac's tunes, including the ones he composed himself. Holding the fiddle beneath the collar of his coat, Pat can keep up a fair pace for dancing, though not too fast. He knows how to make the rolls that surround a strong note with a circle of quick ones and can make a sweet sound with his long bow strokes. But he will never bring out from the fiddle the warm tone his teacher has. As a child, Paddy Mac had learned how to get that tone from three ladies who were travelling the country together, teaching music and dancing. They were staying at one of the big houses near Feakle. On hearing about the blind lad, they offered him violin lessons so that he could make his living as a musician. Before Paddy Mac's time, another blind fiddler, Hartneady, had brought his music from East Galway down into Clare. But it is Paddy Mac who seeds the fiddle playing that blooms for fifty years in the country around Feakle.

A Priest's Housekeeper

It is the first day of November, All Saints Day, 1893, and Michael McNamara is dead. All through summer, Michael's feet and legs had swollen and then his face puffed out, as if he had drowned and was fished out later. He lay exhausted, coughing, until he no longer could. Michael's wife Nora has opened the window and left the body alone for a time so that Michael could find his peace with God. She has covered the mirror and stopped the clock so that people will know, without asking, the time of his death. It is quiet now in the room, as the women bathe his limbs with sure, steady strokes, lifting and arranging the body.

Nora's daughter Kate watches the women as they tend to her father and gets ready the brown habit and the white bedspread, which will cover him. She finds her father's pipe and tobacco and fetches candles to set beside him. Michael's eyes are closed against all this. His beads are wound around his wrists and he is ready. Kate brings chairs, then, because someone will sit with her father, day and night, until the horses bring his remains to the church.

With the curtains closed, it is dim in the kitchen, where the two little boys stand awkwardly, drawn to the glow of the fire. Kate tells them to fetch more turf. There is a sweet loaf baking and someone, perhaps it was her uncle, has brought whiskey and porter, not forgetting port wine for the ladies. Aunt Ellen arrives with cups and her snuffbox. There is hardly a stone's throw between the two households, a huddle of McNamaras, their farms side by side on the drumlin crown that looks down the winding valley of Glenbonniv.

In the evening, people arrive at the door with kind words: 'I'm sorry for your trouble … He was a good man … I knew him my whole life'. Some of the neighbours stop at the door to press a coin into Nora's hand, for the funeral they won't be able to attend. Kate writes down the sum so that the priest can call out their contribution.

Each visitor kneels by the bed to pray before joining the chatter in the kitchen. There is a rhythm between the two rooms, the churn of prayers and the overlapping waves of conversation, the lamplight and the candlelight shifting to the soft tread of neighbours in and out. At midnight they gather for the Rosary, splicing in the special prayer for the dead, and when the neighbours have departed Uncle Pat sits in the room and minds his brother's remains until morning, when it will all begin again.

Michael's death divides the family's life into the before and the after, pushing those left behind into new uncertainties. Their dispersal is gradual, for the children are still young, Hannah and baby Ellie more than twenty years away from their emigration. Nora, a widow at thirty-five, takes over the farm with help from her husband's people, and at twelve and ten the boys can already do much of a man's work. When he comes of age, young Michael will be the farmer and head of their household. It is Kate who must leave.

The Church has been good to them. She will go as a housekeeper down in Tipperary and will send home most of her wages, whatever the Parish Priest is pleased to give her. At seventeen, she is quiet and devout. She could have been a nun, only how then would her family survive? There are many ways to serve God.

During the long hours of work in the silent house, Kate McNamara learns quickly how to organise her time, cleaning all the different rooms, seeing to the laundry and the fires, making the meals her priest likes and keeping the accounts in order. When needed, she performs the rituals of preparing the dead for burial. She would be at Mass every day if she had the time. She learns the polite address for visiting gentlemen and clergy, how to set the tray for tea or for sherry, the gradations of society in a small town. It is not home, but it becomes her home, with the same transfer of loyalties that women make when they marry. Now, her family is the Church and the Parish Priest the head of her household.

Kate is discreet in receiving petitions and conveying them to Father. As intermediary between all classes of parishioners and the divine power of the Church, Kate learns many secrets, but does not gossip. A priest's housekeeper, especially a young girl, must also guard against tittle-tattle. While criticism of priests is impossible, the women who look after their material needs are often regarded as overbearing busybodies, patrolling the parish with killjoy piety. Worse, there have been cases of salacious gossip about housekeepers and their priests. None of this applies to Kate.

On the farm, her mother had taught her how to treat a calf with scours or a man with a sprained wrist. Now, Kate uses her mother's remedies to quell a sore head or a sour stomach. She learns to read the town's movements, of schoolchildren and Mass-goers, countrymen bringing cattle to market. The sounds of bells and cartwheels and brawls on fair day no longer alarm her. Without the benefit of kinship, Kate begins to assert herself among the shopkeepers. She learns to translate her old world of barter—the value of a basket of eggs or a dressed turkey—into the world of money. She begins to understand the trade in status and influence among the various social circles. She listens as the gentlemen lobby the Parish Priest to

It is not home, but it becomes her home, with the same transfer of loyalties that women make when they marry. Now, her family is the Church and the Parish Priest the head of her household.

support their projects, listens when he rehearses his petitions to the Bishop and overhears his negotiations with the convent's Reverend Mother. Kate knows the value of the gifts the country people bring him, the labour that raises the chicken or preserves the fruit. Now she learns which gifts will win them a good word with the sergeant or a wedding date in Shrovetide and how to bargain for a daughter's marriage fee. She is in awe of the women of the parish, whose power plays are subtle and brutal. She learns the ways of this world.

Kate returns to the farm. At thirty-six years of age, she is old to be on the marriage market, but over many years has accumulated a dowry from her meagre wages, together with what her brother will contribute. Nora works the family connections and locates a possible match. The matchmaker has enumerated the many qualities Kate McNamara would bring to the marriage: a hard worker, knows all the workings of a small farm, an excellent cook, and thrifty. He is a farmer from the mountain country the other side of Ballycroum, not far as the crow flies. Pat Canny is forty-five years of age, lives with his widowed mother and a younger brother. When Michael McNamara assesses the property at Glendree, he finds it poor compared with his own farm, but a fair exchange. The wedding is celebrated three days ahead of the penitent season of Lent. There will be no dowry for Hannah or for Ellie.

The Music of War

The sounds of a war escalate from political speeches and comradely bravado to violent explosions and tortured cries. They reverberate through time, merging with the voice of a new nation. Military action is reclassified as murder, loyalty to the losing side as treachery. Sounds of defiance and doubt are pacified and united in songs of pride.

The soundscape of the War of Independence in County Clare is no different. The harbingers of war are heard in inflammatory speeches and secret deliberations, in clashes on the hustings and disputes in pubs and in kitchens. Always present are echoes of past insurrections and seditious movements in songs and stories commemorating heroic resolve and defeat.

Men here sing the music of war to their children, songs of the Fenian Uprising fifty years ago, of the Young Irelanders before that, and that could-have-been victory of 1798, the defeat that turned Ireland into a colonial backwater without a parliament of its own. These songs frame the present struggle for independence and the argument between those seeking to strike a bargain with the colonial masters and those who would rid the country of masters. With the martyrs of the Easter 1916 rebellion their ghostly leaders, a new generation of revolutionaries rises.

When the Irish Volunteers recruit in the rural parishes of East Clare, they know to make a big noise, to show swank and swagger. In 1917, they make their speeches where young men gather, at the church gate after Mass and at hurling and football matches. At athletics meetings, Volunteers march onto the field wearing their new caps and belts. They enter teams in the tug of war, always the most popular event, where onlookers cheer or jeer as one team pulls the other to fall like skittles. The Volunteers win every contest and the defeated lads enlist on the spot. The tug of war promises to make men out of them: to give self-respect to subordinate farmers' sons and make heroes of landless labourers.

There is music in the war in Clare, because music is stitched into people's lives. As each new company of Volunteers forms, they drill in the fields after Sunday Mass. If the musician with the war pipes can't be brought from out from Limerick, local men do the job on melodeon or concertina, even flute. It is not a whole lot different from dancing. Soon there is a company of Volunteers in every parish in East Clare. Drilling is declared illegal, but that doesn't deter the Feakle Company. In fact, the jailing of their Captain, Tadhg Kelly, only inspires more men to join up. With rifles a scarcity, they drill with wooden guns, and pikes fashioned at the forge, while the village fife and drum band—every man a Volunteer—brings them smartly into step.

Returning from one of his recruiting campaigns, Michael Brennan's company of Volunteers rests on the slopes of Sliabh Bearnagh, which divide East Clare from County Limerick. As usual, the officer with the finest voice gives them a song. But instead of a rebel ballad they all know, a new song rings into the night.

'*Arís!*' his companions urge. 'Sing it again!'

This time, they join in the chorus:

> Soldiers are we whose lives are pledged to Ireland,
> Some have come from the land beyond the wave,
> Sworn to be free, no more our ancient sireland
> Shall shelter the despot or the slave;
> Tonight we man the *bearna bhaoil*
> In Erin's cause, come woe or weal,
> 'Mid cannons' roar and rifles' peal
> We'll chant a soldier's song.

Rebels had sung 'The Soldier's Song' in the Dublin GPO during the Rising. Brennan's company, those of them that survive, will sing it the rest of their lives, translated into the Irish language as the anthem of the Irish nation, when it is won.

In 1917, a by-election in East Clare results in a contest between the Irish Parliamentary Party, which advocates a constitutional reform that will return Ireland its own parliament, and Sinn Féin, which demands a fully independent Irish nation. Their candidate is Éamon de Valera, just released from prison for his role as a leader in the Easter Rising. Irish Volunteers stand guard at de Valera's impassioned speeches and canvass on his behalf. On election day, the Feakle Company escorts the privileged few who are entitled to vote, while musicians play to lift their feet along the miles to the county town of Ennis.

After Sinn Féin's landslide victory in national elections in 1918, they set up their own parliament in Dublin. The Anglo-Irish War of Independence breaks out the following year, and from 1920 the British boost their defences with a force comprising mostly unemployed war veterans. A law unto themselves, the 'Black and Tans' respect neither the discipline of the regular British Army nor the laws governing the now heavily armed Royal Irish Constabulary. The nickname refers to their improvised uniforms, which combine the dark tunic of the RIC with the British Army's khaki trousers, but equally it might apply to their brindled duties, which combine soldiering and policing. And, like the black and tan foxhound, they hunt in packs, their prey the Volunteers, now known as the Irish Republican Army. Travelling country roads in lorries bristling with arms the revolutionaries covet, they raid and burn farmhouses where they suspect support for the rebels. What begins with arrests and trials and imprisonment has become a ferocious war of terror.

Even in the mountain areas, people stop visiting one another at night for, under martial law, meetings and social gatherings are outlawed and curfews enforced. But for some, even the threat of enemy forces cannot constrain their passion for dancing and drinking. Mike Donnellan's house stands beneath the brow of Ballycroum, facing north into the hard weather. Between the Canny farm at Curraun and the Hayes farm across the valley in Maghera, Donnellan's is a music house where there

Even with the Tans out patrolling the roads, neighbours will cross the fields to a dance at Donnellan's. True, the windows are covered to conceal the light, but the sounds of concertina and fiddle travel far into the night.

East Clare Brigade members

might be dancing any night of the week if he is in the humour. Even with the Tans out patrolling the roads, neighbours will cross the fields to a dance at Donnellan's. True, the windows are covered to conceal the light, but the sounds of concertina and fiddle travel far into the night. In any case, as the hours wear out the dancers, Mike Donnellan will grow defiant with drink and devilment, and throw open the curtains.

With music and dancing central to country people's social life, it is no surprise that the Tans burn dancing platforms and target instruments when they break into houses in search of their elusive enemy. When a company of Tans enters the farmhouse of Patrick Griffin, a young Volunteer from Ayle, near Feakle, they help themselves to tea and food and mess about with his melodeon before smashing it to pieces.

The jailed leader of the outlawed IRA's East Clare Battalion, Michael Brennan, requests permission to receive a concertina from home, for the IRA internees, once hunger strikes have won them prisoner-of-war status, keep their spirits up singing songs of past rebellions, in between strategising for the present one. Brennan's request is refused.

Alphie Rodgers and 'Brud' McMahon are among the young men who remain active in the East Clare Brigade. As part of a band of guerrilla fighters—the Flying Column—they move from action to action, sleeping in barns, making hideouts in old limekilns or inside haystacks or dug into the ground in woods and fields. Their survival depends on the goodwill of farming families, the women in particular, who make them dinners, treat their injuries and take risks to warn them of military movements. The two nineteen-year-olds keep close to Scariff, where their families are in business, against their commander's order to keep well away, for the British have identified their part in recent deadly ambushes. Their battalion has also attacked the Scariff barracks. A debacle with dud bombs and grenades that left the building and its occupants unassailed, it resulted nonetheless in Crown forces abandoning the post. Now the town bristles with British soldiers who raid and burn houses, increasingly desperate to track down fugitive fighters. Instead of taking refuge in the mountain country, Rodgers, McMahon and their comrade Martin Gildea move only ten miles along the Lough Derg shore to Whitegate. It is a bad decision, because that district is full of English holiday houses, and many locals are on friendly terms with the owners, increasing the danger from informers. The trio bunk down in the old coach house on an English property where a local Volunteer, Michael Egan, is caretaker.

Men of the Flying Column at times will enjoy a dance in a remote area where the people are friendly. But in Whitegate it is too risky for three lads to go out dancing, let alone ride around in a pony and trap so that anyone can see where they are staying. But this is what they do. Inevitably, the British Army's Auxiliary force arrives while the three fugitives are asleep, capture the caretaker along with them and take all four along the lake to Ballina. They torture the prisoners before handing them over to the Black and Tans, who shoot them point blank, without court or priest. Seventeen bullets in each man, on the bridge that crosses the Shannon between Ballina and Killaloe. When eventually the bodies are released, dozens of priests and hundreds of mourners run the gauntlet of the military to attend the Requiem Mass in Scariff, where all four share a single grave.

Can such a story be set to music? Within weeks, the poets have venerated the victims in verse. In Clare, men and women sing this powerful song to commemorate the desperate fight for Irish nationhood and the terror and desolation of that time: 'The Scariff Martyrs'.

'The Scariff Martyrs'

It was seven o'clock in the morning, at the end of a long night's session of music in Melbourne, Australia, with local musicians and visitors from the touring band, The Boys of the Lough. A solemn silence fell when accordion player Joe Fitzgerald stood to sing 'The Scariff Martyrs', his voice hoarse from cigarettes and quavering with passion. Today, the song is best known through recordings of Christy Moore, who learned it from a local woman when, as a young man, he worked at the Bank of Ireland in Tulla. The versions are almost identical, the small differences revealing Joe's deep investment in the song. For Joe's home place lies scarcely eight miles from Killaloe, in the townland of Corragnoe on the slopes of Sliabh Bearnagh, which men of the East Clare Brigade stealthily crossed and recrossed during the War of Independence. In Joe's song, Christy's 'those four youths' become 'our four youths', and instead of 'an awful sight' Joe uses the local expression, 'a lonely sight'. While the song usually concludes with 'young McMahon and Rodgers, brave Egan and Kildea', in Joe's heartfelt rendering, it is 'poor Rodgers and McMahon, poor old Egan and Gildea' who bring the song to its close.

> A solemn silence fell when accordion player Joe Fitzgerald stood to sing 'The Scariff Martyrs', his voice hoarse from cigarettes and quavering with passion.

Oh the dreadful news through Ireland it rang from shore to shore
Of such a deed no living man has ever heard before.
The deeds of Cromwell in his time I'm sure no worse could do
Than the Black and Tans who murdered our four youths in Killaloe.
Three of the four were on the run, they were searched for all around,
Until with this brave Egan he was found in Williamstown.
He was asked if the boys were inside, but to them he proved true
And because he denied the Tans, he was shot in Killaloe.
The sixteenth of November, boys, in history will go down.
They were sold and traced through Galway, to a house in Williamstown.
They did not get a fighting chance, they were captured while asleep,
And the way the Tans ill-treated them, 'twould cause your blood to creep.
Sure they tied them up both hands and feet with ropes they couldn't break,
They brought them down to Killaloe by steamer on the lake,
Without clergy, judge or jury, on the bridge they shot them down
And their blood flowed with the Shannon alongside Killaloe town.
Then they threw them in a lorry, boys, like cinders in a heap.
They brought them to the bally cart, where two days they did keep.
They kept them closely guarded, where no one could them see,

Not even those who'd reared them up from their very infancy.
By faith and perseverance, on the third day they let them go,
At ten pm our martyrs four passed through Ogonnelloe.
They were kept in Scariff chapel for two nights and one day.
Now in that yard of rest they sleep, kind people for them pray.
If you was at that funeral, it was a lonely sight
To see a hundred clergymen and they all robed out in white,
For the likes of our four martyrs in one grave was never seen,
For beneath our flag they tried to save, our yellow, white and green.
I hope they are in Heaven above, that holy place of rest
Amongst our other martyrs, boys, forever there to rest.
The day might come when we might know who sold their lives away,
Of poor Rodgers and McMahon, poor old Egan and Gildea.

Written by the anonymous 'Ogonnelloe Poet'.
Sung by Joe Fitzgerald, Melbourne, 27 January 1993.

Born in a Time of War

When Nurse Doyle delivers Kate Canny of her first child, John (Jack), in December 1912, Ireland is ruled by Westminster and the British administration in Dublin. Locally, British law is administered through the Tulla Courthouse and the Royal Irish Constabulary in their Feakle Barracks. When Michael (Mickie) is born in March 1916, the tide of nationalism is rising fast. Feakle men are among the earliest to join the civilian militia, the Irish Volunteers. At Easter, while the Rising is taking place in Dublin, local men stand ready to fight. After the rebellion is suppressed, a British Army battalion marches into County Clare and those men are arrested and deported to English prisons. The army takes over the Tulla Courthouse and the Workhouse outside the village. Built to house the destitute in the dying days of the Great Famine, the building was abandoned after absentee landlords withheld the rates necessary for its upkeep. Now it seethes with six hundred British soldiers.

By the time Nurse Doyle arrives at Curraun on 9 September 1919 to bring Patrick (Paddy) Canny into the world, Ireland is at war. There were many catalysts. Before he won the seat of East Clare in 1917, support for Sinn Féin's Éamon de Valera had been boosted by anger that the Home Rule Act to reinstate the Irish parliament had been postponed and outrage at the execution of 1916 Rebellion leaders. In early 1918, Clare was declared a 'Special Military Area'. The British Army imposed censorship and curfews, banned meetings, and restricted fairs and markets, pub drinking and even entry to the county, curtailing economic activity and breeding resentment. At the same time, there was a re-emergence of the agrarian unrest that had erupted periodically in County Clare for over a century. In rural Ireland, where over ninety per cent of the population live, Land Acts enabled the division of estates and farmers are taking up the opportunity to purchase their land. In parts of Clare, including Glendree, the process had stalled and tenant farmers were impatient. These agitations had a symbiotic relationship with the nationalist cause, each lending the other validation and energy.

Even after the War of Independence is over and the Anglo-Irish Treaty signed in 1921, establishing the Irish Free State in all but the six counties of Northern Ireland, the strife is not over. The Civil War that follows partition is as vicious and tragic as every civil war. The new government hunts down and interns twelve thousand IRA 'Irregulars' who oppose the Treaty. In the eleven months of civil war, there are almost as many deaths through military action and state executions as there were on both sides of the Anglo-Irish War.

In the Canny household in Curraun, memories of war are overlaid by the everyday struggle to provide for a family. But they are not forgotten.

After the Treaty is signed, the East Clare Brigade's commander, Michael Brennan, stands down his soldiers, saving the area from the Free State's most brutal suppression. But not all his former soldiers comply. The split in political convictions breaks up the fife and drum band, which not so long ago had led Volunteers as they marched up and down the street of Feakle. Everyone knows which families support the Treaty and which hold out for a united Ireland. These convictions are passed down for generations, translating into votes for the pro-Treaty Fine Gael party and the majority for Fianna Fáil. There are many in the mountainous districts above Feakle, where the IRA's Flying Column had hidden out, who maintain their Republican rage. Those who openly dissent are arrested and jailed.

In the Canny household in Curraun, memories of war are overlaid by the everyday struggle to provide for a family. But they are not forgotten.

Mother

His mother's work is a chain of tasks that draws Paddy after her throughout the long day. He wakes with the rooster and, in the quiet of the morning house, hears her feet padding back and forth on the cold stone, the panting of the bellows as she rouses the fire, the thud of the pot as she takes it from fire to floor, inside it the oatmeal that has transformed overnight into creamy deliciousness. The kettle chinks as she hangs it from the crane above the fire.

Kate Canny is gone out into the early light. The buckets squeal at her side as her bare feet swish through the dew and up the hill to the cows. Paddy creeps down from the loft and out to where his mother squats on the grass, leaning in to soothe the cow as she tugs out steaming squirts of milk. Paddy holds an ear to Bridgie's flank, intrigued by the gurgling. Kate insists he stand back. The cow is irritable; it is not long since the calf was taken from her.

Paddy follows his mother to the dairy, where she strains milk into a pan so that the cream will rise to the top. Returning to the kitchen, Kate lifts the kettle to make tea. It is Paddy's task to rouse his brothers so they won't be late for school. He throws himself in on top of Mickie and onto Jack, who wrestles and tickles until Paddy squeals and begs for mercy.

After their father has eaten his breakfast, the children sit for their porridge and tea and brown bread toasted at the fire. When the kitchen is empty and tidied, Paddy helps carry spuds from the rick to plop in the pot for the pig. This is the best time of day, when the others have gone to their work and he and his mother can explore the world around them. Paddy trots beside Kate down the boreen to the well near his uncle's house. The thrushes, too busy to sing, dart in and out of the hedge, for they are making their nests and soon will lay eggs, the same as the hens do.

Before they get to the hens' house, there is a clamour of cackling. The moment Kate opens the door, calling unnecessarily in her high-up voice, 'chick chick chick', the hens swarm out, their sharp beaks attacking the scattered meal. Paddy's job is to take warm eggs from the straw and place each one gently into the egg basket, for eggs is gold, eggs is money. He looks carefully in the corners of the hens' house, because they like to hide their eggs, and Paddy likes to find them.

In the dairy, the air is cool and sour, the room brightened by the lime painted on the walls and on the canvas Pat Canny has rigged beneath the thatch. Carefully, Kate tilts the milk pan from this morning, and with the wooden skimmer coaxes

When the kitchen is empty and tidied, Paddy helps carry spuds from the rick to plop in the pot for the pig. This is the best time of day, when the others have gone to their work and he and his mother can explore the world around them.

a silken flow of cream, splosh, into the crock. She distributes the skimmed milk to the cats, who wind around her legs impatiently, and the calves jostling one another as it splashes into their trough.

Paddy knows that today they will make the churn, because yesterday was wash day and it rained and the clothes had to dry in the kitchen and it was damp and warm like being inside a cloud. There is a luscious slurp as Kate pours her week's collection of cream into the oaken churn, which is the same shape as herself, long and lean. She closes it tight and begins to pound the stick down and up and down again. Paddy watches from his little stool, feeling the churn's pulse through his feet. The plunging goes on and on, Kate's face reddening from the exertion, until suddenly the churn changes its tune from splatter to flop as morsels of butter form. Kate strains out the buttermilk and lifts the pale lumps into a wooden basin, where she beats the butter with spades. Some of it she slaps into blocks to be sold. The rest Kate feeds with salt and softly smacks into smaller pats for the kitchen and then—the part Paddy has been waiting for—she sweeps knobs of butter into delicate curls. These will sit on a plate on the high shelf until they come down onto the table to slather on the baked griddlecake, which his Daddy will declare fit for the Bishop.

It is time for Kate to feed the pig with spuds and buttermilk, the same as she will make for the dinner, along with the fresh butter and some bacon. In the kitchen, Paddy solemnly reaches the cup into the cool of the bin and brings back flour. They will make the bread together. Kate mixes in salt and soda and hollows a well in the centre and pours in buttermilk, just enough to patter into a cake of bread. Paddy is permitted to use the knife, his mother's hand guiding his, to mark a cross through the dough. Then quick into the pot-oven and crown the lid with hot coals.

When Jack and Mickie are home from school and have eaten the leavings of their father's dinner—potatoes and bacon and the vegetables that make children grow—Paddy is no longer the little man who helps his mother with her work, but once more the baby who gets in the way and is too small to kick the pig's bladder about the yard or go with their father to feed the horses. Instead, he stays by the fire, watching his mother as she moves about the kitchen until the kettle hisses for tea and the soft potato cakes sizzle in the pan and it is time for him to call the others inside.

As soon as supper is eaten, the family kneel for the Rosary. Every night there are new mysteries. The Hail Mary, which comes in strings with scarcely a breath in between, is already in Paddy's memory, a song that has no meaning yet, except that there is mother in it and Jesus. Kate shuffles her beads as she gives out the prayers and the others murmur the responses like bees in a hive, until they say the Hail Holy Queen together and then it is bedtime.

'Twas My Father Gave Me the Music

I remember before ever I started to play, my Dad would come in and I'd crave him and I'd rub him down and I'd do everything to know would he take down the fiddle. He'd often come in tired after a hard day's work and maybe he didn't feel like playing that much. But I always got around him and made him take down the fiddle and play, because I had a great love, a great taste, for it. And I was only little more than a toddler this time, but the sound of the fiddle had some effect on me, and when he started playing, I'd start laughing. I'd have to laugh and smile at the very music, at the sound of it. I loved to hear it.

My father used to play the whistle as well; he was fairly handy on the whistle. So we learned a few tunes on the whistle anyway, myself and Mickie, and we used to play them together. And we'd always be sure we'd have a few good tunes for the Hunting of the Wren. And a lot of the neighbours used to come in to learn the few tunes from him. And he was that type of a man, he wouldn't refuse. There was one girl anyway by the name of Kathy McNamara and she used to be coming up to my father for lessons a long time. And of course I was only a small lad and I was doing my lessons at one end of the table and they'd be noting away at the other and they'd be going through the tune, she'd be picking it up and of course I'd be glued on to what was happening. And when she'd go home I could play the tune that she was at it all the night, I would be taking up the fiddle and playing it. Even though he wasn't teaching me at all, like, I was learning. That's how I was started.

And anything I hadn't right, my Dad would look after me and make sure that I got it right. The fella, he had a great interest on me, because he saw I was able to take it, so every tune he had, he would learn it to me and I was able to pick it up. He taught by ear, and I'd be watching his fingers and I'd be listening to the tune as well, and I was able to pick it up and I could play it. Whatever way he played it, I could play it. I suppose I was eight or nine, and I remember when I started I was barely able to get my hand around it. The fiddle was too big for me, if you like. I had my arm full stretch to hold the fiddle. But from there on, I had a great love for it all the time.

I had a go of my father's fiddle for a while, so he'd play the tune, he'd give it to me and I'd play it, so we both managed with the one fiddle for a while, then I happened to get one in Ennis. I kept it hanging up over the fire. 'Twas always there, but the only thing was, from time to time there wouldn't be strings in it. They were gut strings and they didn't hold. In the damp weather

> 'I was only little more than a toddler this time, but the sound of the fiddle had some effect on me, and when he started playing, I'd start laughing. I'd have to laugh and smile at the very music, at the sound of it. I loved to hear it.'
> — Paddy Canny

they stretched, and then they got tight when they got the bit of heat, and you'd have a bit of a job keeping them in the right shape. So you could be out of tune, depending on the weather or the heat of the kitchen.

My Dad was a great man for rolls, he was very tidy in rolls on the fiddle, and 'twas the first thing he showed me, was how they were done. I could do all them things fairly good. And no matter what a hurry he was in, if I was around the house and I was trying to get a tune, he'd make time to see me right, make sure I had it. But he was a great Dad. 'Twas my father gave me the music.

There was a lot of music around our place, too. Really, it was all over the locality. 'Twas nearly everyone played a little bit. The fact that Paddy Mac had so many pupils when he was coming, the music stayed around then. My father went to a lot of house dances here, there and everywhere. And people called him at night when he was gone to bed and he got up and went. He was that type of man. And wherever he was asked to go, he went, regardless of whether he was tired or whether he was overworked or whatever, he always went. My Mam, then, would be trying to hunt them off, but she'd get no heed anyway, he'd go off wherever.

— Paddy Canny

Facing page: '**The Britches**'

'That's as old as the hills. My father used to play it like that.'
— Paddy Canny, 1999

Polkas were often played for the last figure of the set. On the fiddle, they were good, strong tunes for children to start on. At eighty years of age, Paddy plays this tune with the vigorous bowing, accented notes and fast pace suited to dancing. His bowing exemplifies the sweeping up-bow and slurring onto the main beat common among fiddlers in his area. While the standard version of 'The Britches Full of Stitches' is in two repeated eight-bar parts in the key of A, this four-part setting has a tonal centre of G, allowing the high third part to be played without moving the hand from the first position on the fiddle. Paddy embellishes the first part with a run, DEF, the F an ambiguous note between F and F#. Similarly, in the second part, in the run, ABC, his C is somewhere between C and C#. This is the tonal system that young fiddlers learned, their middle fingers needing to find only one position on the fingerboard for F/F# and C/C#. These in-between notes were typical of fiddlers in the early twentieth century.

'The Britches'

Paddy Canny, 1999

Paddy Gets Away

It is the tin whistle that first teaches Paddy's fingers to make music. The Christmas before Paddy goes to school, he and Mickie spot the whistles in the shop below in Feakle, little black flutes with golden writing painted on. They put their heads together and in a moment their threepences are on the counter. The boys know they are musical instruments, but not how to make them work. At home they are astonished when Pat Canny takes up a whistle and plays it.

By the time Christmas comes around again, the two boys have their whistles tamed and a good few of their Dad's tunes, enough to take them out Hunting the Wren on St Stephen's Day. Wearing raggedy costumes fashioned from old clothes, their faces smeared with soot, they join the other Wren Boys visiting all the houses in the district. One of the boys has already caught a wren and tied it to a branch, hoping that, this year, it won't escape. Outside every house the Wren Boys play their concertinas and mouth organs and whistles, then burst into the kitchen, prance around wielding the branch tied with rags and ribbons and the poor old wren and sing:

> The wren, the wren, the king of all birds,
> St Stephen's day he was caught in the furze,
> Although he was little, his family was great,
> Rise up, my lady, and give us a treat.
> Up with the kettle and down with the pan,
> Give us some money and we will be gone.

The kitchens are warm and the tea hot, and if they are lucky there might be a cut of sweet cake left over from Christmas. One of the big lads collects coins from the man of the house to buy porter for the Wren Dance tonight in Mike Donnellan's big kitchen. And tomorrow night, if there is enough money and enough porter left over, they will have the scrap dance. Which is almost certain, for people in these parts love nothing better than a dance.

Glendree may not be a country where farmers easily prosper, but for a child it is full of magical places, each field and stream with its own name and its own story. On the road down to Magherabaun there is a fort where fairies live, where the wind shakes the whitethorn and the grass grows high, because no cow will dare go near it. At Curraun, Paddy knows the names of all the cows and horses and dogs and donkeys and is sorry for the pig when the pig butcher comes, though the transformation from beast to food is thrilling. In the early mornings there is hurling in the

After footing the turf

As he works alongside him, Paddy learns his Dad's songs and how to whistle tunes. Sometimes he will whistle a tune for hours, fast and slow, depending on his task, or carry it all day in his head until he has the chance to bring it out on the fiddle.

field next to the school, and on wet Sundays Paddy goes fishing with his brothers, for the fish won't see you when it's raining.

Now that he is a schoolboy, Paddy begins to learn a man's work. He joins his brothers in the bog, neatly laying out the sods their father tosses up, turning them over when the topsides have hardened and later building footings, little castles that let the wind blow through their windows to dry out the turf. At harvest, Paddy does a full day's work in their meadow and in the neighbours' meadows, until all the hay is saved and there is a mighty celebration. In the autumn, the whole family works together to lift the spuds and, over winter, Paddy helps to feed the animals and clean out their beds and carry hay to the cattle that have to tough out the cold.

As he works alongside him, Paddy learns his Dad's songs and how to whistle tunes. Sometimes he will whistle a tune for hours, fast and slow, depending on his task, or carry it all day in his head until he has the chance to bring it out on the fiddle. Other times, Paddy can't resist bringing the fiddle with him into the field, even when they are making the hay. And his mother will not be impressed at the fiddle appearing out from under a tram of hay. But he is the baby of the family and his father's pet and, somehow, Paddy gets away with it.

For a couple of weeks each summer, the Canny boys go down to help out on their Uncle Michael's farm in Ballyglass, near Quin. The uncle, who has no family of his own, works them hard and there is no enjoyment for them there. But Paddy is very organised in how to escape. He puts his clothes into a bag and hides it in the ditch and when the coast is clear he runs across the fields and all the way to his aunt in Doora. Aunt Mary is Pat Canny's sister and there is always great music in her house. When the neighbours come around, there will be dancing and there will be singing and the aunt will be playing the concertina and Paddy listening to it all. And, somehow, he gets away with it.

No Better Boy

He knows for the first time that exhilaration when the tune in his head is animated by fingers and bow and released from the belly of the fiddle to fly out among the dancers, propelling their bodies.

At ten years of age, Paddy is not taken in by his father's prediction that in Glenbonniv they will find fields full of piglets, just because the townland is called 'glen of the bonhams'. It is the same way with tunes. A polka called 'The Britches' has nothing to do with a pair of trousers and 'Apples in Winter' doesn't mean you will get any, though it is a lovely jig to play. Paddy hugs the case with his new fiddle in it and chuckles along with his Dad. Bonhams!

Pat Canny has promised that Paddy will play at the wedding. It is his first outing as a dance musician and a magical evening. One man's singing so enchants Paddy that he has to change his tune about his mother's family. There can be no doubt, the McNamaras of Glenbonniv have music in them, despite Kate's dim view of her husband's going off to all parts of the country whenever a musician is wanted. And this gives Paddy hope, because tonight he has discovered the alchemy of the dance, when music sets base bodies into gilded motion, forward and back and around, lifting feet from the floor and driving them down again with a stroke of the bow. He knows for the first time that exhilaration when the tune in his head is animated by fingers and bow and released from the belly of the fiddle to fly out among the dancers, propelling their bodies.

'No better boy!' says his father, and his mother is smiling too.

After the wedding, Paddy starts to feel that he must be good on the fiddle, because his father promises to bring him along to play for the sets in other houses. He has lots of tunes now, although nowhere near as many as his old Dad, who can take down his fiddle and play the length of a winter's night, hundreds of tunes, when most people only know a handful. Thinking of the long nights and the drinking and the dark roads, Kate has no enthusiasm for this plan, but her husband prevails.

So Paddy goes off with his father to house dances that are not too far away and other dances at his uncle's house back in Ballinruan, near Crusheen. The dancing starts around eight in the evening. The older people are first to take the floor, their steps precise and their movements economical: beautiful dancers. They note with amusement the likeness between father and son, their two arms scrubbing back and forth in tandem. But while Pat Canny is always watching them, a genial partner in the dance, the boy's countenance is serious and faraway.

Once they have retired to the room to play cards and talk about the weather and politics and whatever old people talk about, the pace picks up and Paddy has to wake up to himself to avoid the boisterous young couples when the lads swing the

Pak Houlihan's house, Glendree

girls till they are giddy and their dresses fly up. At suppertime, he will get tea and bread, which might have jam on it, and his Dad gets his own bottle of drink. They will stay on to listen to the songs and then, if it's a school night, they'll go home. If it's not, Paddy and his father will stay on for a while, for the dancing might go on until seven or eight in the morning, and for that they will need music.

On Sunday evenings at Curraun, neighbours will call in to learn a new tune, or send their children along for lessons, and Pat Canny wouldn't think of refusing them. He has played at summer dance platforms and house dances and weddings to the farthest ends of Feakle and Tulla and Killanena parishes and knows every musician in between. Some of these musicians take Paddy under their wing. At Pak Houlihan's house, across the road from the Glendree School, he is likely to meet any musician from the district and listen to their music. Like Michael McCarthy—Sandy Carthy—from Uggoon. There is a dance platform near his house, made from the tray of an old hay cart, and on Sunday afternoons in summer the Canny boys join the crowd there. Sandy and his sister Kate—Sis, they call her—play their concertinas for the dancers and invite Paddy to join them, for at twelve, he is already a fine fiddler.

Paddy plays with his new friends in kitchens up and down Glendree and Magherabaun. There is never a shortage of couples to take their turn in a set. The musicians work in shifts, too. Maybe Sandy and the fiddler Bill Malley will play for a few sets, then Paddy might join up with Pak Houlihan and his whistle. Paddy's music is bursting out of him as he discovers all the ins and outs of playing for the sets and how to pace himself for the long hours of music. These musicians give Paddy the new tunes he craves and, every time Paddy plays one of them, he remembers the musician who gave it. And if they hadn't a name for the tune, he gives it theirs.

Paddy soon understands that, while in every house there will be a concertina and one or two people who can play it, the fiddle is the most respected instrument. People are especially excited and honoured to have one of Blind Paddy Mac's students play at their dance. Johnnie Allen is the most famous of these, and not only for the ringing tone he gets from his fiddle. He is renowned for having given tunes to Captain Francis O'Neill for his book, *The Dance Music of Ireland*. And when O'Neill sent him 'The Book', as musicians called it, and someone showed him how to read the notes in it, Johnnie got a whole horde of tunes out of it that nobody else has. And, of course, all the other musicians are mad to hear them. But Johnnie Allen has become very shy, as if he is afraid that people won't recognise the value of his art, and he likes to keep those tunes to himself. So, if Johnnie Allen is known to be playing somewhere, musicians will creep up the ditch around the house and steal away his tunes.

Of all the fiddle players Paddy has met, it is Martin Nugent from Feakle whose playing captivates him. Martin is another of Paddy Mac's pupils. Over the years, he has developed his own style of playing and does things in the tune that nobody else is doing. And he has tunes from Johnnie Allen, which come out of The Book—tunes which nobody else in the area has. Martin invites the teenager to play with him at the dances in Paddy's uncle's house in Feakle and at many other houses. Some people say that Martin plays a bit slow for the sets and they're put off by the way he sometimes hums along with the tune. Paddy is simply enthralled by his tunes and the flowing rolls he puts in at unexpected places, so sweet and so lovely. He sticks close to Martin Nugent at every opportunity, is glued to him, and when Martin marries and moves across the county to Lisdoonvarna, Paddy is bereft.

'Sandy's Reel'

Jack Canny, 1994

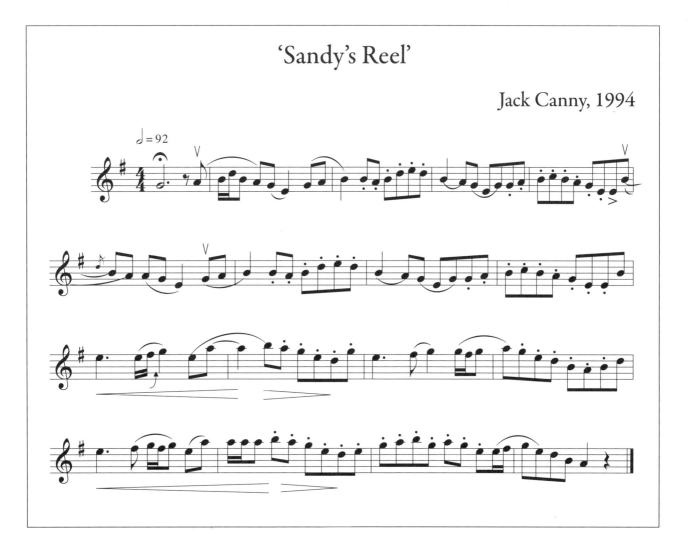

'Sandy's Reel'

Jack Canny learned this tune from concertina player Sandy Carthy and recalled it after he took up the fiddle again, some fifty years after he had stopped. Although he had played the fiddle for only two or three years as a teenager, Jack's playing shows several aspects of the local style, including using a light staccato on separate bows, anticipating the main beat (bar 9) and using a long bow and increasing volume on a phrase rising to the highest note (bars 9–10 and 13–14). Like almost all local dance musicians of his time, including his brother Paddy, Jack uses a double foot tap, his feet alternately marking the four beats in each bar of a reel, matching the dancers' steps. Other musicians in north-east Clare call this tune 'The Cloonagroe', referring to the old townland between the Cannys' farm and the Hayes's. A *cluain* is a meadow among bogs and marshes.

Like a Wave in the Ocean

Michael Coleman

Paddy has fallen in love with Michael Coleman's music. It happened one quiet Sunday evening, when Pat Canny took him to see the gramophone that had arrived all the way from America. They began to hear it nearly a half-mile from Mrs Hennessy's house, which sits snugly beneath Ballycroum, looking out across the valley to Maghera Mountain. It sounded to them like fairy music, or what you might expect fairy music to sound like, for neither had actually heard the mysterious fiddling that lures people away into the other world or bewitches them so that they are compelled to play music day and night.

As the pair approached Hennessy's, the high singing voice of the fiddle and the jumpy thumping of a drum—no, not a drum, something else—came together as a tune. It was magical. In the kitchen, father and son joined the crowd marvelling at the music coming from a box on the table. So fine a thing belonged in the parlour, but there is no parlour in this house. Neighbours were taking turns to peer at the shiny black wheel turning dizzily inside the box, which was built into its own smart suitcase, complete with leather handle. They put their ears to it, but could not work out where the sound was coming from, let alone how.

Even standing right next to it, the music sounded far away, as if from some other world. The thrill of it: to listen to the gramophone was to hear the promise of America, right in this room. At the same time, the music was from home, from here, only better. It was a marvel. When a few couples started dancing 'around the house', laughing at the exhilarating pace, Mrs Hennessy shooed them away from her gramophone, in case they should bump the table and have the needle jump and run and ruin the record.

Young Paddy Canny was spellbound. A fiddle was playing like no other fiddle he had heard and together with it, or not quite together, a piano, he was told. A fiddle playing tunes he had never heard before and so much in each tune, so many notes winding fast around one another, other notes knotting into a kind of stutter. Not a slow stutter, like the one that sometimes holds back his own speech, but a stutter gone again so fast, his ears could scarcely catch it. He wanted to listen to this music again and again, forever. 'Seventy-eight revelations in every minute,' he heard a man saying. Before they went home that evening, Paddy dragging at his father's heels like a calf from its mother, Mrs Hennessy agreed that Pat Canny's son could come again and listen to her gramophone.

Since that day, more gramophones have arrived in the mountain townlands. And after the gramophones, the records keep arriving from women who as teenagers had gone out to America. They will never return, but scrimp their wages to send home money and melodeons and men's suits cut from fine woollen cloth, and sewing machines and gramophones. Children know these aunts only by their parcels.

The aunts' records bring the jaunty fiddling of Michael Coleman and James Morrison and the perfectly matched duets of Paddy Killoran and Paddy Sweeney, all Sligo men, and later, Hugh Gillespie from Donegal and Dublin's Frank O'Higgins. There are flute players as well, McKenna and Morrison and Fireman Barney Conlan, and the Flanagan brothers' band sounding like America itself: modern and fast and new. Most people have a favourite recording artist, but the fiddle still reigns in these parts—as, evidently, it does in New York City.

At every opportunity Paddy devours all the tunes on all the records in any house where there is a gramophone. He studies every tune until he has it note for note and can go home playing it inside his head. He never knew what music could be until he heard Michael Coleman. His one desire, which consumes him day and night, is to play like Coleman, a desire he shares with many another fiddler in Ireland, although he doesn't know it. More than Coleman's intricate embellishments and restless variations, he wants to discover the lovely flow that seems to come so easily and yet is so elusive. Paddy can almost see Coleman's music rising up and falling down like a wave in the ocean.

The greatest lesson Paddy learns from Coleman is humility. A precocious lad, whose playing is far ahead of every other fiddler's in the district, music came easily to him. Now he attempts the impossible, day after day, always striving to be a better boy. Climbing up and tumbling down, rising and falling, in his striving to perfect himself, Michael Coleman's music remains the touchstone, the benchmark and yardstick, against which he measures his accomplishment.

New tunes were always scarce, but suddenly are everywhere. So much music coming in. Pat Canny does not have these new tunes, let alone the techniques Paddy is attempting; he is too old a dog to learn new tricks, he says. Nor is he going to pester his neighbours to listen to their records, when no gramophone has arrived at Curraun. At Paddy's age, he had seized every tune Blind Paddy Mac had put before him and later had gathered every new tune he met, if he liked it. Now, his boy has the chance to learn music the likes of which neither he nor Paddy Mac nor anyone in these parts could have imagined. Pat Canny encourages his lad to keep at it, to learn everything he can from this new teacher, the gramophone.

Of all the fiddlers in the district, Paddy alone is intent upon playing not only

More than Coleman's intricate embellishments and restless variations, he wants to discover the lovely flow that seems to come so easily and yet is so elusive. Paddy can almost see Coleman's music rising up and falling down like a wave in the ocean.

every note of Coleman's tunes, but every cut and roll and slide and stutter that graces them. It is Paddy alone who seeks to emulate Coleman's phrasing, which expands the tune away from the regular, chopping rhythm the district's dancers require. Other musicians take tunes off the gramophone records in the same way they might pick up a reel Paddy Loughnane was whistling in his shop in Feakle or a piper's hornpipe they heard at the fair of Spancil Hill. Those musicians play the new notes in the old style. A lovely flow is the last thing the dancers want. What suits them best is a strong beat like Bill Malley gives them. With his fiddle jammed against his chest and his eyes on the dancers, he hacks at the tune with a flamboyant energy they can't resist. But Bill is not the man to let a good tune pass him by. All these new tunes coming in with the gramophone, some of them are mighty. Like 'Ballinasloe Fair': a good solid tune for dancing.

Facing page: **'Ballinasloe Fair'**

Bill Malley

At the peak of his career, in 1927, Michael Coleman recorded this much-lauded and often emulated 'side'—'Lord McDonald's' followed by 'Ballinasloe Fair'—which earned him a bonus equivalent to five months' wages for the average Irish emigrant worker. No wonder: his performance is a work of art, finely phrased and brilliantly embellished. Coleman's transition into the second part of 'Ballinasloe Fair', sliding up to the high G as the tune changes from A dorian into sweet C major, is sublime, echoed as he slurs from low to high, accenting the on-beat with a smooth, rocking motion (bar 9).

In contrast, Bill Malley's playing of 'Ballinsloe Fair' is vigorous and straightforward. It is clearly music for dancing. Bill's pace, slower than Coleman's, is what local dancers preferred. He keeps the structure simple, playing each eight-bar section only once, where Coleman repeats the second part. Bill plays fewer notes—no rolls or finger triplets—and emphasises each of the four beats in the bar, one for each of the dancer's steps, using mostly separate bows or slurring three notes together. A signature of Bill's playing is his use of strong up-bows on phrases of two or three notes, a common enough practice among fiddlers from around Glendree. He puts shoulder heft into his bowing, strengthening the beat by adding the adjacent open string to the melody note, or by placing a finger across two strings to play two notes together (the non-melody notes written here with smaller heads and no stems). These double stops sound harsh on the highest string, notorious for producing squeaky notes. Musicians of Bill's generation did not buy the expensive E strings that promise a golden tone, but ordinary steel strings like those Paddy Canny used.

'Ballinasloe Fair'

Coleman's 'coda' variation to the last eight bars

Double Act

The two lads have their circuit, they have bikes and they have ways of strapping fiddles to their backs. They travel to dances throughout the three parishes of Killanena, Feakle and Tulla. Paddy and PJoe are serious about the music and serious about themselves as musicians.

At twelve years of age, Patrick Joseph (PJoe) Hayes is still a scholar, but learning a man's work on the farm. He follows his father, Martin, known as Quillan (*coileán*: 'pup'), in the yard and the garden and the bog. It is PJoe's job to count his father's cattle on the mountain commonage, where they might wander off to another farmer's herd. At harvest time, he takes a man's job, his skinny shoulders strengthening with the work. The Hayes farm, on the flank of Maghera Mountain, is bigger than Canny's in size and productivity, and consequently in status. Quillan Hayes is at the centre of social life in his townland. On winter nights, it is around his fire that household heads gather to discuss the politics of the district, the county, the nation and the world, and it is Quillan's assessments that they most respect. Pat Canny is at the centre of social life in Glendree as a dance musician who can be called upon at any hour. He will pass on his skills as a fiddler to anyone who asks, but these days he gets so tired that sometimes he has to teach from his bed.

When old Tommy McNamara, another of Blind Paddy Mac's pupils, passes his fiddle to Quillan, thinking that his cousin's young fellow might learn to play, it is with Pat Canny's lad that lessons are arranged. At fourteen, Paddy is already an accomplished musician. PJoe is already a dancer. When music gives him the dance, he gives it back, tapping out the beat with his winter boots. Even as a little child, he danced to the music from his mother Maggie's concertina. Now, he is eager to make that music himself.

PJoe is Paddy's first pupil. Following his father's method, Paddy begins with an orientation to the notes on the top two strings of the violin. Once PJoe's fingers can find these notes as Paddy calls them out, he puts them together in half a jig. It is not a real tune, but introduces useful patterns for the fingers, something like a girl's embroidery sampler teaches the basic stitches she will need. PJoe never forgets it:

A^2 C A	A C A	A C A	D B
A C A	A C A	A C A	B A
A C A	A C A	A C A	D B
A C A	F^1 G A	E C^2 A	B A

PJoe listens to each note he makes, to be sure his finger comes down in the right place and he marries each note with one rub of the bow. When he progresses to playing real tunes, PJoe takes home pieces of paper Paddy gives him, with the tunes

Quillan Hayes, Paddy Canny,
Maggie Hayes, Mary Hayes,
Philomena Hayes

written out with the names of the notes and numbers for the strings they are played on. He practises until the tunes play all day in his mind, until they live in his dreams and are still playing when he wakes, until the sound of each tune has taken root in his fingers' memory as well as in his mind. He copies the way Paddy taps his feet in time with the tune. Keeping the rhythm comes easily, because he already understands the different ways the body moves to a jig or a polka, a reel or a hornpipe.

By the time PJoe has learned six or seven tunes this way, his introduction is complete. When Paddy gives him the next tune, he doesn't call out the names of the notes. Instead, he plays one phrase at a time and PJoe has to echo what he hears. Then they assemble the phrases into half a tune, then the whole tune, and when he and Paddy play it together PJoe feels the thrill of the two fiddles resonating. As PJoe's fiddling develops, the music he brings out with his two hands coincides with the music in his head, with no thought put into it. Hearing the tune inside and outside at the same time is like stroking one hand with the other, touching and feeling the touch together. PJoe absorbs the patterns in the tunes: the way they go higher in the second part and how snatches of melody are repeated at certain places. Eventually, he finds that he can learn any tune, as long as Paddy plays it through a few times.

It is scarcely a year before PJoe is ready to join Paddy playing at barn dances and wren balls, country-house dances and parties—swarees, as they call them. Paddy first heard Michael Coleman's music in Mrs Hennessy's house and it is there that he returns with PJoe. They are delighted that almost every record that arrives from

America has two tunes—on each side. They set out to learn every tune on every record, but their scheme is not foolproof. While Mrs Hennessy loves music and welcomes the boys when she is in good humour, at other times she will send them packing even before they can get inside the door.

At dances, the boys are always on the prowl for new tunes and have adopted a technique other musical partners employ: each memorises one half of the tune. This is not such a hard thing to do, when only one tune is played for each figure of the set. What is more difficult is to hang onto those half-tunes until on the way home you can whistle or jig it out loud to each other. Before Paddy and PJoe part company for the night, they might take out their fiddles and put the two parts together.

Equally captivated by music and committed to playing together—every day, if they could—Paddy and PJoe develop an intimate friendship and the kind of rapport that musical brothers have, each anticipating the other's next move. From the beginning, PJoe accepts that Paddy has the ambition and the talent to exceed all others, including himself. He has the wisdom to enjoy each step of his own musical journey.

Jack Gets Away

Music was people's main hobby when their day's work was done in the farms. Our main enjoyment was music and everybody was playing some type of an instrument. We all started playing, myself and Mickie and Paddy, when I was fourteen or fifteen, just after leaving school. We were learning jigs at first, for they were a lot easier than the reels to learn. It seemed to be quite natural for Paddy to hear a tune a couple of times and he could take up the fiddle and play it. But I couldn't do it. I'd have to spend weeks at it before I could master it properly. I never devoted a lot of time to music, for I knew I could never get to the top in music. I'd learn a tune and then I wouldn't touch that tune maybe for weeks, until we'd go to a neighbour's house where there were two girls learning fiddle at the time and we used to meet there and do our practising. And during the cold frosty nights in the winter time there was a local fiddler called O'Malley, who used to come in and we'd talk nice to him and ask him to play for a set and we'd all get out and dance the Clare Set to get the frost off of our bones.

'It seemed to be quite natural for Paddy to hear a tune a couple of times and he could take up the fiddle and play it. But I couldn't do it. I'd have to spend weeks at it before I could master it properly.'
— Jack Canny

Jack Canny, 1993
(Dean McNicholl)

In the summer, we had the crossroads dances on Sundays. Whoever was organising it, they'd get all these boards cut, level off a patch of ground just off the roadside, put all the joists down, put all the boards across—it was the same as a floor. There was a platform just down the hill from our place and all the teenaged boys and girls, they used to come down wearing their Sunday best and dance all the different steps and set dances.

My parents got me an ordinary pushbike when I was about fifteen and of course I was happy as a sand-boy going around with my new bike. I used to take it down to the stream and wash all the spots off it, all the mud. We didn't have sealed roads in that time, and they used to get very muddy when the rain would come. I was very keen on hurling, which was the main sport around our place. After I got the pushbike, I used to go to all the local football games and hurling games and sports meetings and whatever was on. The Athletic Club in Feakle was very successful and I brought home a lot of trophies. I loved cross-country running: that was my main sport. The club was run by a fellow by the name Michael Tully. He was a guard, and he got us to clear out our house at home and have a few dances there for the club. And my Dad played and Paddy played and we all played for the sets.

A couple of years later, I met a local chap on the road who was a good track cyclist and I went a bit past him, to see how fast he could go.

He says, 'You're a bit too young yet to test an old timer.'

And a few weeks later he says to me, 'Why don't you have a go at the cycle races?'

'I couldn't,' I says, 'I couldn't keep up with them.'

'Well,' he says, 'All they can do is beat you. You've nothing to lose.'

This chap was a mechanic and he was the local taxi and he used also sell bikes, repair bikes. And I says, 'What do I have to do with this old bike to make it suitable for the racetrack?'

'Leave it to me,' he says. 'I'll fix you up.'

He put on a fixed wheel sprocket, he stripped the mudguards off, he got me a pair of racing handlebars.

'There you go,' he says. 'Go out and get a couple of weeks' training on that,' he says. 'And then we'll see what you're like.'

So after a few weeks, I went to a local sports meeting and I was up against some cyclists out from Limerick, some from Galway, and I got a twenty-yard handicap in the three-mile cycle. 'Whatever you do', he says, 'When the bell goes, don't look back'.

So as soon as the bell went, I gave everything that I had and I couldn't make out why they weren't passing me, and I won the race. Then, after three months cycling, I went out again on the three-mile and the same thing happened: I won. And that started me. The next year, I got a proper racing bike, with sprint wheels, and I did a lot of training and I entered for some of the professional events, and every one I went in, I nearly won them all.

I was after coming from one sports meeting and I was on the main road from Ennis to Tulla, and all of a sudden I saw two guards and I did a U turn.

'O'Malley's'

Jack Canny, 1991

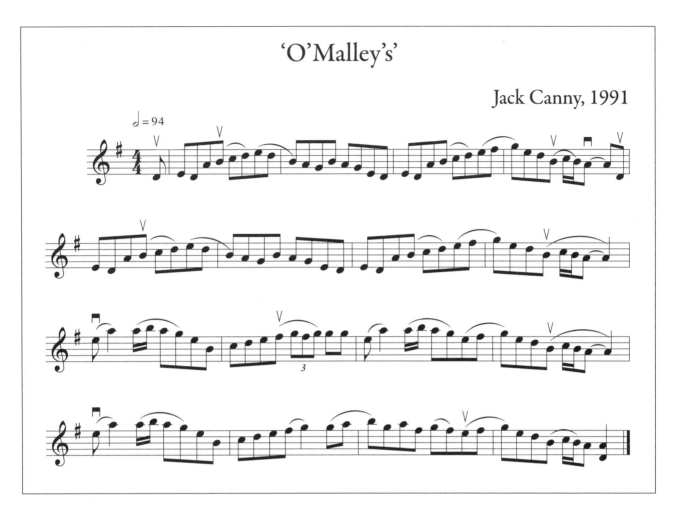

And one of the guards—that was the days when the guards used to ride around on pushbikes—one of them shouts out,

'Where's your lights?'

I didn't answer. They started to put up speed, to catch me. I'd let them get within a hundred yards of me, then I'd sprint ahead and get two hundred yards away from them, then I'd slow down again. And that went on and they couldn't catch me. In the end, one of them shouted,

'Ah, you bugger, we'll get you one day!'

The following year then, I won all the Clare championships and later that year I won an All-Ireland title in the 1,000 metres. I can't recollect how many cycle races I won. I travelled all over Ireland. All my spare time went into cycling. I kept the racing bikes in the hayloft and I made a frame for the bicycle, like an exercise bike, so that I could keep training over the winter months when the roads were bad. I wasn't interested in fiddle music at that time. I lost all contact with the fiddle music. And then I suddenly got a bee in me bonnet and I migrated to England. I didn't have a bike there and I didn't do any more cycling.

I'm the only one in the family that had itchy feet. I suppose we're all built different. Mickie and Paddy, they preferred to live back home in their own country and they were happy to do so. I wanted to travel and I don't regret it.

— Jack Canny

'O'Malley's'

This tune, which Jack Canny recalled as the one Bill Malley played as the first tune for the set, is a version of 'The Eel in the Sink'. Jack sometimes groaned as he played—whether at the effort or as a way of singing the tune was unclear. It was quite common for local fiddle players to sing, hum or groan as they played.

The Bee and the Boo

Mrs Hennessy has a gramophone before anyone in the district has one and everybody wants to hear it. She likes nothing more than a night out dancing and Grogan's big kitchen in Magherabaun is where she likes to go. Mrs Hennessy will bring her gramophone, if someone will carry it for her. Often, that someone is Paddy O'Donoghue (or Donoghue). Paddy's father is Mikey, who attended Paddy Mac's fiddle classes up at Canny's. Mikey swapped out his farm in Glendree for better land below at Ballynahinch, when the Land Commission divided up the big estate there in the 1920s. His mother-in-law lives in Magherabaun and his boy Paddy often comes back up the mountain to stay with his grandmother.

So on Sunday evenings, Paddy Donoghue will take the path up Ballycroum, dodging treacherous pools in the bog, his way-marks the ancient stone tombs. Tobar Gráinne is named for the ancient chieftain's daughter who, discovering that her mother was a sunbeam, drowned herself in the lake: Lough Graney. Some people call the tomb Diarmuid and Grainne's Bed, after another legendary princess, who refused marriage to an old king and ran off with a young warrior, avoiding capture by sleeping out in wild places such as this. Near the top of the mountain is the Mass Rock where, in penal times, people came secretly to worship. Arriving at Hennessy's, Paddy will take the gramophone by its leather handle, promising to hold it above the wet grass, and bring it out over the mountain and down again to Grogan's. Carrying the machine is some work for a child, but Paddy is strong and he knows the mountain the way the rabbit knows his run.

Paddy Grogan being a keen concertina player, musicians are always welcome to play at his Sunday night dances. Paddy Donoghue likes to crouch against the wall as the dancers whirl and clatter, storing away all the tunes the musicians play and all the different ways they have of playing them, for young Paddy is already a promising musician. When Mrs Hennessy brings her gramophone, though, the evenings have a different rhythm. The musicians listen with admiration and great attention, for they are eager to learn the new tunes. At the same time, it is awkward. If they don't get to play, they feel redundant, dismissed; but if they do play, they are newly aware of their shortcomings, especially the fiddle players, for not one of them could match the likes of Coleman or Killoran.

The old people straight-out dislike the new arrangement. They distrust the gramophone machine, with its sinister crackle and hiss. For the dancers, the records are a novelty, but, in truth, the records are not great for dancing sets. It's not the way one tune suddenly changes into another. The dancers don't mind that,

Since Mrs Hennessy began bringing her gramophone, the evenings have a different rhythm. If the musicians don't get to play, they feel redundant, dismissed; but if they do play, they are newly aware of their shortcomings.

even if they notice. It's not even the exhilarating pace, faster than the local musicians play, for they're young and up for it. But each side of the record is either too long or too short for the figures of the set. And then, if the appointed assistant hasn't cranked the gramophone enough—perhaps fearing they might overwind it and break the spring, as Mrs Hennessy keeps warning—it will slow down in the middle of a tune, the music grinding from a wail to a growl. Without musicians right there beside the dancers, there won't be a proper ending when the figure is done and the tune won't change to a fling to end the set. Certainly, it won't be urging the dancers on with a shout or calling out the name of the lad battering his feet on the hearthstone for all he is worth.

At Grogan's, Mrs Hennessy takes charge of playing the records. Among the district's musicians, she is better known as 'The B Moroney' after her first husband, and a female dog. Only she may take the discs from their brown-paper covers and only she may execute the delicate operation of dropping the needle onto the record. But if she is not brought out to dance as often as she wishes, which is more often than anyone else, she is bound to take the boo—the hump, the huff. And then she'll be gone, clutching her records, young Paddy Donoghue trotting after her with the gramophone. Weeks later, or it could be months, when eventually she arrives back into Grogan's on a Sunday evening, they'll smile slyly at The B Moloney: 'Oh, has the boo gone?'

Part and Parcel

There was Yanks home one time, and they were putting in hay, that was a big day's work, there might be three or four cars, horses and cars, and they'd go out and they'd pick up the hay outside in the field and bring it in and they'd put it into a rick. 'Twas a lovely sunny day. And one of the Yanks came out and says, 'Jamesie!'

'Yes, man.'

'We're one short for a set. We're just going to dance a set and we're one short. Will you come in and dance it?'

'Oh, I will, man, I will.'

So he went in and he danced a set and he came out and forked over his hay again. It was part and parcel, the dancing and music.

Another time, they were cutting hay, they used to cut the hay with horses that time, horses and mowing machines. But the blades had to be edged very often, so the old man of the house came out and sat down and was edging the blade and then they'd change it over. And the son was cutting the hay and while he was cutting, he was singing. And he had to sing very loud to hear himself over the noise of the machine. But the father stopped him when he was coming around.

'You're singing that song wrong,' he said.

'What's wrong with it?'

'The air is wrong. That's the wrong air.'

So they spent half an hour talking about the air of the song, and the horses enjoying themselves eating the hay.

That was what music meant, how they appreciated it. It was part and parcel of their being. You'd imagine that there should be music in the bushes, there was so much music to be heard. I mean, you could go out at night, especially a frosty night, and you could hear a fella whistling in the next parish. Often at night and you were out in the countryside you wouldn't hear a sound, only maybe a donkey, or maybe a goat squeaking, but you'd hear somebody whistling miles away. And singing! I used to hear my father singing. Oh, he'd be out ploughing or in the garden or cutting hay, or whatever, and he'd be singing there to his heart's content. 'Twas a normal thing.

— Jim Brody

'The Primrose Lass'

Paddy Canny, *c.* 2000

'The Primrose Lass'

In the townland of Turkenagh, just below Killanena, where Jim Brody came from, they danced the Galway Set. It had five parts to it: reels for the first three, then a jig, ending with a fling. This last figure was very energetic, with the couples swinging separately before joining up to whirl around in a 'basket' or 'Christmas'. 'Johnny When You Die Will You Leave Me the Fiddle-O' was one of the flings they played and 'The Primrose Lass' another. Paddy Canny wrote out this tune in an old diary, perhaps for his granddaughter Eimear, whom he was teaching to play the fiddle. A simple tune suited to beginners, it is good for practising crossing from one string to another and back again. The letters are the names of the notes and the numbers indicate the string (1 for the E string, 2 for the A, 3 for the D). The dots indicate that these notes are played in the higher octave.

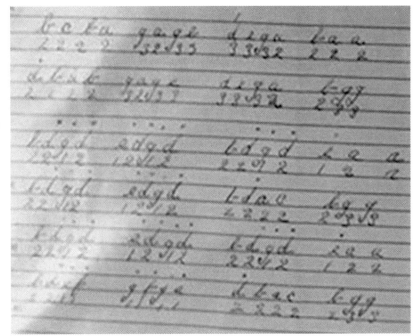

Dancing Out of the House

Helter-skelter out of the house, they all take flight. Paddy Canny, his fiddle and bow hastily stowed, bolts into the haggard with the rest. They hide as best they can, the lads panting with excitement and the girls scared that someone will give out their names to the priest, who strides into the house and silently, menacingly, closes the door. They wait. They can't hear what he is saying but they can hear the outrage. They wait, but he doesn't come out. The cold is punishing. In the end, they all slip quietly into the boreen and head for home.

Of course, they will all return the following week, because they are having the scrap. The fellows organising the dance had put their few bob together and collected a half-barrel of stout from Limerick—else, what kind of a dance would it be—and tonight collected money at the door. From the men, anyway. Now there's enough for more Guinness than there was on the first night. So of course they all go back for the scrap. The men, anyway.

This experience shocks Paddy, although it should not. It still seems to him as though nothing will ever keep young people away from a dance. They will walk six or seven miles to a house party. Others, if they are lucky, can bike it. They go to the 'wakes' for departing emigrants and to the big gamble dances before Christmas, where they might have to wait hours for a dance, while their elders play cards—Forty-five is their game—and winners go home with a dressed turkey. There are more dances during the winter months and a rash of wedding parties before Ash Wednesday. At other times, people visiting a house might simply feel like dancing a set, even if they have to lilt their own music—'gob music' some people call it.

The boys and girls here throw themselves into dancing. Paddy is no dancer. His sport is to go fishing or roam the hills with his beagles in a hunting party with other lads. According to his brothers, dancing is a way to get the feel of a woman. And the other way around. Despite the modest gap between their bodies, a girl can learn a lot about her partner: whether he has clammy hands or bad breath, whether he gallops off the beat or glides you 'around the house' like a fish through water. Whether he keeps up a stream of banter or a sullen silence and whether he has too much drink taken. The men compete for the best looking girl and the best dancer and the girl who, lacking brothers, will have a farm to marry into.

Pity the girl who isn't an able dancer; she might stand all night along the wall. Performing the figures with style and precision is a skill shared between dance partners. There is such pleasure when the four couples move in harmony to make the set's larger pattern, especially when the musicians play simple tunes that they know, tunes with good rhythm. Skilful dancers feel the main beat and the in-between patterns move through their bodies and out their feet. When a phrase catches their fancy, the men batter the flagstone at the hearth, sparks flying from their boots. The young people's dancing is boisterous, with laughter and sweat, shared mostly with people they have known all their life and will know until emigration or death separates them.

When the musicians and dancers take a break, there might be a song, or someone might dance a hornpipe, like Kathy McNamara, who has learned all the steps the Gaelic League prescribes and every year brings home medals from the Feis. Not that the Gaelic League's project of reviving the Irish language has drawn much interest in these parts. Apart from school lessons, everything is in English, at home and in the village shop, and it is English they read in the *Clare Champion*. For Paddy Canny, Irish is the language his grandparents had spoken. Even so, the Irish nests inside the English, taking flight to name fields and streams and townlands, to define the weather or a fool or to dandle a little child.

The 1930s are hungry years in the hills of East Clare, a hardship that can't be danced away. When Fianna Fáil won the election, they kept their promise to make the Irish Free State more self-sufficient, building a wall of tariffs and stopping repayments on the loans that had financed land transfers from British landlords to Irish tenants. When the British retaliated with their own tariffs, the large cattle farmers—no friends of Fianna Fáil—lost their primary market. But the small farmers, whose votes had brought in the new government, lost their income from selling young cattle for fattening. In the six years of this Economic War, they are collateral damage. So mass emigration continues—not to America, where the Great Depression has brought tight quotas but, ironically, to Britain.

The best dances are in summer, when these workers return on their holidays. How Paddy looks forward to his brother Jack's homecoming, his tales from the building sites of London and the strange characters he has met, his contagious, gulping laugh: ah-HUH, ah-HUH! The ghost stories Jack tells late at night, his shoulders jumping at his own suspense, make Paddy just a little nervous passing certain abandoned houses on his way home from dances, for ghosts are far more dangerous than any old fairies. Since Paddy's schooldays ended, he has been playing at dances that mark every season and occasion, or no occasion at all. The district is filled with musicians, he and PJoe Hayes among them. But the dances are melting away.

The Public Dance Halls Act 1935 passes into law with little resistance, complementing the government's censoring of books and films. The clergy have been campaigning for years against modern 'jazz' music and all-night dancing; against the lascivious foxtrot and depraved men who lure young women into motor cars outside isolated dancehalls. The Gaelic League has supported their campaign, for not only is this modern dancing immoral, it is foreign and—even worse—racially impure. Now, public dances of all kinds are banned, unless they are licensed.

It is not only public dancehalls that are affected. Without a licence from the courthouse, all at once an evening's set dancing in a private kitchen is against the law. If the priest won't support your application, there is no chance of a licence. No licence if money is to be collected towards the evening's provisions. No licence for a turkey gamble, or for a household bolstering their finances with a raffle. You can't even

> When a phrase catches their fancy, the men batter the flagstone at the hearth, sparks flying from their boots. The young people's dancing is boisterous, with laughter and sweat, shared mostly with people they have known all their life and will know until emigration or death separates them.

celebrate a wedding in your own house if there's no sanitation. Is there even one house around here that has 'sanitation'? So families have to hire out a hotel in the town.

The Gardaí are inconsistent in enforcing the Act. In certain areas people are willing to chance it, despite the fines or even jail if they are raided and the shame of being named at Mass or in the *Clare Champion*. Once again, the people of the rural townlands are collateral damage, for the Act puts an end to the main entertainment knitting together their neighbourhoods.

Although the truth of it is, there aren't enough women. Take the dances in the Feakle market house: just a small place, but popular. Or was, until the priest started giving out at Mass about drink and immorality and banned his flock from attending. After that, the girls stayed away, and that was the end of the dances.

Young women have other reasons, too, for staying away. They have come to see house dances as rather crude affairs compared to the dances in the towns, where bands play for the foxtrot and women wear elegant frocks. Or so they hear. Going to the little cinema in Feakle is all right, as long as it is not a western, but Hollywood only feeds their fantasies of a better life elsewhere. Sisters come home on holiday from English cities with accounts of their modern life—sanitation just the beginning—and earning money of their own and nights out in ballrooms and so many new friends. The quest for a 'suitable' husband here—one who has inherited the farm—is increasingly unattractive, because the farms themselves yield scarcely more than the most basic subsistence. So many young women leave, and young men, too. The number of bachelors on the poorest farms increases. Who will dance with them now? It is only in Ayle and Drumcharley, townlands not far from Feakle, that house dances continue to flourish. Their secret? Large families with plenty of girls.

Parish priests all over rural Ireland go on a spending spree, building halls where they can supervise dances and harvest the takings. In Feakle, there isn't the money to do this, and instead Sunday night dances start up in the Kilclaren School under the priest's supervision. After a few bob is taken out for the musicians, entry fees go towards parish schemes, like improvements to the parochial house. In the schoolroom, the pupils' forms are pushed against the walls to allow space for waltzing couples and for the Gaelic League's céilí dances, 'The Siege of Ennis' the most popular. Most times, they'll dance a few sets as well. Paddy Canny and PJoe Hayes are one of the musical partnerships popular at school dances all around Killanena Parish, in Douglaun and Drumindoora and Flagmount. The musicians sit on the windowsills, safe from the swirl of the dancers, and play in shifts, often with a melodeon player, whose instrument can be heard above the clatter of feet on the wooden floor.

The school dances are popular with married couples and young people, who consider them more sophisticated than house dances, which they look down on as suitable only for children and old people. The old people return the disdain, for they find no comfort or neighbourliness in the schoolroom. Alcohol is forbidden, apart from a sup for the musicians, and the dance stops at midnight, one o'clock in summer. And where playing music for dancing belonged to the give and take among farming families, now the musicians selected for the job are hired hands.

The quest for a 'suitable' husband here—one who has inherited the farm—is increasingly unattractive, because the farms themselves yield scarcely more than the most basic subsistence. So many young women leave, and young men, too. The number of bachelors on the poorest farms increases. Who will dance with them now?

Ballynahinch

Freewheeling into Feakle on a Sunday evening, past trees turning golden with the season, Paddy Canny has his wellingtons on the carrier and the fiddle strapped to his back. At the fair ground he turns south towards Kilbarron, where the singer Johnny Patterson was born, and pedals past Dromore Hill and the house of the wise woman Biddy Early and the lake into which the priest threw her magic bottle. No one likes to pass here after dark, for fear of her ghost. A couple of miles further and Paddy is on the Ennis Road, heading towards Bodyke. In a few minutes he arrives in at Mikey Donoghue's.

The O'Donoghues were neighbours of the Cannys until 1927, when they moved to a farm among the lush pastures of the former Ballynahinch Estate. The neighbourly connections, and the musical connections, persist. And so Paddy Canny arrives each autumn to help the O'Donoghues at the potato harvest. For Mikey's son Paddy—the same boy who carries 'The B' Moroney's gramophone up over Ballycroum when he's visiting his grandmother in Magherabaun—the days and nights when Paddy Canny comes are pure magic.

Now that the link between playing music and dancing the sets in kitchens and barns has broken, almost all the musicians around Glendree have put away their instruments. But there is always music in the O'Donoghue household. Mikey was renowned as a concertina player until he let his instrument fall apart. After biking it down from Glendree each morning to rebuild the house in Ballynahinch—it was only a ruin, with no door, no windows, nothing—and then getting married and the children starting to arrive and all the work of establishing a farm, there was no time for playing music.

But the music wouldn't let go of Mikey, and within a few years he took up the fiddle. There are plenty of fiddle players around Ballynahinch—Martin Rochford and Mike Doyle and Jimmy Long among them—and they get together to share their music at Donoghue's, for nothing makes Mikey happier than a few tunes of music in the house. Listening to one another play, they might discuss how well a roll goes on a certain note, or whether you're changing the tune too much to take a certain phrase in a new direction. Mikey's father, Mick, had been one of Paddy Mac's fiddle students and had brought him along to the lessons when he was just a small boy. After Paddy Mac came and Glendree was alive with music and dancing, you would think nothing of seeing forty people at a dance platform after Mass. Now, you could walk from Canny's down to Maghera on a Sunday evening and meet nobody on the road. So many young people have left and, with them, the music and dancing. But the misty

> Now, you could walk from Canny's down to Maghera on a Sunday evening and meet nobody on the road. So many young people have left and, with them, the music and dancing. But the misty lakes and soft drumlin hills of Ballynahinch are brimful of music.

lakes and soft, drumlin hills of Ballynahinch are brimful of music.

When Paddy Canny comes to help dig the spuds, he might stay a week or he might stay two, working alongside Mikey, the one with shoulders that could lift a cow from the ditch, the other a tiny little man, but tough. The O'Donoghue children idolise Paddy. They laugh in delight when he catches a bag of spuds or a sack of flour in his teeth and walks it around the kitchen. In the evenings, when the house is full and Paddy playing his heart out, the children sit, spellbound, listening and learning. Over the years, they will all become musicians: Paddy on flute and uilleann pipes, Tommy on accordion and drums, Jim an artist on the Clarke whistle, Mary on fiddle and Bridget a singer like her mother. But, for now, it is Mikey who will jump out of bed in the middle of the night and fetch his fiddle because he has suddenly remembered the turn of a tune.

Now that musicians are becoming liberated from the need always to keep the rhythm hard and strong for dancing, their music runs into longer phrases, with complex variations in rhythm and melody. Mikey maintains that the bare note is poor, that what makes the tune is the cutting and rolling and putting in tribberties: his name for trebles, where three quaver notes on the same pitch take the place of two, making a little bump, or stutter, in the tune. One of the O'Donoghues' neighbours in Ballynahinch is Martin Rochford. Although a sweet fiddle player, who Paddy knows from dances at Ayle, midway between Glendree and Ballynahinch, it is the uilleann pipes that become Martin's great love, from the moment he first hears a piper in the summer of 1936. The following year, he meets Johnny Doran, who might be the greatest of the Travelling pipers, and on his advice buys a

Facing page: **Paddy Fahey tune**

Paddy Fahey plays one of his many untitled compositions with delicacy and precision, using very light staccato notes between legato bows joining two, three and sometimes four notes to bring out the nuances of the melody. The A part of the tune has a simple, symmetrical structure of repeated four-bar phrases made up of two bars rising followed by two bars falling. Where Fahey emphasises the beginning of each two-bar motif with a crotchet, however, Martin Rochford leans on long notes marking the end of the rising passage. Both fiddles are tuned about a semitone below concert pitch and play at a sedate pace (especially Fahey), compared to Paddy Canny, for example. On the recordings transcribed here, both musicians follow the tune with 'The Humours of Scariff', the A part of which has a similar melodic contour.

Paddy Fahey's tunes are notably 'busy', with few notes longer than a quaver, and have a melancholy feel induced by the sliding up to, and a little beyond, the high F, in the minorish dorian mode and the chromaticism of occasional F sharps and sharp Cs and Gs. In his interpretation, Martin's fiddling is neither precise nor delicate and, like Paddy Canny, he does not wander away from the basic key. On the other hand, he amplifies both Fahey's busyness and the tune's melancholy mood. In his hands, the tune has few resting places and he plays his long, legato rising variation at bar 5, an embellishment also typical of his piping, with an emotive surge in volume. Despite differences in their style and interpretation, Fahey and Rochford both conceive of music as related to feeling, to be appreciated by musicians and attentive listeners. Although adhering to the forms of Irish dance music, their music would be impossible to dance to ... and neither would worry about that.

> Now that musicians are becoming liberated from the need always to keep the rhythm hard and strong for dancing, their music runs into longer phrases, with complex variations in rhythm and melody.

'Paddy Fahey's'

Martin Rochford
(Peter Laban)

practice set of pipes for two pounds. As yet unencumbered by marriage and his farm inheritance, Martin is driving himself through the piper's painful apprenticeship when Seán Reid, a piper in Ennis, starts visiting him with tips and encouragement and trips to West Clare to meet Willie Clancy, another piper smitten by Doran's music.

In the spring, Johnny Doran halts his wagon at Ballynahinch on his circuit from Dublin to the coast of Clare and north to Donegal, following the keenest audiences for his music. Johnny plays at the Scariff Fair, at hurling matches and sports meetings, at horse fairs and the Galway Races, where men in fine suits throw five-pound notes into the hat. Musicians listen in wonder at the clear, ringing tone of his pipes and the precision in all his cutting and rolling and tribberties, despite the breakneck speed. Settled farming people need the Travellers, who earn their living by tinkering and horse dealing and music. But that doesn't mean they approve of their neighbours befriending them, as musicians often do. Not that musicians are quite respectable, either, even when they are good farmers from good families and keep regular hours a good bit of the time.

Playing together, Canny and Rochford share an intimate musical conversation. While Paddy's bow work draws out the inner nuances of a tune, Martin will explore alternative settings and endings. Both are intensely emotional players who play their best in this house, where the listeners give them an equally intense and educated attention. They do make an odd couple—the one quiet and sweet-tempered, the other garrulous and argumentative, his cursing and witty ripostes legendary and his tall tales provoking the local priest to ask whether Martin is thinking of turning professional as a liar. And yet Paddy and Martin remain lifelong friends.

The Threshing Mill

The roar of the steam engine erupts into the autumn morning. It has taken a good half hour to get that crackpot of a jennet to pull the machine between the stacks of corn. The two men dig shallow trenches to hold the wheels and at last the threshing mill sits snug. Billy Moloney fires up his steam engine and tugs the whistle, a call to arms for the men of the townland. They arrive with pitchforks and dogs and children, who gawp at the rumbling engine belching smoke, its long tongue of belt running to the threshing mill. Shaped like a square wagon, the huge contraption is painted pink, with red struts dividing it into rooms. Inside them, a mystery. The children don't have to be warned to stand back once the belt starts to turn the flywheel and the motor kicks in, transforming the pretty caravan into a rattling, roaring monster.

Sheaves of corn—oats, more often than wheat—have been saved in stooks and piled into stacks ready for the men to pitch onto the thresher's deck, where Moloney's thresherman stands ready. That man is Paddy Canny, his job the most dangerous on the field today, as he feeds a stream of sheaves into the maw of the machine. It is a rhythm of risk, taking up each sheaf, cutting its binding and shaking it loose, feeding it headfirst with an easy sweep—a shove could cost you an arm—into the rolling drum. All day long, through showers of rain and the wind frisking up dust, Paddy works steadily, his sturdy form unmoved by the machine's vibrations. He stands at the vortex of a noise so great, it can be heard three miles away. And not one sound with one rhythm but a cacophony: the interminable rumble of the steam engine, the hum of the belts whizzing over the flywheel, the raucous clank-clank as the mill shakes out straw, all out of step with the back and forth agitation of the riddles. Loudest in Paddy's ears is the thunder of the rotating drum before him as it swallows the corn and rips off its heads, thrusting them into the guts of the machine to be shaken until they surrender the grain. The drum's roar rises almost to a scream before falling to a growl, up and down, over and over, except when a bundle catches in its throat and it coughs and rattles in protest. The whole contraption jitterbugs about, but Billy Moloney has used his spirit level to check that the machine sits evenly on the ground. One big jolt from a poorly balanced mill and he could lose his thresherman. It has happened.

At one end of the mill, where a chute spits out a shower of straw, two sweating men fork it onto a growing stack. At the other end, grain spills into sacks, another pair of men hauling them away with a one, two, and up on the shoulders. As rats and mice desert the sinking corn stacks, squealing children and yapping dogs chase

> And not one sound with one rhythm but a cacophony: the interminable rumble of the steam engine, the hum of the belts whizzing over the flywheel, the raucous clank-clank as the mill shakes out straw, all out of step with the back and forth agitation of the riddles. Loudest in Paddy's ears is the thunder of the rotating drum before him as it swallows the corn and rips off its heads.

Threshing corn the old way
(David Lyons)

them. Cats crouch on standby. One little boy has a mouse by the tail and waves it gleefully aloft, until it bites his thumb. The child cries out, releases his catch, and the waiting terrier snaps its teeth.

For all but the largest properties, the year's grain can be threshed and bagged in a day. Where farms have just one small field of corn, the threshing might move three or four times before nightfall, each job finishing with a spread of tea and fluffy shop bread and jam made from summer fruits. Then the engine and the threshing mill and the whole carnival of donkeys and children and dogs moves on with the workforce of farmers and their lads.

At the end of the long day comes a special dinner the woman of the house has prepared with help from her neighbours, who have brought extra cups and perhaps a marriageable daughter to show off in her Sunday dress. When the washing and chopping and cooking are almost done, they set out trestle tables end on end and cover them with flour-bag cloths. They place a chair at each corner and lay planks between them to seat the crowd. The men feast on flitches of bacon, taken down from the ceiling and boiled with cabbage, and on the floury potatoes that are piled in mountains along the table, with mustard and HP sauce in the valleys between. At the end of the meal, the men still have an appetite for apple tarts and strong tea.

After the dinner, there is music and dancing on the wooden floor of the hayloft, where once the corn was threshed by hand over winter. Paddy travels without an instrument and, unless he's asked, won't even let on that he plays music. He never declines to play, either, and if there is a fiddle in the house, he plays it, and if there is only a whistle, he plays that. Tonight the fiddle hanging above the fire is taken down and presented to him. The woman of the house brings out her concertina and her son takes up a whistle. It is a long night, with work starting again at dawn, but Paddy is in his element, taking turns to play and to listen, hearing songs new to his ears, exhilarated by the atmosphere of celebration at this last communal gathering of the year.

The days of the meitheal are waning. Farmers might still lend out their sons to help neighbours bring home their turf and lift the potatoes, or for the big jobs in the spring, the ploughing and harrowing and sowing and planting. But the weeks of harvest no longer see groups of men and women come together to strip each farm in turn of its summer grasses, turning it and stooking it to dry, building field haycocks and hauling them to the farmyard, finishing with the big harvest dances. These days are gone now that there are machines to mow and turn the hay. But for the time being, before the combine harvester arrives to take over, the threshing machine, which calls for a workforce of a dozen men or more, reinstates the meitheal. Perhaps this accounts for the good humour that is part of the threshing.

Paddy threshes for Billy Moloney at the end of September and through October, all the way out to Gort and back along the top of Ballinruan. At some places they are mad for music and in other places there is no music at all. At some places they let the men sleep in the house and at other places they are put up in the hay barn, in clothes dusty or rain-sodden, for the threshing continues in the open air, in any weather. Or nearly any weather.

Rooney

Everyone calls him Rooney and, like Mickey Rooney, whose films feature almost every week at the cinema in Feakle, he seems always to be in some kind of a scrape.

No sooner has Paddy Canny got that cranky old donkey to line up the threshing machine; no sooner has Billy Moloney started up the engine and the men of the townland have poured into the field, than the rain comes driving down. Like a curtain, it shuts out the morning and any possibility of threshing corn. The men shift the threshing mill from the haggard into the farmyard, where it won't become bogged, and that's it for the day's work. The trio are not devastated. Billy will get paid just the same for the hire of his machines and can sit by the fire enjoying his breakfast. The donkey is out in the barn chewing corn like it's Christmas. And Paddy Canny? Paddy's day of rest brings him Rooney.

Paddy has heard of Rooney Moroney, a flute player taught by the famous Mickie Cooleen. By all reports he is a big fellow, over six foot tall and strong, very strong, a great asset in a neighbour. And a very good musician. He is related to just about everyone around Drumindoora and he doesn't give two hoots what any of them think of him. They seem to think a lot of things. Just last night, one of his neighbours was scoffing at Rooney's idea of farming.

'Rooney cares more for his music than he does for his farm,' he said, and the others nodded assent or shook their heads at such foolishness. All through April, when everyone was planting their spuds, Rooney would be bringing his flute into the garden and playing away without a care. It was the middle of May (the middle of May!) before he put down his spuds. The corncrake was already nesting in the fields, and you could hear it croaking, this man was saying, croaking at Rooney: 'Crack-crack, crack-crack! Too-late, too-late!'

That got a laugh. But Paddy was thinking, wasn't that the sort of thing he'd done himself: taking the fiddle out into the garden or hiding it inside a tram of hay, for the moment when a tune would come to him and he would have to play it? Musicians, Paddy knows already, are looked down on in many quarters. Long ago, all dance musicians were itinerants, a lowly, landless caste: strangers, who evoked distrust as well as fascination, for they could fuel riotous behaviour in otherwise steady men and women. And yet, last night, the same men who looked down on Rooney were only delighted to dance to music.

Mick Moroney is a wild man, they said, and loves his liquor. Everyone calls him Rooney and, like Mickey Rooney, whose films feature almost every week at the cinema in Feakle, he seems always to be in some kind of a scrape. One time the priest stormed into a house and ordered all the dancers out with the fear of hellhounds after them. Rooney hung back, for the half-barrel of porter had been tapped and he

'The Mills are Grinding'

'The Mills are Grinding'

When East Galway's Ballinakill Traditional Dance Players recorded this tune in 1931, they named it for the local flourmill. The tune is related to 'Paddy on the Turnpike' and 'The Bunch of Keys', but this version is local to north-east Clare and south-east Galway, where it is often called 'The Flowers of Limerick'. A comparison of Rooney's playing and the Ballinakill's shows him keeping the basic shape of the melody, but reimagining it as his own. His tune is less repetitive, the melody's range expanding at the beginning of each part, the turn flowing in longer phrases, little touches that are altogether lovely. Rooney played a Clarke's C whistle.

was concerned it should not go to waste. The farmer who met him stumbling home the following noon told that story.

'I was out mending a wall,' he said, 'And didn't Rooney sit beside me and play music for me? That's all he's good for, playing music.' Paddy's ears had pricked up again. He has that same hunger to play music and yet he knows that playing music can't be all he is good for.

Once the meitheal has broken up for the day—gone home to build their Arks, perhaps—Paddy scarcely waits to drink his tea before heading out through the downpour. Cap down, collar up, borrowed whistle inside his jacket, he arrives at Rooney's door. There he finds a man like none he has ever met, who welcomes Paddy as if he were an old friend, expected right at this moment. No sooner has Rooney said 'God bless you' and brought Paddy inside than the pair are sitting at the hearth breathing life into their instruments. The day is scarcely long enough to play all the tunes they both know and for Rooney to play tune after lovely tune that Paddy has never heard. And talk. The big man, it turns out, is no priest-defying rogue, but as placid and easy-going as you please, as good at talking as he is at playing his flute.

Rooney tells Paddy about the time long ago when he would go out in all weathers to lie up in the ditch outside Johnnie Allen's house—Johnnie, who'd gone all quare after O'Neill sent him 'The Book' with his name in it and wouldn't share the tunes he had got from it. The sound of the fiddle came up out of his chimney and into the ears of Rooney, who stole those tunes away. Out of the chimney and away into Rooney's penny whistle, the Clarke's C, which is called a flute.

Rooney has opinions about music and musicians and Paddy is eager to hear them. Rooney remembers where he got all the different settings of a tune and why a fiddler might end it one way and a fluter another and where one player might add in a little flavouring of his own. This he does himself, not putting in extra notes, but shifting them around a small bit so that the tune sounds fresh. All of his music sounds sweet to Paddy's ears, but when Rooney plays Pat Canny's tunes with notes that aren't the correct ones, the ones his father got from Blind Paddy Mac, it troubles Paddy.

Rooney has his own troubles with musicians who would 'boil the music', putting in so much extra that the rhythm driving the tune gets lost in the crowd of notes. This opinion gives Paddy pause, too, because isn't he doing just that, embroidering the tune the way he has heard it on gramophone records? Paddy puts aside that doubt, because he is nineteen years old and in love. With Michael Coleman.

His Master's Voice

Paddy Canny would not be the first lad to throw himself into the fire of obsession, not even the first in his own family. Hadn't his brother Jack spent years working at his cycling: first the sprint and then the road races, tinkering with his bikes and chasing himself up and down the rough roads and riding across the country to compete, until he became an All-Ireland Champion? And before that, hadn't their father found a fiddle teacher and coaxed from him every tune he had, with the zeal of one newly converted? Pat Canny's venture had brought people together, first the group of fiddle pupils and then the dancers they played for. Paddy's is a personal quest. His Dad always said he was good and now Paddy has a model for how good he might get.

Michael Coleman's recordings have fallen like a meteor into Paddy's world, their brilliance illuminating the music in ways he could not have imagined and at that stage of life when the mind has the audacity to grasp at the unknown. Although Paddy learns tunes and techniques from every record he gets to hear, it is Coleman's music that most enthrals him. At first, it seems strange, to be listening so intently to this ghostly presence, coming from America, where an Irish lad might become a star. But, without an actual musician in the room, Paddy has no qualms about interrogating Coleman's playing over hours of intense listening, whenever he gets the chance. Michael Coleman becomes his teacher.

The first thing that stuns Paddy is the way Coleman changes the tune, not just between the first and second or third times he plays it, but all the way through. Everything changes. Paddy gets the dizzying sense that the possible combinations of bowing patterns and ornaments and variations on the melody might be boundless. It takes the floor out from under him. He had always been certain that the tune that was given you, or that you took from another musician, was the tune. And if someone played the melody differently, either they were wrong or it was a different setting from somewhere far away. Now, the tune begins to shimmer. The melody might go this way, or that way, or somewhere else. How would you know the limits of this uncertain world without falling off the edge?

Then there are the many ways Coleman embellishes the tunes. All his life, Paddy has followed his father and other older musicians, with no instruction about how to hold the bow, let alone how to get these special effects. Pat Canny had shown him rolls and cuts and Paddy had watched and listened and copied until he heard *Tá sé agat!*: 'You have it!' From Martin Nugent, he had learned the different places you could put in those rolls and how a longer bow could produce a sweeter tone.

> Michael Coleman's recordings have fallen like a meteor into Paddy's world, their brilliance illuminating the music in ways he could not have imagined and at that stage of life when the mind has the audacity to grasp at the unknown.

To milk every last drop of Coleman's genius, Paddy has to listen in a new way and has to be his own judge of whether or not he has it right.

Until now, a tune simply transferred itself into his memory after a couple of hearings. Then he would take up the fiddle and bring out the tune in whatever key he chose. On the record, there is so much more to listen for that Paddy's listening is reduced to fleeting fragments: to phrases and notes and the notes between notes. He listens especially hard to work out the little stuttering notes Coleman puts in so often—sometimes on the same note, sometimes a run of three notes, sometimes jumping up and back—tiny little notes that you can scarcely hear.

Paddy is mesmerised by Coleman's bowing: the way it reveals the contours of a tune, dividing or slurring together notes so that some stand out and others draw back—and then changing that pattern the next time he plays it through, as though telling the same story in different voices. The years Paddy has spent with Martin Nugent have taught him that in fiddle playing, the bow is everything. It is not something you can pick up simply by watching another fiddler; you have to listen to the sound they get and work out how to reproduce it. He learns to soften his hand so that he can change the direction of his bow quickly and smoothly.

Listening to Michael Coleman is both thrilling and exhausting in what it demands of Paddy and it is only in retrospect that he appreciates how much he has learned. In the process of disciplining his fingers and bow arm to master all these complexities, he has developed a whole array of ornaments and ways of phrasing a melody and the bowing patterns that bring them out. These now form a menu from which he can select to polish any tune. Eventually, Paddy's listening expands outwards again so that he can immerse himself in the sound of the whole tune, as he had on that first day at Mrs Hennessey's. It is as if, having bent close to the gorse to take in the flower's sweet scent and note the way its petals form a bonnet framing a little face, he stands back to take in the glory of the whole golden hillside.

Eventually, Paddy finds he is able to achieve stylistic and technical feats unimaginable to his father's generation. And, sometimes, when he brings the fiddle with him and plays along with the record, keeping the same time and the same notes and almost the same bowing, for the space of three minutes, he might almost be Michael Coleman.

'Ballinasloe Fair'

'Ballinasloe Fair'

Ciarán Mac Mathúna (1925–2009) made this recording in Crusheen, thirteen miles west of Glendree, in January 1955, when he was starting out with Radio Éireann's Mobile Recording Unit. It is believed to be the earliest available solo recording of Paddy Canny, who at this time was still strongly influenced by Michael Coleman's repertoire, technique, tempo and interpretations. On the other hand, Paddy's rhythm is smoother than Coleman's syncopated bounce and typical of his area, although also a little uneven, for one aspect of Paddy's expressiveness is an occasional change of pace. In accordance with local taste, Paddy makes fewer melodic and rhythmic variations than Coleman. And where Coleman plays an uplifting eight-bar variation to the second part only as a kind of coda to the whole track (see p. 35). Paddy is inspired to play it every time. Where Coleman habitually begins his finger triplets (represented as two semiquavers followed by a quaver) on a down-bow, as most northern fiddlers do, Paddy Canny prefers to start with an up-bow, like most fiddlers in the southern counties. The effect is lighter: a delicate, unobtrusive staccato. Where Coleman increases volume only in the final 'coda' variation, Paddy increases volume at the highest point of the melody and accents the lowest points by lightly touching the open string below, giving a subtle drone effect (represented here by notes with smaller heads and without stems).

No Better Boy   61

Under the Bridge

As it barrels down, the sup chums look for shelter before tackling the road up to Glendree. Under the bridge, where the stream divides the townlands of Feakle and Baurroe, there is just enough room to crawl in together.

Going down to the fair in the dark of the morning, making the deal and bringing home the money—that is Pat Canny's job. This morning, Paddy goes with him, flourishing his stick to keep the cattle moving along the three miles to Feakle—young animals which have never been on a road before, nor smelt such inviting pasture across the ditch. At the fair ground, Paddy listens as Pat Canny negotiates with the buyers. The first man is so amiable, he seems to have known his father all his life. An offer is made and rejected as though it is a simple courtesy between friends. Pat Canny tells his son that it is unwise to accept the first offer. Better to wait and see what the day will bring.

Pat Canny greets his friends as they pass by. Paddy minds the cattle. It seems like hours before the next buyer makes an offer. It is lower than the first, which shocks Paddy. A blocker, his father explains. They work with the dealers to drive down the prices, so their first offer will look better. Sure enough, the first man returns and repeats his deal. Pat Canny is friendly as can be, but declines. And then, it seems, the real business starts when another dealer offers a price that is not great, but fair enough. Pat Canny spits in his palm, there is a slap of hands and the deal is done, a coin returned to the dealer to bring them both luck.

When the cattle are loaded and driven away, Pat Canny heads off for a pint. Paddy's pocket jingles with the coins his father has given him. He takes a turn around the hawkers' standings. Is sixpence too much for a pair of rabbit snares? He decides to make them himself with a bit of old wire. Paddy falls in with some Glendree lads and they slosh through the muck to the pub, where Mrs Bohan is perfecting a row of pints and the dinners are coming out from the kitchen. As the afternoon turns into evening, they sink pint after pint in one long round.

Sooner than Paddy can believe, it is closing time. Outside Bohan's, the cold of the night and a shower of rain slap their faces. As it barrels down, the sup chums look for shelter before tackling the road up to Glendree. Under the bridge, where the stream divides the townlands of Feakle and Baurroe, there is just enough room to crawl in together.

Soon they are laughing about Master O'Connor at the Glendree School, how he never worked out why his scholars were so brilliant, every one of them completing their six sums a night and most times getting them right. As children they had formed a meitheal to copy and correct one another's homework before school. For the task, they had hidden a bottle of ink and a pen under the bridge below the school.

The bridge at Feakle

Paddy is in fine form, and when his turn for a story comes around he tells one from his brother's store. How Jack was walking home from a neighbour's house and there was this great big rock with a four-foot drop beneath it. They all know the one. In the dark, you could go right over the top without even knowing. And that is what Jack's companion did: right over the edge. And wasn't there a donkey standing below, taking shelter from the wind! The man fell right onto its back and it took off, braying like the hounds of hell were after it and the man on top crying, 'Help, help! The divil is running away with me!'

The lads laugh and bray like donkeys and screech, 'The divil is running away with me!' When they put upon Paddy to sing for them, it is a donkey song that comes to mind. As the rising stream laps their boots and the stones amplify Paddy's resonant bass, they all bellow the chorus:

Oh, a good old friend and a kind old pal was this old ass to me.
Many's the night he brought me home when I was on the spree.
Though he's highly bred, he's badly fed, since I don't own much grass,
He's a hare-um scare-um, a divil-may-care-um, a great big roaming ass.

Next morning, Paddy faces his mother's displeasure on top of his own sore head. The full reckoning comes on Sunday, when the priest denounces the young men carousing after the fair, who saw fit to be singing at a late hour of the night, disrupting the village and disturbing people's sleep. An affront to the whole Parish, it will not be tolerated! Paddy is mortified, too ashamed to show his face at Mass in Feakle for nearly two years. In the meantime, there are other churches in other parishes—to go without Confession, without the Host, is unthinkable—but how can Paddy make amends for the humiliation he has brought upon his family?

'The Great Big Roaming Ass'

Oh, to look at me would you e— ver think that I was in my prime? Me clothes are torn and my shoes are worn and my age is for— ty nine. Oh, too much time I've spent a— lone, but I like for to be at home. The on— ly one that I have now is a poor old, shook old one.

'The Great Big Roaming Ass'

Few people today have heard Paddy Canny's rich singing voice. He sang this song towards the end of a long night of music at Lena's bar in Feakle, around 1970. The crowd quietens somewhat to listen to this song about a small farmer's lonely bachelor life. Jim Brody, who played the tape for the author, had been reminiscing about Lena's and what a great spot it was for music and how he would go down there after Sunday Mass for a few tunes with Joe Bane and some others. When Paddy finishes the song and resumes playing the fiddle, the noise in the bar rises once more to a din. Jimmy was disgusted: 'What's wrong with people that they'll listen to someone singing and they won't listen to music?'

Gone

Around the Canny homestead there is no sound of whistling or of singing; no voice at all, only the wind whipping leaves from the apple trees and soft sounds from the garden as the earth gives up spuds to the two men working along the drills. No sound from inside the house, where Kate watches the pot for the dinner she will put down a half-hour from now. A widow of six weeks' standing, she feels herself an old woman now, sitting when she should be working, worrying about the future despite knowing there is no point in that.

There had been signs. Her husband tired out after a day's mowing in the meadow, knocked by a day in the bog. And then bringing in the hay. At seventy-four years of age, could he not have given his sons the toughest work? Mickie and Paddy are grown men now, as strong as—no, stronger than—their father. Like every man she has ever known, like her own father when he was sickening, her husband was loath to let go the reins, felt he had to take the lead in everything. And now …

He was taking up the hay and it was too much for him. The two lads were bringing it in and forking it up, and their father was above in the hay shed, taking back the hay, a hard job. He got weak and fell and they brought him down. The doctor said it was the heart. In bed for a week, he grew weaker, until the priest came and his breath went and then … gone.

The air in the room had contracted, then, making them aware of their own breathing as they knelt beside the bed. Paddy bolted from the house. Later they found him lying at the top of the quarry, his face turned to the earth, still crying. Kate knew he would take it hard, to lose the father who had given him the music and encouraged him always. 'No better boy', he would say, when Paddy struggled with his music. No better boy.

So lonesome after that.

Kathy the Governor's American Wake

John 'the Governor' McNamara is the district's authority on any subject that might be found in a newspaper or a book. That is how his daughter Kathy supposes he got the name, and the need to distinguish him from all the other McNamaras hereabouts. It is the Governor the district's farmers call on to settle their fireside disputes about the world beyond Magherabaun. At the same time, they think he would be better off farming his land than sitting around reading an old book. The farming life, however, is not his true calling. Nor Kathy's. Because she is the youngest and the pet, Kathy never had to join in the heavy work at harvest, only take out the bread and the tea. With older sisters to help in the house, she had more time to practise her dance steps and play the fiddle. The sisters were sent to Pat Canny for fiddle lessons—another sign of the Governor's eccentricity, for most girls are satisfied with a chance at the concertina or melodeon, instruments more suitable for females. The money for a fiddle is better spent on a son. But the Governor no longer has a son.

Returning from London on her way out to America, Kathy was looking forward to visiting her old fiddle teacher and his son. Before she left Magherabaun, Paddy had been working on tunes from the Coleman and Morrison records. She remembers him as a little boy, eavesdropping on her fiddle lessons. Such a precocious talent. Almost the first news she learns is that Pat Canny died at harvest time, only a few days before Paddy's twenty-first birthday. When Kathy visits the Canny household, she finds a desolate scene. Paddy barely raises his pale face to greet her. There will be no music in that house for a long time.

This is the mood in the autumn of 1940: worse news coming after bad. In London, the streams of Irish workers who had joined British defence works are now faced with rationing, air raid drills, eerie nights of blackout and then the relentless bombing. From the cellar of the hotel where Kathy worked, they could hear the nightly explosions, hear buildings crashing down, and in the morning go out on the street to see firemen dragging hoses up precarious ladders, craters where roads should be, women in shock pawing at mountains of brick. When they sent the children away to America, Kathy made up her mind to follow. She was on the boat from Liverpool to Dublin just as soon as she had bought her ticket on the last but one passenger ship to New York.

John the Governor is shocked that Kathy should think of leaving for America in these times. But none of her father's warnings deter Kathy, not even the five hundred merchant ships German U-boats have sunk this year on the Atlantic

> When Kathy visits the Canny household, she finds a desolate scene. Paddy barely raises his pale face to greet her. There will be no music in that house for a long time.

crossing. Not even the thought of her friend Katy Shea, whose parents still called her Baby. The telegram had arrived a whole month after she left Magherabaun: 'Katy dead, buried at sea'. Visiting Katy's parents, she sits for a minute on the bench outside their house, taking in the vastness of sky and the green fields sloping down the mountain and all the way across to Sliabh Bearnagh. She remembers two giddy girls sitting here, dreaming of departure, planning to make something of themselves.

The priest is accusing emigrants of deserting the family of Ireland, young women the worst offenders. The government is urging every citizen to work harder to keep the economy afloat. No one should abandon ship in the nation's time of need. Despite Ireland's neutrality, there are calls for all citizens to be 'ready', whatever that means. They call it The Emergency and there are shortages and rationing. In London, Kathy knew what shortages and rationing and emergency were about.

Nothing now will change her mind. In America, Kathy will meet her sisters, Della and Minda. She will make her living and choose her own husband and raise her family in a modern world. At home, that prospect does not exist. Elizabeth—or, rather, her husband—will inherit the farm. With no dowry, no land and a family tainted with her brother's consumption—the bad drop, they call it—what match could there be for Kathy? The life of a farm wife is not what she wants, anyway. Kathy will leave all that behind, as she did when she went to London. And this time, she will take her fiddle.

Kathy has said her farewells at every house up and down Magherabaun and Glendree, where she has rehearsed her memories and her plans. Little girls listened with envy and anxiety, the lads crestfallen to see one more girl leaving. Kathy realises that almost all her school friends have emigrated.

Afterwards, Kathy finds the details of her American Wake difficult to bring to mind. Everyone she knew would have come to the house. There would have been music and dancing and old songs and reminiscences. They would have left before dawn, in ones and twos, some in tears. What she does remember is Lisbeth waving at the gate, her father geeing up the horse as they left for the Limerick bus, the giddy sense that her old world was rushing away behind her. Not a word from her father, who was holding the reins. Then his wooden figure, turning for home. Over his shoulder, 'God be with you', and he was gone.

> Little girls listened with envy and anxiety, the lads crestfallen to see one more girl leaving. Kathy realises that almost all her school friends have emigrated.

Goodbye, Johnny Dear

Swallow's Travelling
Circus arrives in
Limerick, Johnny
moonlights with the
circus band, wins a
contract, buys his way
out of the army and
into the wonderful
world of circus.

In 1840 a boy who will create songs that the Irish cherish for generations is born at his father's roadside forge in Kilbarron, Feakle. Three years later, his parents die and their children are scattered among family connections. Johnny's good fortune is to be adopted by his uncle in the county town of Ennis, a relative haven in the coming years of the Great Famine.

After the Famine's devastation, visitors passing through rural Ireland find desolation and silence, where once there had been singing and dancing, fiddling and piping. The seasonal songs of work are gone, along with the clacháns, small communities that had subsisted on potatoes, until there were no potatoes. The pipes are silent, the itinerant pipers gone. The music and laughter of dancing boys and girls is silenced, for the surviving young have emigrated. Even the women's keening for the community's dead has been silenced. The countryside is empty and silent as the grave.

At fourteen, Johnny Patterson becomes a drummer boy in the British Army's Limerick regiment. Irish is Johnny's mother tongue but now he translates himself into English. For five years, quarantined from the surrounding desolation, he cultivates his musical talents, learning the soldiers' songs. And then he is ready. Swallow's Travelling Circus arrives in Limerick, Johnny moonlights with the circus band, wins a contract, buys his way out of the army and into the wonderful world of circus.

Not far along the road, Johnny volunteers a solo act and steps into the ring for the first time. His first joke reaches across the gap and the audience is with him. He sings a familiar old song and they join the chorus. Mr Swallow recognises a star and Johnny becomes 'The Irish Singing Clown'.

It is a family of sorts, a tribe that collaborates to create a world of illusion in towns around Ireland: raising the pole and the heavy tent, assembling the seats, setting up the ring, then transforming themselves into acrobats and rope-dancers. And there is that girl, Selena, dancing on horseback. Between one thrilling spectacle and the next, the clown keeps the ball rolling. Johnny creates an outfit embroidered with the harp and shamrock, in the colour of Ireland, of renewal and rebirth, the colour of the fairy world and the colour of American money.

Johnny finds that he can write his own songs. He recalls his childhood friends gathering to sing at 'the stone outside Dan Murphy's door' and his courtship of a Kerry girl, Bridget Donahue. In 'Goodbye, Johnny Dear', he conjures the plaintive voice of a mother losing her son to emigration, projecting his own longing for such a mother's love.

By the time he turns thirty, Johnny has married the bareback rider, Selena, and they are touring in England with the first of their three children in tow. A talent scout from the great American circus, Cooper and Bailey's, offers him a one-year contract. Selena continues her circus career and the children go to his sister in Killaloe. Johnny sails to America, first class.

By 1876, the Irish population in America has exploded and so has the popularity of circuses. Johnny is a perfect fit. It is not surprising that the Famine immigrants, now middle-aged, are drawn to songs of longing for mother Ireland. In truth, few have a home to return to or a means of getting there. Johnny's songs are a consolation and there is a chorus everyone can sing. His songs mirror a population assimilating to American ways, but proud of being Irish and resentful of crudely

comic stage characters. Johnny sings out of his own experience as an itinerant worker, a suitor, an emigrant, a father.

It is as a father that Johnny is undone. At the zenith of his career, at forty years of age, his younger daughter is killed in a circus accident in England. It blackens Johnny's life and drives him into the bottle. The inconsolable loss that was shrouded within the orphan child erupts so violently that it cannot be turned inside out and put to music. Johnny drinks to that.

Johnny Patterson has become one of America's most celebrated and well-paid entertainers of his time. But he wants to go home. Back in Ireland, he buys a house in Belfast and reassembles his little family before taking to the road again. He is still a celebrity here, but Ireland's culture has changed radically. The Catholic Church prevails, with a new emphasis on piety and respectability. The indigenous culture of his youth, and the language that gave it voice, are almost extinguished. While Johnny is on tour, Selena dies of tuberculosis and the

'Goodbye, Johnny Dear'

Johnny Patterson

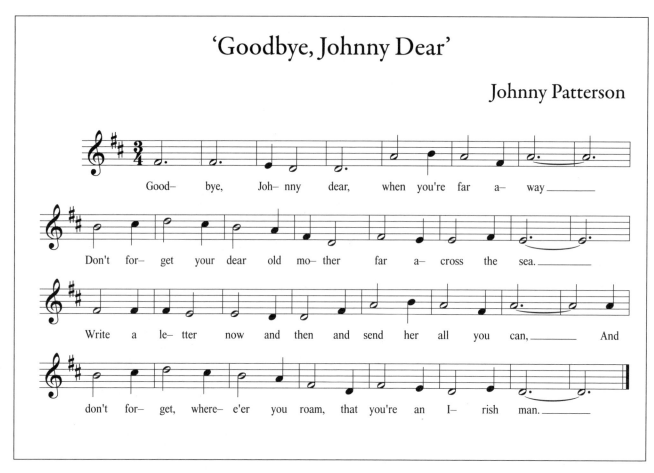

children are returned to Killaloe. Johnny has lost those he loved, time and again. He drinks to that.

Circus performers are outsiders, adored on the stage, shunned in society. But they are rarely rebels. A supporter of Parnell's drive to reinstate Ireland's national parliament, Johnny proudly wears the harp and shamrock and refuses a request to add the Union Jack. Following Belfast riots between loyalists and nationalists, Johnny writes a song advocating unity and understanding. Ireland is not ready for such sentiments. Touring County Kerry, where nationalist politics and agitation for land are on the boil, he sews a crown beside his harp and shamrocks. At Tralee, 'Do Your Best for One Another' is the death of him. In the fight his song prompts, an iron bar fells him.

In his songs, Johnny Patterson embraced mothers' love, dancing, kindly uncles and warming turf fires. When news of his death reaches his circus mid-show, the audience kneels in his honour while the band plays his lonesome song.

> Just twenty years ago today, I grasped my mother's hand,
> She kissed and blessed her only son, going to a foreign land;
> The neighbours took me from her breast and told her I must go,
> But I could hear my mother's voice, though her words were faint and low.

Spring

Winter is black as ice, bleak as the Arctic wind tearing down from the bogs. The family at Curraun is diminished, the circle of their nightly Rosary closing around the gap that is not spoken of. Jack is home at Christmas and then gone again to his life in England, where he has left the terror of the London Blitz for a market garden in Somerset that looks out across the sea. He is building a greenhouse there, settling down.

The world at Curraun never stops changing. The wind blows, the apples fall, the pig is killed, the whitethorn turns from stick to leaf as if in a day. The place is alive, but the life has gone out of Paddy, who is downcast and distant. The work takes over, as it always must. He and Mickie whitewash the house and inside the dairy, mixing the lime in a bucket of water and slapping it on with wide brushes. Paddy takes no pleasure in the transformation of each wall from grey to dazzling white as the lime dries. All through the day, he goes at it hard, seeking exhaustion. He shadows himself, scarcely noticing his brother, head down and silent, or his mother, thin as a rail.

Paddy has returned to the church at Feakle. Besides accompanying his mother and brother to early Mass on Sundays, he is at first Fridays and first Saturdays every month. Every time there is a Mass in Feakle, Paddy will be there, and every night he has his prayer time. Paddy also knows the comfort of dogs and cows and horses: warm animals that know nothing of human troubles, but sense the trouble in him. The house reverberates with the lack of music. Paddy has barricaded his mind against it.

The spring of 1941 is brilliant. Morning mists rise before bright, clear days that sharpen the green haze of new leaf. Paddy scarcely hears the birds going mad in the hedges.

He scarcely hears the brindle heifer's bellows until Mickie calls him to the barn. She is frightened and exhausted from straining to birth her first calf. The nose is out, and the forelegs—a good sign—but she seems too weak to continue her labour. The brothers work together, reproducing their father's soothing voice and gestures. With ropes fixed to the calf's dangling fetlocks, they pull steadily, not too hard, matching the cow's contractions, resting when she rests, until chest, then shoulders, then the whole sack of new life slithers out.

Winter is black as ice, bleak as the Arctic wind tearing down from the bogs. The family at Curraun is diminished, the circle of their nightly Rosary closing around the gap that is not spoken of.

Plans

Plans. Paddy clenches at the thought. Without their Dad, how can they make plans? That would be leaving him out, leaving him behind, when plans are always his to make. Paddy cannot face a future without his father, the one who understands when no one else does. Understood.

Kate Canny is determined that her sons will succeed in life. That means each must get his own farm of good land. Curraun is Mickie's now and he will inherit his uncle Michael Canny's farm in Ballyglass near Quin, where he worked in the summer as a teenager. But where would Paddy get land? They put their heads together, the three of them, and come up with a plan. Kate manages it so that each of her sons gets a fair deal and Paddy will not have to emigrate or work as an unpaid labourer, like most youngest sons. The past decade has been punishing, just to keep their heads above water. Now they will have to work even harder. For land, you need money.

They can rely on Jack to keep sending a few bob until the time comes when he marries. But there is little money coming out of this farm, which produces scarcely enough to feed the three of them, let alone a new family when Mickie should marry. The brothers will work together, Mickie the farmer and Paddy his helper. When money comes in, Mickie will divide it equally between two savings accounts, each holding a future.

They exploit every resource they have. First, the quarry. They keep the contract with the Clare County Council to maintain the stretch of road between Glendree and Maghera. They dig out the dykes so that the roads don't flood. They excavate stone and haul it to the roadside. A mile from here, a century ago, starving families built the Famine Road from Feakle to Glendree. Seven miles long, the only straight road in the parish. Now, the brothers do the same, smashing the rock with hammers, pounding it into road metal. After that jarring work, it is a wonder Paddy is ever able to play music. In the winter, the brothers fill potholes with the crushed stone and spread it along the road, where the iron rims of passing carts press it into the roadbed.

Like every family in the district, they have turbary rights to a stretch of the Glendree Bog. They win another contract, to supply turf for the County Council. After they finish harrowing the garden and planting the spuds, Mickie and Paddy cut turf, many times more than is needed to keep their own fire burning. Every year they take up hay knives and open the bank a few feet more. And then another few feet. One brother slices the sods and tosses them off the sleán to the other, who

The brothers are like a team of horses pulling together, each knowing the exact weight of the other's strength, the light and shadow of their mood.

East Clare, 1940s

spreads them in rows. Then they swap. After weeks of cutting and spreading and turning, they build a forest of footings to dry in the wind, before building stacks and thatching them against rain. At the end of summer, they bring it down off the mountain. It takes three or four donkeys to carry the turf in baskets—donkeys that will take off in all directions, anywhere but the path down to the bend in the road, where the County Council lorry will collect it.

Years ago, Pat Canny and Kate bought a few fields of land down towards Tulla. The Rampeens, they call it. Now that the Economic War with Britain is over and the market has opened up again, they graze dry cattle there. And the farmers thereabouts are amazed to see Paddy and Mickie out foddering those cattle, each of the brothers carrying on his back bearts of hay as big as haycocks, bigger than the men themselves, so that anyone watching—and neighbourly eyes always are—would see two whole trams of hay heading up the hill, such is the strength of them. The brothers are like a team of horses pulling together, each knowing the exact weight of the other's strength, the light and shadow of their mood. And, at an age when many have given up the ghost after a lifetime's slog, dawn until bedtime, Kate Canny continues to work.

The Cuckoo

The whole country is alive again, the hillsides brightened by blackthorn and gorse, the hedges by hawthorn and cow parsley. Wildflowers are bursting out among the brambles and elegantly unfurling bracken. At last, Paddy visits PJoe one Sunday evening. He doesn't take the fiddle, for he has no desire to play, and even to think about it draws him back into a deep emptiness. But when PJoe presses his own fiddle on him Paddy finds that he can do it.

PJoe's Aunt Delia has promised to send a gramophone from America, but there is no shipping it now, because of the German submarines all across the Atlantic. In the meantime, Paddy and PJoe resume their visits to Mrs Hennessey or to any house where they can listen to the gramophone. They are hungry for every morsel they can glean from the records.

The two friends learn to block out the piano accompaniment, which often gets left behind. When Paddy hears recordings by James Morrison and Hugh Gillespie, the guitar backing beguiles him: light strumming that does not overwhelm the fiddle, with syncopated rhythms and strangely percussive chords seasoned with the smoky swing of jazz. Paddy cannot get 'Dick Cosgrove's', a reel Gillespie plays, out of his mind. A restless, moody tune, with the guitar pecking on the beat and striking the chord on the off beat, exactly in time with the fiddler. What is more, Gillespie's fiddle is tuned a mellow semitone below concert pitch, the tuning Paddy and his friends prefer.

> If he is to rise to the altitude where Michael Coleman's cuckoo sings, Paddy must learn how to move his fingers higher up the fingerboard, where no fiddler he knows has ever gone.

Facing page: **'Murray's Fancy'**
Young Michael Coleman was a dancer, as good at step dancing as he was on the fiddle. Slightly built and agile, he could jump like a young deer. As a teenager, he won medals for it, his trousers so tight they were an attraction in themselves. In 'Murray's Fancy', Coleman dances around the fiddle with seemingly effortless facility. He plays the tune four times, each time somewhat differently, especially in its second half (where the cuckoo calls, indicated here by ⬤), in which he plays elaborate variations high up on the fingerboard at a pace much faster than most fiddlers, let alone dancers, could cope with. But this is not music for dancing. It is a virtuosic display reminiscent of pipers' extravagant variations in the programmatic composition, 'The Fox Chase', and similar to the classical 'air and variations' form. Indeed, Michael Coleman's wide-ranging musical interests included classical music concerts and an acquaintance with the violinist Fritz Kreisler.

'Murray's Fancy'

Michael Coleman, 1921

Coleman's final variation on the second part

The first time they hear the hornpipe Michael Coleman calls 'Murray's Fancy', they are flabbergasted. There's a cuckoo in it! From that day on, Paddy pursues this hornpipe, along with his renewed ambition to play as well as Coleman. The label on the record tells Paddy it was recorded in 1921, twenty years ago. Michael Coleman is already a man of the past, living out his years in a two-room basement apartment in New York. But in Paddy's ears, Coleman's music is eternally fresh. In 'The Cuckoo' hornpipe, as Paddy calls it, Coleman plays breathtaking passages where so many notes, slurred together in triplets, cascade like a waterfall. The second part goes impossibly high, the little cuckoo peeping out of it, like a cuckoo in the bushes, which can be heard but not seen.

If he is to rise to the altitude where Michael Coleman's cuckoo sings, Paddy must learn how to move his fingers higher up the fingerboard, where no fiddler he knows has ever gone. There is no one he can ask how to do this. At first, he tries simply stretching out his left hand, which is easily large enough, but it is awkward then to find the notes that follow. Soon he gets the knack of moving his whole hand up, just a little way, and discovers that the cuckoo sings much more clearly there.

Returning to the tune over and again, Paddy hears new pathways through the melody, new patterns in the rhythm. He works out ways to bring out those patterns with his bow and with finger ornaments. In the past few years, Paddy has developed skills that help him, not only to reproduce the sounds that Michael Coleman makes, but also to convey the nuances his inner ear has recognised in the music, to the point where the fingers on the bow and those on the fingerboard respond directly to this inner music, without conscious direction. This is flow.

Getting a Band Together

The World War is over, and Ireland's Emergency, but the youth of Tulla parish are leaving the district at an alarming rate, sometimes two or three in the same family going off. There are no jobs for them here in Ireland. Not that Paddy Canny and PJoe Hayes are thinking of leaving the farms where their families need them. At some time in the future, PJoe will inherit a good farm at Maghera, while Paddy is committed to the family project of acquiring better land. So they continue to work, the tunes playing in their heads matching the rhythm of their boots on the muddy ground. For in February 1947, the weather is so bad it is almost impossible to get the ploughing done.

The lads get themselves and their fiddles together as often as they can. There is very little dancing going on where they are. Any girls who haven't emigrated would much prefer the Astor Ballroom in Scariff, or the dance halls in Gort and Ennis, where the big bands play waltzes and foxtrots and the musicians are got up in dinner suits with starched shirts and dickie bows. Not the sort of thing Paddy and PJoe can see themselves wearing.

A few years ago, Paddy joined Martin Rochford's Ballinahinch Céilí Band. Martin had wanted the same blend of fiddles, flutes and piano as the Ballinakill Céilí Band from East Galway, which he had heard on the radio. A few of Martin's neighbours were in the group and his friend Mr Reid came out from Ennis to play the piano. As Martin had no interest in playing for dancers, they performed only at a handful of local concerts. Between the kettle drum and the big bass drum Martin got out of the local fife and drum band, they could scarcely hear themselves play half the time.

Most of the musicians Paddy and PJoe played with at house dances have put away their instruments. But some of the music houses have kept on, and that is where Paddy most enjoys playing—where people will listen to the music and value what he gives them. O'Connor's is one of those houses. They are mad for music there—Danny Connors and his brother Ciarán, and the mother—stone mad for music. As often as he is invited, Paddy goes to them at Cragroe, down past Drumcharley church, for a night of music. Sometimes Teresa Tubridy, the schoolteacher's daughter in Tulla, will invite them to her house. Teresa gets on the piano, Danny sings a few songs, then Paddy takes out the fiddle and Jim O'Donoghue his flute and they have the great old crack.

On one of those evenings, Teresa has a proposal for them. Her sister Maureen Commins is a music teacher in Limerick, where she has been involved in setting up

PJoe and Paddy continue to work, the tunes playing in their heads matching the rhythm of their boots on the muddy ground. For in February 1947, the weather is so bad it is almost impossible to get the ploughing done.

Tulla Céilí Band at the Oireachtas, 1947 (l to r: P. J. Hayes, Francie Donnellan, Paddy Canny, Seán Reid, Jack Murphy, Jim O'Donoghue, Willie Clancy. Front: Paddy O'Donoghue)

the Féile Luimnigh festival of music and dance and drama. There is to be a competition for céilí bands and, with only a few weeks to go, she is worried they won't have enough competitors. Maureen asked Teresa if she could bring down some sort of a band. What do they think? The lads are interested and suggest bringing in Garda Bert McNulty, a good man on the fiddle.

'I'm in!' says Bertie, when they ask. 'And I can get you Aggie Whyte.'

Before he transferred to Tulla, McNulty was stationed in Ballinakill, a part of East Galway where everyone seems to play music. Aggie Whyte has been with the Ballinakill band since she was a schoolgirl, making recordings with them and playing on the radio. There is crystal clarity in each note she plays and of course she has all the Ballinakill's great tunes. Aggie is in. Jim Donoghue says he can get a neighbour of his, Jack Murphy, who plays the flute and plays it well. Now they have their band.

'I've another one that I have to bring in, and that's PJoe Hayes,' Paddy Canny pipes up. 'We play good together, and he has all the tunes that I have.'

Paddy should have spoken earlier.

'We'll have to leave him out, because we already have three fiddles and we wouldn't be able to keep four fiddles in tune.'

'We'll keep them in tune, all right,' says Paddy. Besides, there's no better band than the Ballinakill and aren't they thick with fiddles? So Teresa sends Danny Connors up to Maghera. And now the band is formed: four fiddles, two flutes, and the piano.

Their first rehearsal is in the Tulla Courthouse, but something is missing—apart from some warmth. There is the feeling that, these days, a céilí band might need an accordion. Teresa says that the bands at all the big céilís have them and it would put a bit of body into their music. None of the others has even heard an accordion. There are no accordion players around Tulla, anyway. John Minogue, who works for his aunt Nano at the Commercial Hotel across from the courthouse, knows of a Joe Cooley from Peterswell, near Gort, who played at his father's house one night. A mighty box player, John says.

'We'll look for Cooley, so.'

Jim Donoghue and Danny Connors cycle over the mountain and into East Galway, where they locate Joe Cooley, busy ploughing on Lahiff's estate. That is heavy work for horse and man in the wettest February Joe can remember (although he is only twenty-one). Joe finishes the job and comes down to O'Connors, where they keep him for the week before the competition, thrilled to have such music in the house.

The band practises in the hotel, where Nano has given them the upstairs room with the piano. Teresa can play the kind of vamping accompaniment they have all heard on the American recordings. She keeps strict time and understands how to match her chords with each shift in the tune's melody. Just as well, because this is a new experience for the other musicians. None of them has even competed at a feis.

Teresa has the application sent in under the name 'St Patrick's Amateur Band', since their event falls in the week of St Patrick's Day. With so many tunes in common, the musicians soon have them shuffled into sets that sound well together. They practise those sets until everyone is playing the same notes almost, changing smoothly from one tune to the next and finishing with a full stop. At Féile Luimnigh they win the competition, hands down.

Mr Reid

Paddy and PJoe
have scarcely
rehearsed their story
before Mr Reid's eyes
are shining at the
prospect of nurturing
a group of first-rate
musicians. Already, he
sees this as a way to
raise the standard and
the reputation
of traditional music
in the county.
In the country!

The band—now the Tulla Céilí Band—is moving ahead. They played their first dance at the Scariff Marquee last summer—nine till three in the big tent, dancers rowdy from the sports field and the pub and the carnival booths—and took home twelve shillings and ten pence each. But with céilí dancing at only one in fifty dances around the county, they have had to hold their own fundraising dance. Aggie is sticking with the Ballinakill band and Bert is busy with work and now Teresa Tubridy is heading to England. They need to find another pianist and manager.

The O'Donoghues, Jim and Paddy, recommend Mr Seán Reid, a gentleman with a top job in the Clare County Council's Engineering Department. He plays piano and fiddle, but his passion is for uilleann piping and not only for his own playing—a lifelong project, as any piper will tell you—but as matchmaker and sponsor to pipers everywhere. In Dublin, after his graduation in Belfast, Mr Reid took up the pipes and then threw himself into reviving the piper's club there. He would save the art of piping in Ireland, if he could, and the whole of traditional music, which he can see is heading for extinction, the same as the country-house dances that had nurtured it. He envisages a time when every household in Ireland has a musical instrument and someone playing traditional music on it.

But would he be interested in their little band? To find out, Paddy Canny and PJoe Hayes cycle through the rain to the Reid house in Ennis. A man of forty years opens the door, his wispy hair already receding from a bulging forehead, his manner unassuming and sympathetic.

'Come in, come in!' he urges. 'You're very welcome.'

The lads add their wet-woolly smell to the vapours of varnish and rosin in the crowded front room and stand awkwardly while Mr Reid empties chairs of their cargo of books. So many books! Mrs Reid brings tea and sweet cake, carefully placing the tray on the work table, between a gutted fiddle and a practice set of pipes similar to the one he has lent Paddy Donoghue.

Never one to forget good music, Mr Reid recalls their performance at Féile Luimnigh almost two years ago. Paddy and PJoe have scarcely rehearsed their story before Mr Reid's eyes are shining at the prospect of nurturing a group of first-rate musicians. Already, he sees this as a way to raise the standard and the reputation of traditional music in the county. In the country!

Mr Reid is a driven man. Taking neither tobacco nor drink, he works all day for the County Council and in the evening trains at the boxing studio or with the cross-country running club he started. Sometimes, he will arrive home from work only to leave ten minutes later to transport his band to a dance that will keep him out all night. It is no wonder his colleagues at the County Council find him a little absent-minded. Other evenings he will spend in his front room, among the stacks of books about music and Ireland—all of which he has read—playing music or teaching or mending instruments. Such *grá* has he for the music that, listening to a record, he will close his eyes and vanish into it. He will drink neither tea nor coffee, will not even butter his brown bread, but would feed the country from Mrs Reid's kitchen, along with the growing brood of young Reids. The county's musicians revere him.

Mr Reid's energy and dedication galvanise the young men of the Tulla Céilí Band, which now includes Willie Clancy and his flute. Mr Reid will work his contacts in the Gaelic League and the GAA to get bookings, coach the band from the piano at rehearsal and, on the night of an engagement, gather them into his Morris Ten, the instruments in the boot or tied to the roof, along with the sound gear, for there is no point playing in dancehalls without amplification. With three microphones on the stage, the musicians learn to restrain their usual banter.

At the opening of the Killanena Hall Joe Cooley arrives with his usual laidback bonhomie, self-conscious in the new suit, bow tie wagging from his pocket. Encountering his friend Paddy Canny, he looks sceptically at the dickie bow, perky beneath Paddy's chin. As if to a starter's pistol, the pair grab each other by the shoulders. Each with the strength of a bear, they rollick back and forth and suddenly are rolling over and over on the new maple dance floor, the pride of the parish and lavishly sprinkled with soap crystals to speed the dancers' steps. Eventually the two men clamber to their feet, slapping one another heartily to brush off the snowy flakes.

At times like this, Mr Reid feels let down by the band's country manners and youthful horseplay. His plan had been to present themselves as stylishly as a ballroom dance band. At the Oireachtas in Cork, where they won both the competition and a commission for a radio broadcast, they had looked and sounded first class. And

Seán Reid

now look at this pair: they might have been caught in a blizzard. With the other musicians now laughing and slapping away at them, Mr Reid quells his distress and heads for the piano, hoping that for once the instrument will be in tune.

The new year of 1948 sees Seán Reid—or John Reid as he is known at the County

Council and by the national broadcaster, Radio Éireann—battling the prejudice of both institutions against traditional music and musicians. Going for the radio broadcast is a trial in itself. John Minogue has generously hired a van to take the band to Dublin, where its arrival ten hours later outside the GPO creates a stir: men carrying black cases appearing one after the other onto the street as if for a holdup. In the studio, the lads follow Mr Reid's instructions and move the chairs close together, near the piano. When the station's music director, Mr O'Hanrahan, enters, he protests that this new arrangement is unworkable. Mr Reid stands his ground. O'Hanrahan slams out of the studio, bellowing at the addition of an accordion (an accordion!) when there had been none at the band's audition in Cork. Sneering that the flute players can't even tune their instruments, he vows it will be many years before the Tulla Céilí Band gets another broadcast. The boys look rattled, but Joe Cooley settles the accordion upon his crossed legs, unperturbed. What would a man like that know about music? The red light goes on and Mr Reid strikes two stiff chords to cue 'The Humours of Tulla'.

The broadcast is a triumph, say the legion of listeners in County Clare, and the young men of the Tulla Céilí Band walk tall. Mr Reid is pleased with the band's progress, but wants more for them. Handy with the pen, from the 'I should be thankful' to the 'yours faithfully', and unbowed by his encounter with the Director of Music, he requests a second broadcast, a full half hour this time, and confirmation within the week, if you please.

Certainly not, comes Mr O'Hanrahan's reply. Dismayed, Mr Reid enquires politely: was it their style, speed, rhythm, particular instruments or players? Allegedly, the instruments were not in tune, the ensemble was poor and the piano arrangements doubtful. Doubtful! At Féile Luimnigh, the adjudicator had praised their 'very discreet' performance and advised soft and sweet music for their radio broadcast. But they were not one of 2RN's orchestral groups, sugar coating Irish airs with pretty harmonies. Soft and sweet gets nobody onto the dance floor. All the same, Mr Reid is disillusioned by O'Hanrahan's hostile response, for aren't they engaged in the same project of bringing Irish music to the Irish people?

No such project occupies the Clare County Council, where Reid's new position as Acting County Engineer is in jeopardy unless he abandons his association with musicians and dancing. How can he exercise control when he is mixing with every Tom, Dick and Harry at the crossroads? Although offended by his employers' ignorance, Mr Reid relinquishes his seat at the piano. He sits, disconsolate, at the back of dancehalls, but will not destroy the band by withdrawing their transportation. Eventually, he is found out and his demotion follows. But with it comes the freedom to play music and lead the band as he criss-crosses County Clare in his black Morris, bringing music and musicians to the people.

The car, however, is not as reliable as Mr Reid, nor are the treacherous roads that are his department's responsibility. They only just make it on time to the Carrigaholt Christmas Céilí, after a puncture on the way. And then on the way home, at three o'clock in the morning, doesn't the spare tyre give out! A hard frost crusts the road to Kilkee, down which Paddy Canny rolls the tyre the six miles to the garage, whistling in the darkness to the rhythm of his good shoes. Five men huddle in the

Joe Cooley and Paddy Canny

Morris, too cold to sleep, until Mr Reid sees a light snap on in the desperate hour before dawn. At the farmhouse, he asks for a breakfast and the band thaws out with eggs and hot tea. By the time the car is fixed and Mr Reid has delivered the musicians home, the day is almost gone.

Mr Reid accepts that it would not be worthwhile to bring the band to Dublin for an audition and knows that they will never get another broadcast without it. But he is not the man to be defeated. Convinced that radio broadcasts build a musician's reputation, he secures auditions for three solo performers, selecting Willie Clancy and Joe Cooley, who are working in Dublin. Paddy Canny, the third candidate he puts forward, is reluctant, but Mr Reid will bring him to the studio and look out for him in Dublin. It is a great opportunity.

Willie Clancy, the best flute player in County Clare, is not selected. Joe Cooley's big-hearted 'Bucks of Oranmore' is rejected. Paddy Canny is the only one chosen.

Paddy on the Wireless

The year has turned to 1949 before Paddy is called to Dublin for his first broadcast. In his thirtieth year, he is strong enough to take on any work at home, but the city is foreign to him, and daunting. He is relieved that Mr Reid has organised everything, including an accompanist. He has managed to book Eileen Lane, who backs the fiddler Seán McGuire for his radio broadcasts. Paddy, who is in awe of McGuire's acrobatic technique, is impressed.

In the recording studio, the air is dead. There is no window, no liberty. When he checks his tuning against Eileen's chord, Paddy hears every hair of his bow clutch the steel strings, but no resonance. It is eerie, the way the room swallows sound. Paddy's chest is so tight, he has to gasp for breath. He barely has time to bless himself and stand to attention at the microphone when the red light comes on and off they go. Fifteen minutes is a lot of music—Paddy has timed it out by the clock at home—a couple of jigs and then back to a couple of reels and then a couple of hornpipes, finishing up with a few more reels. But before they reach the end of the first tune, time has fallen away. They get through it grand.

> Fifteen minutes is a lot of music— Paddy has timed it out by the clock at home—but before they reach the end of the first tune, time has fallen away.

The men from Radio Éireann must agree, because Paddy gets another call. After this broadcast, he and Mr Reid are invited for 'the one' at the Town Bar. The station's boss is there with his colleague, Ciarán Mac Mathúna, and Mr Reid's friend from the Piper's Club, Paddy McElvaney. Mr Reid grumbles that the radio gives so little time to traditional music: nine hours for the whole of last year. He actually counted. The radio station boss disagrees. Mr Reid concedes that he wasn't including the Light Orchestra's arrangements of 'Irish folk music'. Paddy has known Mr Reid to ride his high horse before. What surprises him now is how well the radio men take it, Mac Mathúna anyway. Paddy takes the quiet corner, but the rest of them never let up until 'the one' turns into two pints and then three. At the best of times, Paddy is a half-pint man. Next morning, the head is bad.

For a while after that, there is a problem getting an accompanist, because Eileen Lane (Mrs Stapleton) is busy with a new baby. Eventually, the station engages a pianist for Paddy. Looking back, the warning sign was there when she asked for the music and Mr Reid had to write out every tune. Eileen only needed to know the key. They start with a pair of jigs, but this new woman is so slow, Paddy knows he will never get through his programme. So when they come to the reels, Paddy takes off. The poor woman follows as best she can, but she isn't there at all for the finish. After that debacle, someone suggests Tommy Delaney, a piano player with a band of his own. Paddy loves to play with Tommy, so sensitive to the music and he has a way of playing a part of the tune on the piano, which gives the fiddle some relief. And a lovely man, Tommy Delaney.

To play on the wireless, you have to be good. You have to play something different each time and it has to be timed right. The broadcasts are an ordeal, always. Before he enters the studio, Paddy and his new friend Paddy McElvaney pray for Paddy to get through the next fifteen minutes. He always does. Soon, Paddy is making his own way to Dublin. Three or four times a year, he cycles down to catch the bus for Limerick, then the midday train to Dublin, where he stays overnight. Paddy gets three pounds for a broadcast and a pound of that goes to the pianist. With his hand in his pocket for all the expenses, it comes back to very little for the hours he puts in. When his brother Mickie buys a van, he can do it all in one day, taking the last train back down to Limerick and driving on home. At other times, he will stay overnight to play music with his friends in Dublin: John Kelly in Capel Street or Tommie Potts and any number of musicians from the Piper's Club.

Jack Murphy and his wife Bridget—Kate Canny's sister—live on the Cragg Road that runs down from Glendree to Tulla. Around the back at Murphys, people from up the mountain leave their bicycles for safekeeping, or their pony and trap, when they have business in Tulla. Over a few weeks each summer, it is there they will find Paddy Canny, who one day will inherit the property. His uncle has a business making lime to be sold as fertiliser and it is Paddy who takes the sledgehammer to the limestone boulders, smashing them into stones small enough to feed into the kiln for the long, slow burn. After one morning's work, Paddy leaves for Dublin. That evening, the Murphys are amazed to hear their Paddy, who was here, drawing in the stones that morning, playing such fine music on the wireless. It astounds them.

In the rural parishes, where the electricity is not yet connected, wireless sets run on batteries, which have to be recharged every few months. Hardly anyone has a wireless. When Paddy Canny's name appears in the *Clare Champion*'s radio guide, people think nothing of walking three miles to hear him in a house with a wireless. The O'Donoghues go up to O'Connors, whose kitchen is always packed out, whatever time of day Paddy's music comes on. At the announcement they come silently to attention, eyes fixed on the wooden cabinet.

The music that emerges is unmistakeably Paddy Canny's; you couldn't mistake him for any other fiddler. Young Paddy Donoghue closes his eyes, the better to hear. He imagines his hero sitting before him, as he has sat so many times in his own kitchen. In the stillness, he hears Paddy's playing more intensely than when he is right in front of them, his two feet tapping away, his listeners urging him on: 'Good man, Paddy!' Listening to the wireless, the young O'Donoghue hears the music's ethereal, inward quality, his heart swelling with the long sweep of Paddy's phrasing, as if the music were playing within him. When the fifteen minutes are up, the spell—the *draoícht* of Paddy Canny's music—is broken and the wireless turned off. As the listeners come back to themselves, a lonesomeness settles among them.

Paddy Donoghue says that listening to Paddy on the radio is like listening to God. Others call him the king of music. Bill Malley, the fiddler from Magherabaun, is more pragmatic. Always wanting to know where Paddy is getting his new tunes and eager to discuss his radio performances, Bill prefaces his remarks with

When Paddy Canny's name appears in the *Clare Champion*'s radio programme, people think nothing of walking three miles to hear him in a house with a wireless.

'Garrett Barry's'

Paddy Canny, 1959

'Garrett Barry's'

Paddy plays much the same version of 'Garrett Barry's' as his friend Willie Clancy, whose father had it from the piper Barry. In playing jigs, Paddy's tempo is stricter than in reels: an even, rolling rhythm played with long legato bows. He emphasises the tune's melodic shape by increasing the volume towards the highest note, then softening on the way down. The variability of his second-finger notes is evident in the first bar, where the F is lower on the way up to G and higher on the way down. Paddy Canny slides from the note below, often using two fingers, as in bar 2, the second imperceptibly taking over from the first. Paddy could also bend a note, simply by rolling his finger (B flat onto B, F onto F sharp). He accents the lower note, often slowing the tempo a little, before catching up again: a subtle shaping. At the end of the tune, Paddy plays a lovely two-bar 'coda', which, along with the low phrase leading back to the beginning of the tune, is almost identical to the way Tommie Potts finishes the tune.

'I'll only comment on the ones I know'. And Paddy listens, for he puts value on Bill Malley's opinion and is curious, because he has never listened to his own playing the way his radio audience has.

It is a significant achievement for any musician to play on the radio. Since Radio Éireann opened in 1926, there have been few soloists playing traditional music— Leo Rowsome the piper was one, the fiddler Frank O'Higgins another and, more recently, the maestro Seán McGuire. Now, that elite circle has opened to include Paddy Canny. Every listener knows his name and every traditional musician knows his music. Fiddlers in particular listen carefully to the drone effect Paddy gets, to the delicacy of his rolls and the light touch of his finger triplets, drawn into the emotional journey of each tune. Paddy Canny is a star.

In the city, Paddy is besieged by noise and hurry: mayhem at the railway station, the thunder of motor cars and belching buses, the footpaths a rush of men in long coats and women in high heels. Evenings of music and talk are stimulating and then exhausting. He never stays more than a day, two if there's a hurling final to watch. At home, he finds respite in the bog, up past the cutover turf banks engraved with the mark of the sleán and beneath them, dark pools shimmering with moss. He pictures that day when the Glendree boys followed their beagles and for a moment a pelt glowed through a bush of gorse—*an madra rua*, the red-haired dog—and then conjured its own disappearance. They had thought it some wild magic, but it was only survival.

Are You Anything to Pat Canny?

'Are you anything to Pat Canny?'

His father is in the grave these thirteen years, but to hear his name stabs Paddy as if it were yesterday. Not that the man means anything but well. An old man, although not as old as Pat Canny would have been, he has a kind face. Paddy will have to explain. But the man has stopped sweeping the foyer and is into his own story: how they had worked together around Nenagh, where the band is playing tonight. As the man brings out his memories, Paddy, too, is back in those times, when his father would go down in the autumn to dig the spuds in Tipperary. How Paddy had grieved, as a child, to see his father walk out with his bundle—no such thing as a bicycle then. Picturing the men lined up like spailpíns, hoping the big farmers would hire them, Paddy feels the shame of it.

Paddy remembers his mother going out to people—ordinary people like themselves, poor people—who would be crossing the mountain, going who knows where, maybe to look for work. They might call in at a house on the way, and they would be starved, they mightn't have seen a bit to eat for days. Turning up at the Canny house with no shoe on them, nothing. Paddy can see his mother taking a cake of brown bread and cutting it up, giving each of those people a cup of milk and a cut of that bread.

'That's the times we lived in,' Paddy tells the man. 'We had nothing.'

And look at us now, he thinks, with our clean white shirts and our jackets and ties. Paddy would like to stay a few minutes longer, but PJoe Hayes is giving him the nod to follow Seán Reid's piping tunes with a selection on the fiddle before the supper break is over.

Paddy misses Joe Cooley's solid, easy-going presence in the band. At the same time, he is thrilled with Paddy O'Brien's accordion music and his treasure chest of tunes, many of his own making. And the new man PJoe has brought in, Jack Keane, is an exuberant drummer and already the life and soul of back-seat camaraderie on the long car journeys. The band is playing better than ever, two nights a week and always home in time to milk the cows, for dairying is opening up and some of the musicians are giving it a go.

Under Seán Reid's leadership, the band has grown more ambitious, too, and more professional. They are punctual and well dressed. There is no smoking, no drink or chat until the reprieve of supper, around midnight and again at two or three in the morning, after 'The Soldier's Song' has brought the dancing to an end. Each year brings more engagements as the interest in céilí dancing grows. Here

> 'That's the times we lived in', Paddy tells the man. 'We had nothing'. And look at us now, he thinks, with our clean white shirts and our jackets and ties.

in Nenagh, many of the dancers have joined new branches of the Gaelic League and have graduated from their céilí dancing classes. Although, tonight, with 'The Waves of Tory' breaking all over the hall, the teacher has had to calm the waters when couples kept ducking under the same wave and crashing heads.

In towns like Nenagh, the halls are spacious enough for hundreds of dancers. A steady electric glare has replaced the Tilley lanterns that still light rural parish halls and swing in the dancers' wake. Paddy recalls the intimacy of Sunday evening school dances, sitting in the windowsills with PJoe beside him, fielding the back-chat from friends and neighbours. When they look down from the stage in this hall, they might not recognise anyone.

Seán Reid is still at the piano. Poor old Mr Reid; what he had to put up with to play music. Cracks had begun to show in his tightly managed schedule of long days supervising building works, followed by a crowded calendar of sports and evening meetings and long nights out with the band. In the end, he relinquished the band's management: taking bookings, negotiating prices, preparing musical programmes and maintaining the number of musicians. He still drives, though, sometimes alarming his passengers by steering with his elbows while he plays a tune on the whistle.

The man he tapped on the shoulder is PJoe Hayes. Like Paddy Canny, PJoe is as devoted to music as he is to his farm and his family and his religion. On top of that, he is committed to nurturing the living entity of the band. He gets along with everyone, from musicians to ballroom owners to the dancers themselves. Although shy by nature, he will keep a man to his bargain, whether it is the provision of the meat tea before the dance or a musician's undertaking to learn a new tune. PJoe has an ear for a good tune and a genius for putting together sets that energise the dancers with each change of tune and key. His precise sense of rhythm is expressed through his whole body, from his single foot-tap to the turn of his shoulders that signals a change of tune or the dance's conclusion. Under his leadership, the Tulla Céilí Band has the zest and the swing that had made PJoe so popular at house dances.

> Like Paddy Canny, PJoe is as devoted to music as he is to his farm and his family and his religion. On top of that, he is committed to nurturing the living entity of the band.

Mrs Crotty

Late in the night, Mrs Crotty and Paddy play tunes he learned from his Dad or got from the gramophone records, along with ones that are special to West Clare. Paddy blooms in the warmth of Mrs Crotty's good nature and his music flows easily.

That desperate cough when the engine is killed is unmistakeable. But what is Seán Reid's Morris doing at Curraun? Since daybreak, Mickie and Paddy have been working in the garden to prepare the ground for the oats and the spuds and all the different vegetables they will grow. According to Mickie's plan, with the ploughing finished, today they will start harrowing, using the long reins to keep the horses in line as they drag the heavy spikes through the clods. It is hard going for men and horses. But there is Mr Reid standing in the road in an attitude that speaks of urgency.

Ciarán Mac Mathúna, in his new job with Radio Éireann's Mobile Recording Unit, is coming down from Dublin to record musicians at Mrs Crotty's pub. Today. He has a machine that makes 'tapes' of music, which will be broadcast later on a new radio show he has lined up. It's to be called *Ceolta Tíre*—folk music, music of the country people—and he wants Paddy to be involved right from the start. Today.

'I'm afraid I can't,' says Paddy, indicating the horses and the harrow and his brother.

But Mickie tells him, 'Go on away!'

It is fifty miles along bad roads to the port of Kilrush and well into the evening before they arrive at Crotty's pub in the market square. Paddy hesitates at the door, reluctant, as always, to enter a crowded room. But Mrs Crotty welcomes him warmly and in moments he is seated inside the circle of musicians. Denis Murphy is up from Kerry and the West Clare fiddlers are here: Junior Crehan and Johnny Pickering and Hughdie Doohan. There are flutes as well: young Michael Tubridy, home from Dublin, and Paddy Breen, and the Sligo-man Mike Preston, who has recently joined the Tulla Céilí Band. With musicians like these, they are guaranteed a great night of music.

It is only when the music is flying that Ciarán sets up the microphone and many hours after that when he gets Paddy and Mrs Crotty to put down a few tunes together. Paddy has met Mrs Crotty once or twice, for when Ciarán Mac Mathúna and Seán Reid are together, she is bound to be with them. And when Paddy bumps into Ciarán in Dublin, she is the one person Ciarán always talks about, for he loves Mrs Crotty and he loves her music. She can be heard playing her concertina at fleadhs and at the Piper's Club in Dublin and on the radio, always with the same ease and dignity. Mrs Crotty is twice Paddy's age and her health is poor. Yet, when she has an attack of angina, she will take the tablets that are always in her pocket and after a while will be back into the music again. In deference to her musicianship and gracious good sense, the musicians in the county have voted Mrs Elizabeth Crotty President of the booming Ennis branch of Comhaltas Ceoltóirí Éireann, the recently formed association of Irish musicians.

Late in the night, Mrs Crotty and Paddy play tunes he learned from his Dad or got from the gramophone records, along with ones that are special to West Clare. Paddy blooms in the warmth of Mrs Crotty's good nature and his music flows. Although they have only played together once before, Mrs Crotty remembers the tunes they played that night in Ballynacally. She is a comfortable woman to be with, always good-humoured, and has a way of getting him to talk that no one else has. Paddy's fiddling tucks in beneath the concertina, weaving little runs and rolls around the framework of the tune, but this time leaving out the triplets that often punctuate his playing. There are no frills in Mrs Crotty's music; only the doubling of notes when the tune goes high and she plays the low octave along with the melody. Often, she will come to a full stop for emphasis at the end of a phrase, something Paddy will do in speaking as well as in playing. There's a magic between the two of them when they play together.

One tune they play is 'Touch Me if You Dare'. For the recording, they join it up with another old tune, the 'Morning Star', although both Paddy and Mrs Crotty prefer to play only one tune at a time, the way it was done long ago.

It is the morning star that shines on the Morris as it make its way back through the silent streets of Ennis. Ciarán and his crew return to their beds at the Queens Hotel, their first recording session complete. As Seán Reid has a job to go to, he rouses a hackney driver to take his car on up to Curraun. A mile from home, the Morris runs out of petrol. Paddy walks back to Denis Moloney, whom they passed on the School Road.

Mrs Crotty and
Ciarán Mac Mathúna

Could Denis drive Paddy down to Feakle for a can of petrol?

What are neighbours for?

When at last Paddy arrives home, Mickie is working away at the harrow. It isn't every brother who would let a man go off to play music, to stay out carousing all night with no money in it. What can Paddy do, but change his clothes and go out to Mickie in the garden and follow the harrow the whole day?

The Coleman Cup

After the announcement, Paddy can scarcely believe that he has done it. He is the All-Ireland Champion of 1953. And the remarks on the adjudicator's sheet are almost as valuable. Such praise from the man he holds to be the greatest fiddle player in Ireland.

In the corridor, the musicians are lined up in their jackets and ties—except Aggie Whyte, of course. There is a solemnity to the waiting, like going to Confession. Some check their tuning; others strain to hear the musician playing behind the closed door. The competitors are called in one at a time.

It is Paddy Canny's turn. With rows of forms empty of pupils and a line of windows framing only sky, the room is too large for the three men in it. Behind the teacher's desk, one of the adjudicators is writing notes. He looks up. This must be the great Seán McGuire. Paddy has heard he is adjudicating at this year's *Fleadh Cheoil na hÉireann*, the All-Ireland Festival of Music, but he wouldn't know the man. He has only heard him on the radio, listened in awe to his wondrous feats on the fiddle. The adjudicator asks for his programme of tunes. Immediately, Paddy is back at the Glendree School, Master O'Connor demanding his answer to a curly question and Paddy unable to bring the words, despite knowing the answer. It is the same now as he stutters the names of tunes he has played a thousand times.

But Paddy has learned how to compose himself. Hasn't he done so time and again before the merciless red light at Radio Éireann, to say nothing of heedless crowds at carnivals and restless dancers waiting for their supper while the 'ace violinist' plays a few selections? Playing for the people is one thing; playing for one of his peers—no, for a musician who is without peer—is something new. It may be that his whole life has led to this moment: the years of learning, years of painstaking imitation of recordings and many more years perfecting the tunes until the music flows from his fingers and beneath his bow in exactly the way he hears it in his head. Paddy gathers himself. What else can he do but lift his arm, bring down the bow and begin? He begins.

After the announcement, Paddy can scarcely believe that he has done it. He is the All-Ireland Champion of 1953. And the remarks on the adjudicator's sheet are almost as valuable. Such praise from the man he holds to be the greatest fiddle player in Ireland. And, for the first time this year, there is a trophy for the winner, named for that other hero, Michael Coleman. If only his old Dad, the first of his heroes, could be here to see that.

Aggie Whyte (Mrs Ryan, now) is here beside him. She has come second to Paddy but couldn't be nicer about it. She surely won't have long to wait before the Coleman Cup comes her way. Seán Ryan from across Lough Derg in Tipperary is another who is playing like a champion and composing tunes of such beauty they deserve a trophy by themselves. The Tulla band came nowhere in their competition, but the boys celebrate as if they had all won together, almost carrying Paddy to the pub. Paddy O'Brien has won a cup too. He is a genius, in Paddy Canny's estimation. What can't he do on his shiny B/C box, even making rolls the way you would on a fiddle? And Paddy Canny's old friend, Joe Cooley. Back from England and playing in the band alongside Paddy O'Brien, Joe has taken the second prize. The two could scarcely be more different, Joe with his press-and-draw style, sweetly articulated and soulful, Paddy with his drive and smooth virtuosity, a shower of notes in each push of the bellows. And yet the two play away together, chalk and cheese getting along just fine. The way Paddy and PJoe do, their contrasting approaches adding up to more than their sum.

There is hardly a musician in Ireland who doesn't know about Comhaltas Ceoltóirí Éireann's annual feast of music. There is no better chance to pick up new tunes and hear how musicians from elsewhere tackle the old ones, the chance to meet others who share a passion for music. They are all in it together, no matter about the competitions, and there is the greatest of music to be heard in the bars and on the street. Music everywhere. The musicians who come over from London are used to playing together in pubs, but for many in Ireland it is their first time playing in a group, the first time to feel that exhilaration of hearing your own music amplified by others. And it might be the first time they hear Paddy Canny, not on the wireless, but here among them in his moment of triumph.

The musicians who come over from London are used to playing together in pubs, but for many in Ireland it is their first time playing in a group, the first time to feel that exhilaration of hearing your own music amplified by others.

Off to Jamaica

The pair join the cream of New York's Irish musicians to play in dancehalls and bars and at all the house parties and Irish county associations they are invited to.

It was Dr Bill who persuaded Paddy Canny to make this trip to New York. Bill Loughnane, the Feakle doctor, is a tonic in himself. He will bring along his fiddle to cheer his patients, who swear his music does them more good than an assload of tablets. A tall man with a strong handshake and a big laugh, Dr Bill makes his way confidently in the world. He knows most of Coleman's tunes on the fiddle and plays alongside Paddy in the Tulla Céilí Band. In Lena's bar in Feakle, the Doctor urges diffident musicians to play and loudly congratulates them when they do.

In New York, the charismatic Doctor is in his element. A handy hurler himself, Dr Bill has brought with him five sets of hurleys for the Clare GAA club and gets to throw in the ball at the match in Gaelic Park. He talks up Ireland and hurling and music and County Clare on television and radio programmes, to newspaper reporters and at meetings with the dealers of Irish culture and politics. 'He'd talk his way into anything and talk his way out of anything,' says Paddy. At first, he is embarrassed when Bill says it was hearing Paddy Canny playing on the radio that brought him home from Dublin to Feakle, but after the third or fourth time, he is used to it and takes it as the cue to play a set of tunes. Without Bill Loughnane, Paddy would be lost here. In his own estimation, he is a bit too quiet for the job, no good at playing in front of people and worse at conversation with strangers. That is no impediment, though, when the pair join the cream of the city's Irish musicians to play in dancehalls and bars and at all the house parties and Irish county associations they are invited to.

The dancehalls are fascinating, with their strange hybrid of céilí dancing and modern moves, which at home you would never see mixed together. At Bill Fuller's City Center, the newest generation of Irish immigrants temper their appetite for all that is American with a little nostalgia. Two thousand fox-trotters glide around the floor to the swing of the latest hits. But when the big band takes a break (the Musicians' Union is strict about this), traditional musicians replace them on the stage. Then the dancers form sets for 'The Siege of Ennis' and couples circle the hall to old-time waltzes played on the big Paolo Soprani accordion. And when the dancers take refreshments from the bar to sit at tables around the hall, they might lend an ear to Paddy Canny's playing or join in the chorus of one of Dr Bill's songs.

Paddy has aunts in New York, his mother's sisters, who left East Clare early in the century. Since then, twelve million Irish immigrants have passed through Ellis

Island and many of them are moving up in the world. The aunts have apartments of their own now and this month Hannah has moved in with Ellie so that the boys can come and go to suit themselves. In exchange, Paddy walks Hannah's little dog each day, making his way from lamp post to lamp post along the streets of the Bronx.

After one long night of music, the pair are barely warm in their beds when the doorbell rings. It is Paddy McMahon, from a Killanena family they both know well. He has come to take them out for the day, so up they get and off they go to Jamaica—the racetrack in Queens, that is. McMahon has a hot tip, so Paddy hands over his money and, against the odds, the horse comes in. Five hundred dollars! The only real money he sees for the whole trip, given that his earnings from concerts barely cover the airfare over. All that money to sit up, terrified, the whole night and then discover that they had only got as far as Canada and would have to do the whole going up and coming down once more. If the huge crowd at their send-off concert at Shannon Airport could have seen Paddy arriving in New York, his face as green as the box of shamrock he carried, they might think he had better stayed at home.

With neither bit, bite nor sup all day, Paddy and Dr Bill are set for a celebration. They find a restaurant and salivate over the steak. Do they want small, medium or large? 'Large!' says the Doctor. The dishes are huge and yet the T-bones cover them. There are vegetables, too, but they don't feel like vegetables. They go for the steak. Paddy eats his way down one side and up the other side and still he can't finish. Looking across the table, he sees that Dr Bill has swallowed the whole lot. At home, Paddy might feel uneasy at such extravagance. But tonight he lives the dream of abundance that is America.

New York House Session

There is a house in Flushing, in the New York Borough of Queens, a timber house painted white, with a few steps up from the yard. A family house. Inside, a staircase climbs from the spacious hallway to the floors above. More stairs descend into a vast basement. There is a piano here and chairs set around it, a reel-to-reel tape recorder, the best you can buy. Facing it is another room and more chairs. There is a cloth covering Mary Quinn's supper table and a spacious kitchen where the family and their guests, Paddy Canny and Dr Bill Loughnane, have just finished their meal. There is a sudden commotion upstairs: a door closing, excited voices, footsteps coming down. More musicians have arrived.

This is the house that Louis Quinn built to hold his dream of family and prosperity and a life filled with the music of the home he had left behind. New York's Irish music scene is thriving now, in step with the economy. A feast of fiddlers, the older generation now, still play the Irish dancehalls and meet in bars and at parties in Brooklyn and the Bronx. And in amongst it all is Louis Quinn, a fiddle player of renown and an ambassador for Irish culture. He is a dynamo, promoting his friend Ed Reavy's compositions, setting up an organisation for Irish musicians, putting together the New York Céilí Band, sponsoring a stream of immigrants until this house has become an Ellis Island for Irish musicians. Then there is his radio show, *The Shamrock Hour*. One week, he will be playing his fiddle for children dancing an Irish jig, right there in the studio. The next, he will bring in a guest: 'Here's Paddy Canny now, from County Clare, gonna play some reels!'

And here is Paddy now, to play some reels in Louis Quinn's basement at one of

Louis and Seán Quinn

his regular music nights. With his audience of old friends and new seated and still, Paddy makes his characteristic, awkward introduction, scrubbing the bow across pairs of strings to confirm his tuning. Then he begins 'Lord McDonald's', the reel Michael Coleman recorded here in New York City in 1927, the bosses at Columbia Records so thrilled at his brilliance that they handed him a bonus cheque for five hundred dollars for the set. Coleman, who would not compromise his art to play in dance bands.

The room's acoustics are excellent, thanks to the knotted pine panelling Louis's foreman James 'Lad' O'Beirne has made, the same Lad O'Beirne from Coleman country who is equally a genius on the fiddle and as a composer. Tonight he is on the piano, his gently plodding vamp and strong bass keeping the rhythm steady. No rush. Paddy turns to 'The Luck Penny', named for the sum a buyer returned to his seller at the old fairs, before the big cattle marts came in. It is a sweet old jig, which everyone here must know from Paddy Killoran's recording. Killoran is here tonight, too, to listen to this acclaimed fiddler from Clare.

As so often in Paddy's playing, one passage, a velvety legato that enfolds whole phrases in a single sweep of the bow, is counterpoised by another in petit-point staccato. When he finishes, a man cries out 'Wonderful!' and there is wonder in his voice. A woman exclaims, 'Paddy Canny! That's the old Paddy Canny would play that!' It is Eileen Seery, affectionately recalling all the nights of music with Paddy and with the Tulla Céilí Band, before her husband, Paddy O'Brien, brought his family to this new life in New York.

'What'll I do now?' Paddy asks, or asks himself.

'Do you play Paddy Kelly's?' The request is lilted.

Die di- ddl- y eye - ten- dee - dle Die di- ddl -y eye - ten - dee - dle

'I don't know. I might.'

Paddy sketches a phrase, and another, to remind himself of the tune, before launching into a rolling sea of notes, his bow crossing the current of the piano's pulse, smooth sailing alternating with a shower of notes precisely picking out the melody, as if in a dialogue between the darker, stronger statement of the melody's theme and its higher, lighter response. This light and shade is typical of Paddy's playing. He slides up to the pivot point of the keynote then and rests on the poignant flattened seventh.

A few tunes on, Paddy brings out 'Joe Cooley's Reel' and this is the moment he clinches his hold over the audience, when he adds his own touch to the tune they all know well.

Men shout and yelp and when Paddy finishes there's a joyful 'Y'hoo!' from none other than Joe Cooley. For Paddy's great friend Joe, who left the Tulla band for

Paddy sketches a phrase, and another, to remind himself of the tune, before launching into a rolling sea of notes, his bow crossing the current of the piano's pulse, smooth sailing alternating with a shower of notes precisely picking out the melody, as if in a dialogue between the darker, stronger statement of the melody's theme and its higher, lighter response.

'Paddy Kelly's'

Paddy Canny, 1956

America the same year as Paddy O'Brien, is here, for the time being, in New York City. Joe didn't write this tune, but he fell in love with it, a story he often tells. How he and his brother Séamus returned from a night of music and wrestled with remembered fragments the whole night long until by morning they had patched together the reel that once was called 'Put the Cake on the Dresser' but now is simply 'Cooley's'.

Paddy plays another jig—he is always at ease playing jigs. Musicians around East Clare might call this one 'The Old Petticoat Loose' or else 'The Geese in the Bog'. When Louis Quinn's boy Seán recognises it as a version of 'Brian O'Lynn', he is invited to play that jig and then, because they would never let him go at just the one tune, he hurries into 'The Western', a hornpipe Coleman recorded. And then, because Paddy O'Brien has a different version of that hornpipe, Paddy plays it with all the flourishes and chromatic runs that are his signature on the accordion. And of course, he can't be let play just the one, so he gives them Paddy Kelly's majestic four-part reel, an expansive reworking of the tune Paddy Canny played earlier. Paddy Kelly composed this tune for his friend as a farewell gift on his emigration, calling it 'Paddy O'Brien's Dream', although that name never stuck. Paddy O'Brien and Paddy Canny picked up many of Kelly's compositions when they played Sunday nights in Galway City with Kelly and Paddy Fahey and the rest of the band, lilting those lonesome East Galway tunes all the way home in the car. They had always felt an affinity with the music of that area.

When Paddy Canny has warmed up again with a pair of jigs, he brings out one of the simple reels his father taught him. He begins by sketching the melodic shape of the tune,

then fills it in: 'The Humours of Scariff'. When Francis O'Neill collected this tune for his *Irish Dance Music: 1001 Gems,* the fiddler had no name for it, so O'Neill called it after the village where he had broken his journey to Feakle for a glass of porter. When he balked at the taste, his driver blamed the previous week's 'mission', when the fire-and-brimstone Redemptorists had paralysed the town, in a suitably teetotal way, leaving the publican's porter to sour.

Paddy slides onto the high F natural at the end of the first phrase, squeezing it to emphasise the flat seventh note that marks the bittersweet dorian scale, but on the repeat he slides up to the F sharp. Fiddle players in Paddy's home territory, as much as in Paddy Kelly's, season their music with this ambivalence, sliding in and out of melancholy, with more subtlety than is available to a fixed-note instrument like the accordion.

The topography of Paddy's playing is a complex landscape that includes rolling hills of swelling volume and sometimes speed at heartfelt moments, with breathing space at beauty spots, and twisted pathways accomplished by the bow hand's invisible pressure. Paddy learned to hear musical contours from listening to Coleman's recordings. Coleman, who said, 'All the sadness of my life is translated into sound'.

Paddy's next tune is 'The Humours of Lissadell', another of the reels Paddy Killoran recorded. As a dance-band leader, Killoran played a clear, rhythmic style to suit the dancers. He owns a bar not far from Quinns, already familiar to Paddy and Dr Bill, and is setting up a company, Dublin Records, to record Irish musicians. It is no surprise that his business partners, Jim and John O'Neill from Labasheeda, County Clare, have already asked Paddy Canny to record for them. Paddy can do it himself, or ask a few of the lads to join him, whatever he likes.

In his choice of tunes, Paddy has deferred to the extraordinarily talented Sligo fiddle players who have made New York City their home, while displaying his own accomplishment in performing their repertoire. Equally, he has brought to these most sophisticated of Irish musicians the simple dance tunes he learned from his father. He is in his stride now, playing another of these, his volume swelling as the melody rises, withdrawing on the way down. At the end, Paddy's bow crashes the strings discordantly. He often does this, as if to shrug, like a man caught crying, 'Ah, 'tis nothing'. Francis O'Neill called this reel 'O'Reilly's Greyhound', after the man (and his dog) who gave it to him, but Paddy didn't get the tune from O'Neill's book.

'Do you know the name of that one, Paddy?' a man calls out.

'The Outdoor Relief.'

'What?'

> The topography of Paddy's playing is a complex landscape that includes rolling hills of swelling volume and sometimes speed at heartfelt moments, with breathing space at beauty spots, and twisted pathways accomplished by the bow hand's invisible pressure.

'The Outdoor Relief, we used to call it at home.'

'Oh, yeah. "The Outdoor Relief".'

The man chuckles as if unconvinced. Maybe he is thinking of outhouses, because to anyone from the West of Ireland, it is no laughing matter. In the dying years of the Great Famine, the Outdoor Relief was a scheme to provide food for the starving and destitute who could not find shelter in the overcrowded workhouses.

Paddy swings into more of his father's feisty single reels: simple tunes, but in Paddy's hands both wistful and joyous, vivid with emotion. He brings out another of Coleman's elaborately embroidered tunes, illuminating 'Trim the Velvet' with his own brilliance. This is the reel that brought the house down in Carnegie Hall, the tune which will become the signature for an Irish radio programme and which finishes tonight's recital. Larry Redican and Andy McGann, who have brought Paddy in on all their bookings for the month, are here with Paddy Reynolds and Ed Reavy. Paddy Killoran has his fiddle with him. All these great fiddle players. Instrument cases appear as beer and whiskey are dispensed and cigarettes proffered. People from home are surrounding Paddy Canny, who stands to face the small talk before the music can begin again.

Friends and Rivals

The Tulla Céilí Band is now so famous that country people all over Ireland are buying their records, in the old 78 rpm format, because few of these listeners have an electric gramophone. The recordings were made in Dublin after Paddy Canny got back from New York. In fact, PJoe renamed one of the jigs 'Paddy's Return', although everyone else still calls it 'Kitty Lie Over'.

As leader of the Tulla band, PJoe Hayes has found his vocation. A good organiser, he knows the band's worth in the market and commands top money, meagre though that is. He takes it upon himself to arrange the tunes in sets, expanding the repertoire as each new member brings in their own tunes. PJoe synchronises the music for each of the dances on the programme—when to change to a new tune, how many times to play each one—so that the band finishes when the dancers do, with no ragged endings. This goes down well with the committee men of *Conradh na Gaeilge*, the Gaelic League, who are strict about which dances are performed at their *céilídhe mór*, nights of pure Irish dancing and music. They have their programs timed to the minute and will not tolerate foreign abominations like waltzes or quicksteps or—heaven forbid—set dances, despite the fact that set dancing was the only dancing country people knew, and loved, across several generations. PJoe will call on Paddy Canny or one of the others to play in the intervals between dances, for an unbroken evening of céilí dances would be exhausting for everyone.

For several years, the band has had regular bookings at the Astor Ballroom in Scariff, where they are billed as 'the famous Tulla Céilí Band'. But their fame needs to spread further, for each year sees more céilí bands competing for bookings. PJoe advertises their expertise in the national *Irish Press*:

> TULLA Céilidhe Band, playing Céilidhe and old-time waltzes, featuring Joe Cooley, Ireland's ace accordionist; and Paddy Canny, fiddler, holder of Michael Coleman Cup. Will quote for Engagements anywhere in Ireland. Apply to the Secretary, P. Hayes, Maghera, Caher Feakle, Co. Clare.

The extraordinary thing is that céilís have become so popular. When the band first got together, the Gaelic League and the GAA (Gaelic Athletics Association) were the only ones holding them. Now, there is a Marquee in just about every village and town in Ireland, a couple of weeks of summer fun and games with hurling matches and dodgems, chair-o-planes and derby races. Every night there is a dance in the big marquee, usually a pop band for the youngsters and showbands for

The Tulla Céilí Band is now so famous that country people all over Ireland are buying their records, in the old 78 rpm format, because few of these listeners have an electric gramophone.

couples and always one or two céilí nights, which are fun when you know the dances, and always a good mix of people.

Comhaltas Ceoltóirí Éireann started as an association of traditional musicians organising their own festivals. Now it is a movement promoting traditional music throughout Ireland. The annual fleadh cheoil is growing, too, attracting tens of thousands over the Whit Weekend in May. The most popular events are always the céilí band competitions, where the crowds are so fiercely partisan, you would think

they were at a hurling final in Croke Park. It is hard to believe that they care so much about music when, only ten years ago, the same people wouldn't cross the street to listen to Irish music. Every one of them knows which is the best band. In Clare, half of them know it is the Kilfenora Céilí Band and the rest are certain it is the Tulla. The truth is, the Kilfenora have brought home the trophy for three years straight, beating the Tulla by a whisker. Not that the musicians themselves can't be friends. Didn't the Kilfenora and the Tulla play in one big band at last year's fleadh in Ennis? And when the Kilfenora beat them again, weren't the Tulla musicians guests of honour at their celebration dinner?

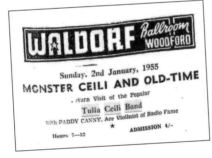

The 1957 fleadh is in Dungarvan, Co. Waterford, the long weekend's events following the pattern of previous years: Saturday is devoted to provincial finals, Sunday to a parade followed by the Bishop's official opening, the schoolchildren's pageant and a lecture lauding Ireland's native music and ruing its neglect, followed in the evening by a concert and a céilí that lasts until dawn. The national finals are held on the Monday, followed by the prize-winners' concert and another all-night céilí. The crowds in the streets of Dungarvan may have disappointed the organisers, for attendance has been just a fraction of what was expected after last year's massive turnout in Ennis. Still, there isn't a spare seat in Dungarvan's Town Hall this evening, or a spare inch along the walls. Three hundred bands have competed and now the Tulla and the Kilfenora are lined up for another showdown, along with a couple of other finalists. The MC has finished his speech, congratulating the musicians for their great work in restoring the music to the hills and the glens of Ireland, keeping that grand Irish, Christian, Catholic tradition alive, for it is the greatest fortress against foreignism that we can have. And so on. The Kilfenora have played already, hundreds of their supporters roaring and stamping their feet at the end of each set of tunes.

Now it is the Tulla Ceili Band's turn. The musicians are exhausted and at the same time jumping with nerves. Yesterday they recorded a half-dozen sets for Ciarán Mac Mathúna's radio programme, then played for the céilí until 4 am. On these fleadh weekends, no one wants to go home to bed. This evening, PJoe is buzzing with anticipation. He has had the band practising in his kitchen these past six weeks, more training than they have put in for any competition yet. They

have played well in the heats and he is certain—or almost certain—that this year, they'll win.

The Tulla barely take in the din from their supporters as they take their seats on the stage. They play the best they know how: the front-row four-fiddle line-up of Paddy and PJoe and Dr Bill Loughnane and Jack Shaughnessy; the flute players Michael Preston and Seamus Cooley; and staunch Seán Reid at the piano. Since they lost both Paddy O'Brien and Joe Cooley to America, Paddy McNamara and his brother Joe have brought their accordions into the band. Joe Mac, who still has an old G and D box, plays an octave below Paddy in the high part of the tune. This adds a richness and depth to the unison ensemble that none of the other bands can emulate. At the back of the stage, Jack Keane, always an ebullient drummer, swaps to the block in the turn of the tune, tapping out the rhythm like feet battering on flagstones, one sharp 'clock' on the wood for every single note. The crowd loves it. But who knows what the adjudicators will think?

The hall is instantly silent when at last the MC approaches the microphone. Some new band from Galway, the Lough Lurgan (who has even heard of them?) has come second. This could be tragic. Or … yes … the Tulla Ceili Band has won! The band has exploded into a jumping, laughing knot of embraces. There are tears among the supporters, now swamping them, every man of them keen to buy a round and then another one. The musicians are no teetotallers, like the Kilfenora crew, but they will have to go steady on the pints, for tonight they must take the stage again at the winners' concert and, after that, take the long road home. For the time being, they float across the square to the pub.

Tulla Céilí Band, 1957
(l to r: Paddy Canny,
P. J. Hayes, Joe McNamara,
Jack Keane, Paddy McNamara,
Michael Preston, Jack
Shaughnessy, Seán Reid)

Kiltannon

Paddy Canny loves Kiltannon. He loves his farm. He loves the land and he loves the work. He loves the cows he milks morning and night. He loves the chestnut horse he still keeps, to pull the plough and the harrow. He loves the caves where the river has carved out a wondrous gallery in the limestone rock. All day he whistles tunes and when his day's work is done he brings out the fiddle and plays.

Paddy has found his place and will never leave Kiltannon. There is no need for him to go out to America, like his friend Joe Cooley, who had been working on building sites in Ennis. Seán Reid had found him the jobs and then lost them for him by calling him away to play music in the middle of the working day. And Paddy O'Brien, maybe the finest musician he knows, has left Ireland. Neither of his friends had land to keep them here.

If not for his mother, Paddy might have had to join them. Even as she moved deeper into old age, Kate has made a final effort to see her two sons settled on good farms. Long expected, Mickie's inheritance has come to pass and he has taken over his uncle Michael Canny's farm and moved down to Ballyglass with his young wife Eileen and their children. Mickie handed up the farm at Glendree to the Land Commission, swapping it for a piece of land next door to the uncle's farm. So he is well established. Placing Paddy in a good farm of his own was more complicated.

Kate was always good to manage. She has a family connection with John Clune, who had a farm down near Tulla, where his wife has a drapery shop. Kate's mother was Nora McCall from Ballinruan and Nora's mother was Bridget Clune and John Clune is from that family. Kate approached John, and when he decided to sell the place, Paddy got first dibs on it, to keep it from passing to outsiders. The price was fair, but between the two of them, Mickie and Paddy had only two-thirds of it. All the years of cutting turf and bringing it down, the years of quarrying rock and pounding it into road metal, the drain digging and the road mending, the clearing of land and ploughing for well-off farmers. All those years with the eyes of the district on them, noting that the Cannys wanted to better themselves. All that work to generate the money in their two bank accounts. On top of that, Mickie had sold the grazing land at The Rampeens, where the brothers had carried burdens of hay to their cattle. And still, it wasn't enough.

Kate Canny had one last resource to draw on: her sisters, Hannah and Ellen in New York. Ellie has had great success in her interior decorating business and the sisters come home every few years. Kate wrote and her sisters sent the money and the deal with John Clune was done.

> Paddy has found his place and will never leave Kiltannon. There is no need for him to go out to America, like his friend Joe Cooley, who had been working on building sites in Ennis.

The gate lodge at Kiltannon and the milking parlour Paddy Canny built

So Paddy has gone down the six miles from Glendree to Kiltannon. He and Mickie have fixed up the old cottage, replacing the rotten thatch with slates from Nenagh and restoring the inside. It's nothing fancy, but snug enough for Paddy. Once the gate lodge to the Molony estate, the cottage stands beside enormous iron gates, the rusting posts and elegant finials begging for a coat of paint. They will have to wait, for Paddy has other plans. He has started off with dry cattle—beef cattle—while he builds up a milking herd, each year keeping the heifers of his best milkers. He uses an old ruin of a cottage as a milking parlour, but will build them a palace with milking machines, for there is electricity on hand. He has the whole thing in his head.

Paddy farms the land and it gives back, whether it is a crop of oats or the vegetables in the garden or the lavish pasture. The rich soil rewards every project. Paddy works as he always has: no rush, no hurry. Steady, methodical, all day long. On winter evenings, Pat O'Halloran, who lives in a once-grand house at Kiltannon Cross, might call in to share his stories about the old Molony estate where, for generations, his family were blacksmiths. He knows the family's official history: the two bishops, one with £150 on his head, the family turning Protestant to keep their estate, the roads and schools they built, their support for their workers during the Famine, the burning of their Georgian mansion on 15 September 1920. Pat knows the unofficial history of that day, too: the band of IRA fighters coming down from the hills, entering the house when the owners were absent, piling chairs beneath the great staircase, throwing matches into the petrol and burning three storeys of grandeur to a ruin. The family moving to the farmhouse, not so grand, hoping that one day they would see their treasures returned, for someone in their employ, being in on the plan, had squirreled them away for safekeeping. Who knows where those treasures are now?

Paddy knows he will never enjoy the status of families who have lived here for generations. That is the case in every place. But an industrious farmer is not out of place in Kiltannon. People here seem to appreciate the improvements he is making and his willingness to lend an ear to their complaints about the weather and the government or to put his massive shoulders to work when an animal is caught in a drain. Just recently, he met Paddy Fitzgerald and his son Joe, who were driving their cattle down from Knockjames on bicycles. The two farmers stood talking in the road for a good half-hour, Paddy Canny all the while holding a bag of cement under each arm. This strength serves him well. People here do think it strange, though, that Paddy would be in his house all alone and playing music late into the night. Some have stood in the road by the huge iron gates, listening. Paddy never speaks about his music, never even lets on that he knows anything about music, and so the matter is not discussed. At the same time, everyone knows that Paddy Canny plays on the wireless and has gone out to America to play music and has won prizes for it.

Facing page: 'The Caves of Kiltannon'
Water has made secret paths through the soft limestone of north-east Clare, carving out caves, which were regarded with awe. In a local story, a man seeking hidden treasure entered a cave in Glendree, never to be seen again, although passers-by could hear him playing a fiddle. The caves at Kiltannon are another magical place, where Paddy Canny would go fishing and bring his family for picnics.

Few musicians in East Clare were known for their compositions, although they were surrounded by the finest of composers, including East Galway's Paddy Fahey, Paddy Kelly and Patrick Moloney, West Clare's Junior Crehan and Tipperary's Sean Ryan and Paddy O'Brien. Paddy Canny's composition, like his playing, has a melancholy beauty. He loved the jig form, which was adopted in Ireland during the seventeenth century, a paradigm in miniature of the gigue, the upbeat finale of the Baroque dance suite. As a child, Paddy internalised the rhythm, structure, and melodic conventions of Irish dance forms, with their repetition of key melodic ideas, especially at the end of each section. 'The Caves of Kiltannon' is in three rather than the more usual two parts, the third introducing a kind of variation. There is an easy flow in Paddy's playing of his tune. The jig is impelled forward by long bows drawing together many notes towards a forceful 'full stop' (bar 8), the same way that he punctuates his speech. Sliding onto notes is prominent in this tune, especially in the opening bar, when he lingers on the A and slowly squeezes up to and a little beyond B flat. At other times, his Bs are sharper, a piquant ambiguity also present in varying F notes, the presence of F sharp moving the tune's G dorian mode towards the moody melodic minor. These tonal shifts are an important aspect of Paddy Canny's expressive vocabulary.

One balmy evening in the summer of 2000, Paddy invited me to come out from Tulla, where I was living, and to bring my fiddle. At the gate lodge, Paddy and his wife Philomena brought me through to the sitting room, where the windows were open and the sweet tang of newly cut hay came in to us as we played. When it was my turn to suggest a tune, I asked for 'The Caves of Kiltannon'. Paddy was delighted and called out to Philomena, who was in the kitchen, making tea.

'Mammy, she plays my tune!'

'The Caves of Kiltannon'

Paddy Canny, 1997

Movies of Happiness

Paddy Canny loves going to the movies, especially if they are westerns. In Feakle they were held on a Monday night at *Scannain na Sonna*: Movies of Happiness. Paddy would walk down with his young cousin from next door, the 'other' Paddy Canny, arriving early for the best of the shilling seats, in front of the rows of children who always cheered when Mr Humphrey cranked up the petrol generator to start the show. On the way home, the two Paddys would discuss the rights and wrongs of the story, the dry country out there in America, the feats of riding and shooting, and the beautiful horses.

When he moves to Kiltannon, Paddy goes to the best picture house in the district, John Byrne's, only three miles away, in Tulla. From Kiltannon Cross, he will collect Mikey McCarthy, who lives with his father in a barrel wagon out on the bog road. Mikey isn't able to speak well—you might call it a speech impediment. He is happy to sit beside Paddy at the pictures and there is never anything on that might upset him. The Film Censor has seen to that: no horror, no kissing, no sex or swearing, nothing that might offend the smallest child in the audience.

When his father Jim McCarthy dies, Mikey walks the few miles to Kiltannon. The poor man is crying when he arrives at the house. Fathers dying is something Paddy knows about. He brings Mikey inside and does what he can for him.

Nothing so Beautiful

There are fourteen pubs in Tulla. John Minogue's is the one with a piano upstairs, where the musicians who formed the Tulla Céilí Band rehearsed when they were just starting out. In the decade since then, John has continued to support the band. He has always loved music and even took lessons from Paddy Canny for a while, so is happy to lend his upstairs room for tonight's recording session.

Johnny Byrnes's tape recorder is turned on and the musicians scarcely introduced when Paddy flies into the first tune, registering Seán Reid's piano vamps only as an extension of his own tapping feet. The tune is 'Garrett Barry's', a jig Paddy loves to play. Back when he was starting on the fiddle, there were more jigs than reels, and the jigs that his father gave him were lovely. At home, he likes to play jigs for the comfort in them. He has developed 'Garrett Barry's' into a performance piece and uses it now to polish the various techniques he will apply in tonight's programme of reels. On each repetition, Paddy changes the melody in small ways and, at the end of the tune, makes a much bolder variation, like the one his Dublin friend Tommie Potts plays, to turn the tune around.

The long and short of rolls and grace notes and trebles, the finger triplets in many varieties, the alternation of smooth and staccato passages, and the use of drones to colour a passage with harmonic warmth: all these Paddy has adopted into his vocabulary of embellishments. These techniques, embraced by the Sligo fiddlers recorded in America, especially Michael Coleman, are also integral to uilleann piping. Paddy knows the music of pipers well, from Martin Rochford and Martin's hero Johnny Doran, from Paddy O'Donoghue, Seán Reid and Willie Clancy, and the famous Dublin piper Leo Rowsome, who comes down to Clare to give concerts and mentor other pipers.

Tonight Paddy is in good form and good humour after an exhilarating Whit Weekend at the All-Ireland Fleadh in Longford. Every time the Tulla Céilí Band was due on stage, PJoe had to search the whole town for Paddy Canny, and every time he would be in some pub, playing with Peter O'Loughlin, the two truants charging at the music like lunatics, a crowd urging them on. And at Paddy's shoulder, Johnny Byrnes, a thin man with thick glasses and the most committed fan of traditional music Paddy has met. Johnny had shared a flat in London with Willie Clancy, when Willie was playing the flute, and knows great music when he hears it. He has arranged with Mick Connolly to record his son Séamus, a brilliant musician who has just won the Under 18 fiddle competition. Before heading to Killaloe, Johnny, softly spoken and earnest, asked Paddy, why doesn't he swing

The long and short of rolls and grace notes and trebles, the finger triplets in many varieties, the alternation of smooth and staccato passages, and the use of drones to colour a passage with harmonic warmth: all these Paddy has adopted into his vocabulary of embellishments.

through Tulla and record him? Paddy heard himself stuttering, unable to bring out a response. It happens when someone wants something of him or when he is confronted by any kind of authority. Seán Reid stepped in and said he would organise everything and so the deal was done.

Paddy plays another jig, 'Whelan's', while a string of music lovers file into the room. He changes into 'Gallagher's Frolics', in the same key and very similar in melodic structure, with winding variations and wider intervals that have a greater sense of movement, of freedom, as though Whelan's has grown wings and shouldered its way out of its tight melodic container.

'Good boy, Paddy!' his audience responds.

Now that his listeners have settled, Paddy launches his first reel. 'Andy McGann's' was composed by Andy's friend Lad O'Beirne, who had accompanied Paddy on that memorable night in Louis Quinn's New York basement. It is a cheerful, catchy tune in the unusual key of C, which reminds Paddy of how he used to transpose tunes down from D to match the old concertinas at kitchen dances.

Paddy's hand is quiet on the fingerboard, making notes with such economy that the broad bunch of his fingers seems scarcely to move. Unlike most fiddle players outside East Clare, Paddy uses dynamic variation to colour his tunes, the volume swelling as a passage rises and subsiding as it falls, for he hears the contours of the tune as emotional changes. He emphasises a rising passage with a long sweep of an up-bow, adding pressure with his forefinger to increase volume, subtracting it as the urgency subsides, a technique heard but not seen. Sometimes he enriches a note by lightly touching the open string below or above the one where the melody plays.

Johnny Byrnes

Paddy is immersed in the flow of his music. In his two years at Kiltannon he has had the luxury of playing every night for as long and as late as he pleases. This past year, he has been busy with his music. There was the big night at the end of February when Ciarán Mac Mathúna and his recording crew came to Feakle. In March, Paddy was supposed to go on the Tulla Céilí Band's American tour and record an album in New York. He didn't go. He was sorry to let the boys down, but he couldn't do it. The last time was almost too much of a good thing. And in March, Paddy's cows were calving and a field of oats had to be sown. PJoe Hayes has a father, a younger brother and a sister to work on their farm but at Kiltannon Paddy is on his own. And it was Lent. But, since the band came home, Paddy has been travelling to céilís every weekend and playing in concerts to promote Comhaltas Ceoltóirí Éireann and then at the All-Ireland in Longford.

At home, Paddy prefers to play one tune at a time. At competitions and on stage, in the band and in the recording studio, he will play a set of two tunes, sometimes three. Tonight he plays the tunes one at a time, only varying this with a couple of sets he has from Peter O'Loughlin and one from Michael Coleman, for it seems almost against nature to play 'Bonnie Kate' without 'Jenny's Chickens'. Most of tonight's reels are from the American recordings, especially Coleman's.

Now that he has warmed up, Paddy tackles 'The Cuckoo', which has enchanted him for nearly twenty years. In the second half, there are technical challenges that require him to move his hand to a higher position, while at the same time making complex variations to rhythm and melody and alternating between two strings to bring out the 'cuckoo' call. Paddy has long since moved on from trying to create an exact copy of Coleman's recording. Paddy approaches the tune with great energy, but at the same time with balance. Neither staccato nor legato passages dominate and he has smoothed out Coleman's jagged hornpipe rhythm. When he gets to the cuckoo call, he gracefully 'tips out' the notes of the falling third. He plays the tune four times and each time varies it, especially in the dramatic second part, although his variations are less flamboyant than Coleman's. Where Coleman plays boldly, his tone strong and even, Paddy's volume comes and goes, echoing the tune's shifts in pitch and intensity. At one point, when he comes to the cuckoo's call, Paddy's volume drops suddenly, like a storyteller's hush, commanding attention. To give weight to a particular note, Paddy will delay it by sliding up from below, or by playing the note below it very briefly, like a grace note. Either way, it is always a subtle shift, a seamless drawing of one note into another that suspends the music in a moment of anticipation. In 'The Cuckoo', this happens at the start of the tune and at every repetition:

whereas Michael Coleman always strikes the note right on the beat:

Paddy's 'Cuckoo', with its brilliance and its pathos, moves his audience. John Minogue, embracing his role as midwife to the proceedings, has offered praise at the end of each tune, along with those who have crept up the stairs to listen: 'Lovely, Paddy!' 'Good man!' 'Beautiful!' But when Paddy comes to the end of 'The Cuckoo', John can express only wonder: 'Wisha, glory!'

When Peter O'Loughlin makes his entrance, exuberant after his wins in the fleadh competitions, the atmosphere changes. He raises his eyebrows at Paddy:

'How's the crack?'

'*Ta go maith*,' says Paddy. It's good.

Paddy releases Seán Reid from his duty and plays a string of solo reels, free of the piano's plodding constraint and not always helpful harmonies. Paddy and Peter try out a couple of reels together, then charge into 'The Steampacket' and 'The Milliner's Daughter', exploding into the sunlight of G major, the strongest key for the flute. Theirs is a new musical partnership and Paddy is still discovering the freedom a flute player gives to the fiddler and responding to the flute's different ways of bringing out the same tune. Supported by Peter's emphatic rhythm, Paddy's playing is expansive and confident. Matching and swapping embellishments, the pair bring out joyous music.

Next day, when Johnny Byrnes and his tape recorder arrive in Killaloe, Séamus Connolly begs to listen to the recording of Paddy. He is astounded by what he hears. Technique is something Séamus is well drilled in and he recognises this in Paddy's playing. But that is only the foundation of what Paddy has produced: the sweet, pure voice of the violin, singing; the poignant note of longing that, even at fourteen, Séamus appreciates. Never has he heard anything so beautiful.

Facing page: 'The Cuckoo'

From the opening bar of 'The Cuckoo', it is evident that Paddy Canny's approach and sensibility are very different from Michael Coleman's in 'Murray's Fancy'. Where Coleman plays hornpipes with a bouncy ebullience, Paddy's bow strokes are gentle and sweet, his phrasing elegant, often in groups of three notes. At Paddy's somewhat slower pace, the tune becomes not only a thrilling technical display but also an emotional journey, expressed in Paddy's sliding onto notes, his more nuanced legato bowing alternating with light staccato phrases, and his surges of speed and volume at high points in the drama, particularly in the B part, with its cuckoo call and virtuosic displays. Not that he shirks the technical challenges; in fact, in the third repetition Paddy introduces an extremely demanding variation of double-stopped octaves.

Where Coleman's tune changes restlessly throughout, Paddy plays the A part almost identically on all four repetitions. There is one exception. The third time he plays the tune, in bar 11 of the A part, Paddy takes one particular variation of Coleman's and amplifies the motif. He must like the sound of a tune momentarily stuck on repeat. Not only does he emphasise it loudly here, but it turns up again and again, including in 'Banish Misfortune' and in 'Sean sa Cheo', where it delighted his audience at Carnegie Hall.

'The Cuckoo'

Paddy Canny, 1958

Paddy Canny's variation to the B part in the third repetition

Michael Coleman's variation to bar 11 and Paddy Canny's adaptation

London, 1958

As the band launches into their signature tune, 'The Humours of Tulla', Peggy McMahon feels the crush of the crowd besieging the stage. People around her are not dancing, but crying: people she knows from dances in Ennis at the Queens and Paddy Conn's and new friends she has met here at the Galtymore in Cricklewood and other dancehalls where the Irish gather. She can see tears even in the musicians' eyes. But beautiful, vivacious Peggy is not crying. She has thrived in London, working at an upmarket restaurant owned by the British airline and going out dancing at weekends, or any night, really. Since Peggy met PJoe Hayes at the end of her first holiday home to Crusheen, their letters have slowly grown more intimate. And now, three years later, here he is in London. Peggy is proud of PJoe and the Tulla Céilí Band, the big splash they are making. She has taken the week off work and will go to every one of their dances.

This is the biggest crowd Peggy has seen at the Galty—five thousand, somebody said—and that's before the men arrive after closing time at the Crown, just along Broadway. On weekday mornings, dozens of them gather outside that pub for the 'call on', hoping to be picked for a day's casual labouring. At weekends, they prime themselves for a big night at the Galtymore. They have come to London from Irish towns and farms in search of work and money and, perhaps, the romance to be found in the dancehalls that are a sanctuary for the Irish in London. A tidal wave of emigrants has left Ireland since the war ended, many of them gravitating to the lodging houses of London's north. For the young women especially, the Galtymore is the queen of the dancehalls, glamorous beyond their childhood dreams, with its silky dance floors and chandelier lighting, galleries upstairs where you can sit with a drink and a friend. The two halls here—one for céilí dancing, the other for modern—are full of possibilities.

On the stage, PJoe is steering the band, driving the music with the swing and energy that shift people off their seats. At the same time, his eyes follow the beacon of Peggy McMahon as she progresses around the room, twirling her skirt and laughing for the pure joy of it. When the band plays their newest tunes, changing from 'Imelda Rowland's' into 'Cregg's Pipes', the dancers roar and whoop. Peggy knows these tunes already, from the *Echoes of Erin* LP, recorded earlier this year in New York. When the record arrived from PJoe, Peggy bought a gramophone to play it on. A huge thing, she had to get the coalman to bring it on his truck.

The band is in top form tonight, exhilarated by their reception after a difficult start to their first British tour. The journey over was tough: the train to Dublin

They have come to London from Irish towns and farms in search of work and money and, perhaps, the romance to be found in the dancehalls that are a sanctuary for the Irish in London. A tidal wave of emigrants has left Ireland since the war ended, many of them landing up in the lodging houses of London's north.

Trafalgar Square, London
(l to r: Jack Shaughnessy,
Dr Bill Loughnane, P. J. Hayes
and Seán Reid)

and the mail boat to Holyhead, then the night train to Birmingham, with a change along the way. They were bowled over by their digs in Birmingham's magnificent Cobden Hotel and, in the bar, by the profligate hospitality of their countrymen, labourers who had crossed the water to build canals and roads and railways. So many pints lined up in front of them and no chance of doing them justice, although they certainly tried. One man boasted that his wages are ten times what he might get in Ireland. It was no idle boast: every musician will return to Ireland with £25 or £30 in his pocket, more than three times the weekly wage at home, where a night's playing will earn them a single pound.

That first night, the band's sound had blurred from too much alcohol and not enough sleep. The dancehall entrepreneur John Byrnes, who offered them this tour, would not be pleased unless they lifted their game. They have a kind of manager in Sonny Mullins, who owns Gort's Classic Ballroom, where the band often plays, but it is PJoe who coaxes the lads to settle down and pace themselves for the nights ahead. By the time they arrive in London, the musicians are hitting their stride.

It is years since Bobby Casey left the band and made his home in Camden Town. He shows the boys his London, taking them to bars packed with the Irish, from Clare and Galway and other places. When he picks up his fiddle, they are mesmerised by the richness of Bobby's music, his languid rolls and luxuriant variations, his music colourful and soulful, the way he finds sadness in the merriest of tunes. West Clare is in his music and will never leave it. Such a contrast to the pared-back versions they play in the band.

Sometimes Paddy Canny goes missing, just as Sonny and PJoe are running the band through the night's programme. 'Paddy's found the church,' says Dr Bill Loughnane, the newest of the band's four fiddle players, who knows Paddy's ways.

Wherever he lands up with the band, Paddy will seek out the quiet of a church and the comfort of prayer before the rigours of a night's performance.

The Tulla has become one of Ireland's most successful céilí bands, bringing the sound of progress to small country places and the sound of home to emigrants. Band members have included some of the greatest Irish musicians of the era: Bobby Casey, Willie Clancy, Joe Cooley, Paddy O'Brien. One by one, they have left for Dublin or London or New York. The band rides this wave of emigration, too, for it is among those who have left Ireland that their acclaim, and their earnings, have been greatest. They have witnessed the tidal push–pull of hope and loss from both sides: young people at home, longing for a way out of poverty and loneliness; those same youngsters, as emigrants, lonely and longing for home. Despite their nation's failure to provide for them, these migrant workers are proud to be Irish. In the music and dancing and drinking and romancing in London's dancehalls, they experience both consolation and a more acute yearning. Swimming against this tide of homesickness, the Tulla Céilí Band will be back in Clare for Christmas.

All-Ireland Champions

'Time's up, boys! We'll have to adjourn now until Monday.' This is not what they want to hear. After all his balancing and fiddling with the equipment, with time ticking away and ticking away, Peter Hunt has recorded only two tracks for them. And they have to get Seán Reid's car back to Ennis tonight. Monday won't do at all.

It has been a bit rushed. Peter O'Loughlin drove the old Morris, picking up Paddy Canny and PJoe Hayes on the way. In the car, they had a chat about what tunes they might play. At the studio in Stephen's Green they met up with Bridie Lafferty, one of the best accompanists in the business, who plays with the Tulla Céilí Band when Seán Reid can't make it to céilís in Dublin. It was meant to be as simple as that: drive to Dublin, meet Bridie, record a few tunes and drive home again.

Paddy Canny is dismayed, for he is the one who agreed to make the tape for Jim O'Neill in New York. Last year Jim's company recorded the Tulla Céilí Band on their triumphant American tour and now O'Neill wants Paddy's tape as a matter of urgency. There is £10 in it for each of the musicians. Not bad for a day's work— or would be if they weren't here in Dublin with no tape completed and only a few bob in their pockets for a night's lodgings. Maybe Seán Reid should have booked the studio for more than the single hour, but that's what the people in New York wanted: an hour of music.

A few phone calls later, Paddy tracks down a Galway man, Harry McCourtney, who works at Eamonn Andrews' recording studio in Henry Street.

'I'm off to Galway tomorrow,' says Harry. 'I can't stay with ye, but I know you're stuck, so ye can have the studio. There's a young fellow there can turn it on and turn it off and that's all he knows about it. He'll see ye right.'

Saturday morning sees the men striding along O'Connell Street, instruments tucked under their arms, overcoats and hats declaring them dressed for the city. At the Post Office they turn into Henry Street with Bridie beside them. They are fresh and keen, and in the studio the tunes pour out. There was no need to rehearse. Since Peter joined the Tulla Céilí Band, the three of them have often played together. Paddy runs through the first bars of each tune for Bridie to get the key, and off they go. They split the sets evenly: duets of Paddy and Peter O'Loughlin, duets of Paddy and PJoe, and the rest with the three of them together. The young lad turns the tape recorder on and turns it off and by six o'clock in the evening, the job is done and the Morris is on the road back to Ennis.

When they receive copies of the LP, they are surprised at the title, *All-Ireland Champions—Violin*. Perhaps Jim O'Neill was still expecting Paddy Canny to make a solo recording and never got around to changing the name. But it is a fact that every one of them has won an All-Ireland: Paddy in the senior violin and in a quartet that included PJoe, and who could forget the Tulla Céilí Band's victory two years ago? Peter has won twice in the senior flute as well as in a duet with Aggie Whyte, and Bridie has an All-Ireland for a duet with Paddy O'Brien back in '53. These All-Ireland titles have become their calling cards, for the Comhaltas competitions are widely recognised now and bestow considerable prestige.

All-Ireland Champions is a remarkable achievement: three young farmers from County Clare achieving an artistic and social status granted to very few in Ireland. In its long-playing format, the record is marketed to the urban, middle-class consumers of Ireland's traditional music revival, who have access to the modern multi-speed gramophone. In fact, this is one of the very first long-playing albums of Irish music to be recorded in Ireland.

The 'violin' of the title echoes *veidhlín*, the name older country people still give the fiddle. It excludes Peter O'Loughlin and, indeed, the record company has included only one of his duets with Paddy. Perhaps they are holding back the rest for another album. A decade younger than Paddy, Peter is a star in his own right— or Peadar, the name he uses at fleadhs, where the Comhaltas officials encourage musicians to use the Irish version of their names.

Facing page: **'Rolling in the Barrel'** and **'In the Tap Room'**
'They all sound the same!' complain those who dislike Irish music. But sometimes the tunes do sound the same, or almost the same. In East Clare there appears to be a local preference for pairing tunes in the same key and often with the same melodic shape and harmonic structure, the second tune differing in rhythmic emphasis, or extending the melodic range, or using the same notes in different patterns. It can be a satisfying practice when the musicians playing recognise and savour the subtle shift as one tune rolls into the next.

'Rolling in the Barrel' was one of Pat Canny's tunes, 'In the Tap Room' a more elaborate setting of the same tune. With an almost identical melodic shape, they differ in rhythmic emphasis. Early-twentieth-century recordings from America featured tunes in sets to provide contrast and to fill a 78 rpm side, and the practice gradually became ubiquitous in Irish traditional music. In the Tulla Céilí Band, PJoe Hayes recognised the importance of contrast, both to enliven the dancers and to help the musicians catch the change into the next tune. On the *All-Ireland Champions* album, the set finishes with a third tune, 'The Earl's Chair', an East Galway composition named for the rock in Derrycrag Wood where an earl was reputed to have rested while out hunting. It provides a complete change—of key, rhythm, mood and melodic shape—and a most agreeable uplift to musicians playing this popular set.

All-Ireland Champions is a remarkable achievement: three young farmers from County Clare achieving an artistic and social status granted to very few in Ireland.

'Rolling in the Barrel' and 'In the Tap Room'

Paddy Canny, 1984

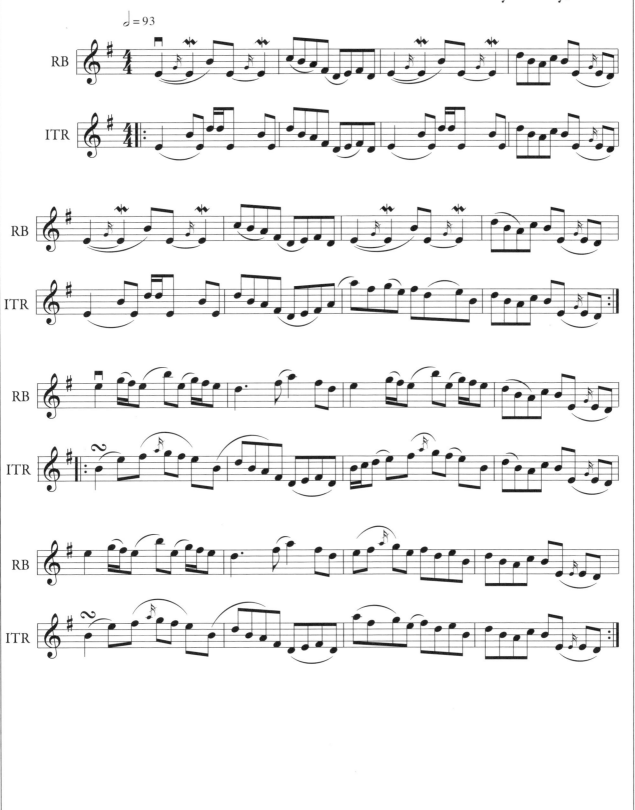

Peter, who plays pipes and fiddle as well as the flute, often travels from his home in Kilmaley to Ballinakill for evenings of music with Aggie Whyte and her friends, among them the ace flute player Eddie Moloney. *All-Ireland Champions* includes numerous tunes from East Galway and Peter is pleased that a set Aggie and Eddie have recorded, 'Kitty Gone a-Milking' going into 'Music in the Glen', comes first on the album.

The record's twenty-four tunes are drawn from the current favourites in the musicians' collective repertoire, garnered over many years from a vast network of musicians and recordings, a trove of tunes and comradeship unavailable to their parents' generation. The trail of these connections leads not only into East Galway, but also across to West Clare and North Tipperary, to Ennis and Dublin, London and New York, and to every town in Ireland where musicians swap tunes at a fleadh. While most of the tunes have been recorded before, new tunes composed by their contemporaries, Sean Ryan from Tipperary, Pat Moloney from East Galway and Ed Reavy out in America, are recorded here for the first time.

The musicians have kept the céilí band convention of beginning with prompt chords on the piano and follow the usual format of recording tunes in pairs but, compared to the syncopated rhythm, dramatic melodic variations and bright tone of the American recordings, their notes are more evenly articulated, their variations more subtle, their tone sweeter: a mellow, inviting sound. Although the pace is nearly as fast as the musicians would play at céilís, their music sounds unhurried.

The second side of the album features duets from Paddy and PJoe, the two fiddles resonating richly, an effect heightened by Paddy's subtle use of drones. The pair has played together for nearly thirty years and it shows in the way they balance out their different ways of executing a tune, the way a couple might learn to accommodate each other's quirks and grievances until at last they can finish one another's sentences and agree to disagree. On *All-Ireland Champions* each of their styles can be distinguished within their unique combined sound. Paddy's sliding onto strong notes, his tricky triplets, the long bows drawing multiple notes together and the swelling volume as the tune rises to a climax—all are offset by PJoe's sparsely ornamented bow strokes, which maintain the sprightly rhythm and keep the structure of the tunes firm.

Paddy and PJoe have played music together all the years of their youth, free from the responsibility of running a farm and raising a family. These times are coming to an end. Paddy has turned forty and PJoe is not far behind. PJoe's father is in his eighties now and past managing the Hayes farm. And Peggy McMahon is still waiting in London.

> The trail of these connections leads not only into East Galway, but across to West Clare and North Tipperary, to Ennis and Dublin, London and New York, and to every town in Ireland where musicians swap tunes at a fleadh.

Double Wedding

After the nuptial Mass in the Pro-Cathedral, two hundred guests join the celebration at the Queen's Hotel in Ennis. The Tulla Céilí Band plays for dancing, as they have for so many weddings here. The photo in the national newspaper shows PJoe Hayes and Paddy Canny, handsome and proud, their brides smiling for the camera from behind the matching tiered cakes. But there is something unusual about this wedding photo, for the two brides are wearing suits when, in 1961, every girl who can wears a white bridal gown on her special day. Peggy McMahon has bought just such a dress in London. So beautiful. But she cannot wear it, for Philomena Hayes has refused to wear a white dress and can't be persuaded. At thirty-six she would feel foolish in such an outfit. And so Peggy does not wear her beautiful gown, only a tulle veil and a stylish evening costume, and her long-awaited wedding day is spoiled. Likewise, her dreamed-of honeymoon. After one night in a Limerick hotel, it is back to Maghera and a quiet evening in her new home, while PJoe goes off with the band.

Over the seven years of their courtship, Peggy and PJoe have had their ups and downs. They have met only during Peggy's holidays at home and the band's whirlwind weeks in London. During the long months in between, they exchanged letters until PJoe called it off, despairing of ever providing the standard of home his fiancée deserved. PJoe was wretched, especially when he learned how devastated Peggy was. But a more worldly-wise friend advised PJoe to modernise. The Hayes's cottage, like most others in the district, consisted of a kitchen, with small rooms at each end for the parlour and the parents' bedroom, and a sleeping loft above. No running water, no bathroom, no toilet of any kind. That was what Peggy had agreed to, to the incomprehension of her London friends. She was delighted with the gesture and the renovation: a bathroom and extra bedrooms and a back kitchen with gas and running water. The engagement was renewed.

Some years back, when Mickie was thinking of marrying, the Canny brothers had made similar improvements to the home place at Curraun. He and Paddy had opened up the doorway, so low that you had to stoop to enter the cottage, and completed the job by lifting the huge padstone with their own hands. They raised the walls, made the loft into a second storey and replaced the thatch with asbestos tiles. In the end, it happily accommodated Mickie's mother and brother as well as his young wife and the children who were born in that house.

Now, with Mickie down at Ballyglass and Jack and his family gone out to Australia, it was Paddy's turn to marry. Paddy has just turned forty-two. PJoe is forty years old, about the age that most farmers marry. Philomena, on the other hand, is considered old to marry, although at thirty-six she is much the same age as Paddy's mother at her wedding.

Because many farmers, even in this generation, remain as head of the household until old age, sometimes without even naming their heir, several sons might work for their father until his death. If this situation continues until it is too late for those children to marry, the family will die out. If one son marries, the remaining siblings might be relegated to odd-jobs man or useful aunt, with no prospect of an independent livelihood unless they are able to emigrate or marry into another farm or find work outside. Rural parishes are populated with leftover bachelors, whose status in the community is low, although not as low as their sisters'.

Wedding day, 1961

Philomena knew that this might be her future and there was little she could do about it. She loved her family and the farm and, now that her mother was an old woman, had taken over much of the household work as well as helping PJoe and their brother Liam around the farm. As the daughter who did not emigrate, it was her duty to care for her elderly parents. A shy woman, nervous in company, the farm was her world. What would become of her when PJoe married? She could stay and become a maid of all work for Peggy, who would have the authority to run the household, consulting only her mother-in-law. She could go to her sisters in America, although, at her age would she even get a position as a housemaid? The thought was terrifying.

But then Paddy Canny asked for her hand. Her great friend since childhood, he was always kind and shared her devotion to religion. They had shared many happy occasions in the kitchen at Maghera and on outings with the band. The life he offered was not so different from the one she knew. Philomena accepted Paddy's offer.

At Kiltannon, Philomena grieves at the loss of her home and family. Despite Paddy's urging that she should 'let her off', she resents Peggy, who has usurped her role there. What is more, Peggy has given birth to a young heir who has captivated the old couple. The two women could hardly be more different: the one outgoing, charming and strong-willed, the other quiet and anxious. Phil feels unwelcome at Maghera and, in the end, her bitterness and Peggy's triumph mean that visits between the two households cease.

For Paddy and PJoe the situation is quite different. Companions almost their whole lives, the two men carry on, never speaking of the conflict between their wives. But an awkward distance grows between them and the intimate evenings of playing music together at Maghera cease forever.

Ciarán at Maghera

The Hayes house in Maghera is a music house. When the neighbours and the priest come to play cards and dance sets and when musicians from the band call in to rehearse new tunes, when musicians like Joe Bane come on winter nights for the music and the company, or on any occasion when visitors call in, there has to be catering. It might be tea and sandwiches and a few bottles of stout, but more often Peggy will prepare a lavish spread with meat and salad and brown bread and her renowned fruit tarts.

Since the fame of the Tulla Céilí Band has made PJoe into something of a celebrity, those with a taste for traditional music will seek him out at any time of day, expecting to hear music. One fine July morning, PJoe was about to go out to the meadow, where the hay was cut and waiting for tramming and, when the whole field was done, collecting the trams to build into haystacks: a lot of work, which must be done before the weather changes. Before PJoe could get out the door, the young curate from Killanena arrived with some German visitors to take photos and listen to PJoe's music and drink Peggy's tea. And when those visitors left, another priest turned up wanting to hear a tune, and the hay still lying in the meadow. Another time, the family had just sat down to eat, when Peggy saw a friend from Dublin arriving with his wife and children. Before they reached the door, she had taken a dish and a fork and whisked the ham off everyone's plate so she could feed them.

And now, Ciarán Mac Mathúna has sent word that he wants to record the band at Maghera. Tonight. It is less than a year since her marriage and Peggy's first big night of catering. The band is seven, then there's Ciarán and his technicians, plus the family, some neighbours and friends—there would be twenty, at least. Peggy goes to Minogue's hotel in Tulla to buy whiskey and beer and Guinness and into Murphy's butcher for the lamb. He hasn't any. PJoe's brother Liam saves the day by going down to the Scariff butcher, Carroll's, coming back with a huge leg of lamb. One pound five shillings. The meat has to be cooked then and a potato salad made and lettuce and tomato to go with it and the parlour cleaned and the table there set and a fire laid—for the parlour is chilly—all before the grey van of the Outside Broadcasting Unit chugs up the avenue.

There are two bedrooms in the cottage's extension and they have the piano in one and Jimmy Leydon's drum kit in the other. There are leads running everywhere—it is all electric here now—but Ted Nugent, the engineer, has them all sorted out. Accordion player Mattie Ryan (Ciarán insists on calling him Martin) plays a few

> Since the fame of the Tulla Céilí Band has made PJoe into something of a celebrity, those with a taste for traditional music will seek him out at any time of day, expecting to hear music.

tunes on the accordion before Paddy Canny takes a turn with some hornpipes and the Coleman set, 'Lord McDonald's' and 'Ballinasloe Fair', which he recently put on a record for Gael Linn. When he plays another reel, 'Trim the Velvet', Ciarán is mesmerised.

When PJoe and Peter O'Loughlin play duets, George Byrt's fingers dance jazzily around the piano, shading the tunes with modal chords, the bass notes roving restlessly, driving the melodies towards their resolution. Georgie, as they call him, is the Tulla band's new piano player. The trio makes exciting listening for the crowd sitting in the kitchen and they have to restrain their feet from dancing, for fear their racket might spoil the recording. 'The Dublin Reel' and 'The Mountain Lark' have never sounded so inviting and will surely become favourites with Ciarán's listeners.

Paddy also plays duets with Peter O'Loughlin, before the whole band plays together, set after set, late into the night. It is one of the best recordings Ciarán has made. You can hear each of the instruments clearly: the two fiddles and the flute, the two accordions and the piano, with Jimmy's drums surprisingly synchronised. When they have nearly finished recording, Ciarán persuades old Mrs Hayes to take up her concertina and give them an old waltz.

> For the past seven years, Ciarán Mac Mathúna has been on a mission to promote the traditional music that is emerging from country kitchens and city back rooms into the public space of fleadhs and céilís.

For the past seven years, Ciarán Mac Mathúna has been on a mission to promote the traditional music that is emerging from country kitchens and city back rooms into the public space of fleadhs and céilís. His job, first of all, is to record music on tape and preserve it in the archives at Radio Éireann (now Raidió Teilifís Éireann, or RTÉ). In this, he is only the latest in a long line of collectors who have sought to save Irish music from certain death. Of necessity, those collectors had relied on music notation to document the tunes. Séamus Ennis, the first of RTÉ's 'outside' broadcasters, used acetate discs to record Irish-speaking musicians and storytellers

Facing page: **'Trim the Velvet'**
Michael Coleman recorded 'Trim the Velvet' in 1927, when he was at the peak of his career. The tune is an exhibition piece in four eight-bar parts. Following Coleman, Paddy Canny begins with what today is usually played as the final part. He takes the tune at a slower tempo than usual, bringing out the melody with flute-like clarity, using less sliding onto notes. He keeps his percussive finger triplet mainly to the first part, his main ornament the smoother roll. Although Paddy's playing is breathtaking, it is no mere technical display. Paddy doesn't play airs, but all the expressiveness musicians bring to that form can be heard in the delicacy and tenderness of his reels, as if he has maintained his initial love for the tune (for musicians fall obsessively in love with tunes) and, even after performing it on concert stages in New York and Dublin and all over the country, we can hear that he still loves playing 'Trim the Velvet', just as Ciarán Mac Mathúna and his radio audience love listening to it.

'Trim the Velvet'

Paddy Canny, 1962

in the West of Ireland. Now Ciarán uses magnetic tape for the same task. And these tapes do not sit idly in the RTÉ Archive. Ciarán's shows broadcasting selections from his recording sessions have become hugely popular, expanding listeners' idea of what good music might sound like. Relying on local reputations and authorities like Seán Reid, Ciarán tracks down musicians in many parts of Ireland, although, it is true, he has a special *grá* for the music of Clare and often replays his favourites, who include Paddy Canny, Elizabeth Crotty and West Clare's Junior Crehan. When Ciarán laments that he can neither play music nor sing, people kindly point out that his instrument is his unmistakeable, mellifluous voice.

Now that almost every household in Ireland has a radio, Ciarán's programmes have introduced a new generation of listeners to a wealth of styles and repertoires. He has opened the ears of urban audiences, his sonorous introductions leading them into nostalgic imaginings of fireside music making in country kitchens, his voice smoothing over all trace of the calculations and mishaps, the moments of awkwardness and irritation on long nights of recording—and drinking—as well as the differences in style and accomplishment among the musicians. What urban listeners hear, besides the beauty and strength of the music, is its authenticity: their musical heritage.

> Ciarán's programs give value to their local music and encouragement to musicians to keep playing or to take up again the instruments they put aside when house dances disappeared.

What listeners in the newly electrified rural townlands hear is somewhat different, especially when they know the musician. They hear the emptiness around this music, a silence they would fill if that musician were actually here among them. But Ciarán and the music he broadcasts soon become integrated into their lives. His programmes give value to their local music and encouragement to musicians to keep playing or to take up again the instruments they put aside when house dances disappeared. They listen critically, too, comparing others' performances with their own and picking up new tunes or new settings of old ones. Unlike gramophone records of Irish music, which can be so perfect and so intricate that they might be discouraging, the rural musicians can identify with the music on Ciarán's programmes.

While Ciarán is a champion of rural musicians, he can't champion all of them. Many fail to be selected for recording; others who have been recorded wait in vain to hear themselves on the radio, while those whose music is broadcast earn a certain celebrity. It was different story in country houses long ago, when any musician who contributed was appreciated, as long as they kept the beat.

It is six o'clock in the morning when the van rolls down the avenue at Maghera. It has been a happy night, at times a little rowdy. Someone with too many whiskeys on board made a grab at Peggy's young sister and broke the holy-water font in the hallway. But all is forgiven. The supper was universally enjoyed and Ciarán is pleased with the night's recording. In the months and years ahead, he will draw from it often on his weekly programmes. He is already planning to play Paddy Canny's haunting version of 'Trim the Velvet' in his next broadcast. He ends up using it for years as the introduction to *A Job of Journeywork*.

.

Bowing Out

At Maghera, PJoe is the farmer now, with his younger brother Liam as helper. Work around the farm has not changed much, for as yet they have no car and no tractor and still use horses for the heavy work. But there have been some changes. Their parents have died and a second son has been born to Peggy and PJoe. Weary of the tedium of organising the band's engagements by letter and telegram, PJoe has had the telephone connected. And they have sold a parcel of land so that a television mast can be erected on the top of Maghera Mountain.

Paddy Canny was the first of the musicians to appear on television. In 1964, few families in the district can afford a set, but they have one at Hayes's. The neighbours were invited in to watch the new invention staring at them from a corner of the parlour. Old Mike Donnellan was there, the same man who, during the wartime curfews, had recklessly pulled back the curtain to expose his dance parties to potential Black and Tan patrols. Now, he cowered, distraught. 'Poor Paddy!' he cries. 'He's been taken!' As if the fairies had enticed Paddy to some other world, across the gap that had grown between the band musicians' lives and this older generation's.

Paddy Canny's life has changed, too, with the loss of his own mother. Kate died in the Raheen Hospital for the aged, her body and mind worn out after a long life of endless work. Now, Paddy is worn out by the band's constant travel and rehearsals and milking his growing herd twice a day. He can't expect Phil to take over this work now that they have two young children in the house. In the end, it isn't a hard decision to leave the band. The Saturday night céilís in Dublin were always tough, but it is the television programmes that finish Paddy off. In 1966, RTÉ commissions the band to play for ten programmes of *Club Céilí*. The band's preparation is intense and the recording sessions exhausting. They drive to Dublin on a Sunday morning and in the afternoon tape two programmes, break for a meal, and then go back into the television studio until eleven at night. As well as playing for the dancing, there are duets and solos from the band, and that means more preparation for Paddy. With the cows already at peak milk production and the band booked every weekend for months ahead, Paddy knows it has become too much. Telling PJoe is the hard part.

Driving up the familiar avenue at Maghera, Paddy feels a rising anxiety. Entering the Hayes house these days feels daunting, although, in the band, PJoe has the same even-handed warmth as always. In the past twenty years, a stream of Ireland's greatest musicians has passed through, but only Paddy and PJoe have been in the band since the beginning. Paddy says what he has rehearsed and PJoe is good about

With the cows already at peak milk production and the band booked every weekend for months ahead, Paddy knows it has become too much. Telling PJoe is the hard part.

Paddy Canny, 1998
(Peter Laban)

it, as if he knew already what was coming and had prepared his own speech. He thanks Paddy for his years of commitment to the band, and for agreeing to all that PJoe has asked of him, when his heart was never in playing for dancers. Over the years, they often discussed whether band playing might spoil a fiddler's technique and limit the ability to play a tune with integrity. That was always Paddy's view and PJoe could see his point, although his own clean, rhythmic style had not changed and was the foundation of the band's sound. They part friends.

The weight lifts from Paddy. No more dealing with the hurly burly of cities and towns and encounters with strangers, long nights playing music and long journeys home again, with the threat of bad weather and bad roads and car trouble. Even the banter with the boys in the band had started to wear thin. He is so tired.

Paddy begins to miss seeing the boys. He misses Georgie Byrt's jokes and the intimacy of praying the Rosary on the way home from céilís. He misses the camaraderie and the wonderful musicians and the great days they've had out of it: the adventure of getting the band together, winning the All-Ireland, the crack in England every year. Recalling their excitement as teenagers when a new record arrived in the district and the freedom of cycling through the hills to a night of music, he misses his friendship with PJoe. How glad he had been to have a friend who shared his passion, PJoe always leaning forward in his music, anticipating the beat, the secret of his spell over the dancers. How he would lean to meet the next challenge, trusting people and enjoying their company. And then Paddy himself, holding back the beat, shying away from crowded places and people's expectations and their judgements. Once, the pair of them had balanced each other out, so that their music and their friendship had both light and shadow and a devotion that neither took for granted.

Paddy consoles himself with farm work and the embrace of family life. As time passes, he finds that he doesn't feel like playing music, any more than he feels like going out. There is a heaviness he has not felt since his father died.

Following page: **'Sergeant Early's Dream'**
PJoe Hayes got this tune from the New York fiddle player Kathleen Collins, who lived for some time in Loughrea, East Galway, with her then husband, accordion player Joe Burke. Paddy Canny uses the title Francis O'Neill gave it, referring to O'Neill's fiddle-playing colleague, James Early. Both play the same setting of this tune, but, where O'Neill has the tune in A dorian, they play it in the now generally used key of D dorian, which stays within the first position on the fiddle.

Given the two musicians' history of playing together, it is not surprising that their approach to the tune should have much in common. Both take it at a fairly sedate pace, PJoe especially, and team it with other tunes in the same key, so that their two tracks contain five D dorian reels. This suggests that PJoe, who likes to provide contrast in sets designed for dancing, retains the local taste for tunes in the same key when he is playing for listening.

Both musicians were long past their youth—PJoe is in his sixties, Paddy in his late eighties when each of these recordings was made—but each retains the style of his heyday. PJoe's sound, although much inflated by reverb, maintains his uncluttered clarity in presenting the melody and a strict tempo through the regular chop of his bow. Where PJoe faithfully follows the tune's rhythm, Paddy tells the story of its melody, with subtle phrasing that overrides the regular beat, a greater use of embellishment and his emphatic marking of the end of a section (bar 8) or a phrase (bar 19).

'Sergeant Early's Dream'

Lonesome

Lonesome is as lonesome does: it is a transformational force. It is lonesome when a young man loses his beloved father. It is lonesome farewelling a cousin who is emigrating. It is lonesome listening to music from home when you have left that home behind. The baby's first cry for breath after losing its sustenance in the womb is lonesome. The cry heard in women's keening at funerals in rural Ireland was like this, too, a downward-sliding wail. In lonesome music, this cry transforms desolation by touching deep, lifelong hurt. Touch is also the word for the fairies' power over human life, and music with the lonesome touch has a spiritual power to enchant and to haunt: *draíocht*.

Music with the lonesome touch is not a style and not a feeling. It is a force that moves us, the musician and the listener. Although it sounds differently in different music cultures, lonesome music is universal. And it is embedded in the life-world of small farmers in the mountain townlands above Feakle. To those who have known such music from childhood, hearing it now is overlaid with nostalgia, for it is a trigger that sets off simultaneously warm memories of youthful dancing days and sadness that those days have vanished, along with their youth. When the dancing stopped, the future for many of those dancers and musicians, the ones who did not emigrate, was a life of struggle, with no chance to marry and few entertainments within reach.

In north-east Clare, it is mainly the older fiddle players who make music with the lonesome touch: bittersweet, melancholy music that comes from a deep emotional engagement with the music and is expressed in the rise and fall of volume, in long sweeps of notes within a bow stroke and in the way they will squeeze a note to make it cry, sliding onto it and delaying its arrival. This lonesome quality is particularly evident in Paddy Canny's music and in Martin Rochford's, but is a quality recognised and reproduced by many another fiddler in the area.

Other features of fiddling in this part of East Clare (and in some adjacent areas) are a preference for tuning the fiddle a semitone or more below concert pitch, producing a darker, mellower tone that complements their taste for tunes in the 'sad' keys—the minor or aeolian mode, the dorian mode, and the mixolydian mode—when the vast majority of Irish dance tunes are in the cheerful major or ionian mode. They might modify a tune that is generally played in a major key, like 'My Love is in America':

> Music with the lonesome touch is not a style and not a feeling. It is a force that moves us, the musician and the listener. Although it sounds differently in different music cultures, lonesome music is universal. And it is embedded in the life-world of small farmers in the mountain townlands above Feakle.

by playing the third and seventh steps of the scale, made with the second finger, about a semitone flat, as Martin Rochford did when he played the tune for Jos Koning in 1975:

When the tonal centre and ending note of a tune is D, as it very often is, on the third step of that scale, instead of the expected F#, these musicians will play a note about halfway between an F natural and an F# and at the seventh step, about halfway towards a C natural instead of the expected C sharp, producing what Western musical convention identifies as 'sadness' or, as accordion player Paddy O'Brien expressed it, 'that old, plaintive touch'.

To today's ears, these notes simply sound flat—as they are, when compared to the same notes played on the accordion, for example, or the piano, where every note's pitch is fixed according to a tuning system called 'equal temperament' (because each note is separated from the next by an equal distance). In the course of the twentieth century, piano accompaniment and accordion-dominated céilí bands changed the sound of traditional music in Ireland. Younger fiddle players adopted that intonation. But those who learned to play before instruments tuned in equal temperament entered their sound world have retained an older system of tonality, similar to that of *sean nós* ('old style') singing in Irish and the 'just tuning' of the uilleann pipes, which allows each note of the scale played on the chanter to ring sweetly against the low drones, but will always clash with instruments tuned in equal temperament, the third and seventh notes in particular sounding flat.

This older tonality is at the heart of early-twentieth-century fiddling in northeast Clare, in East Galway and West Clare as well as in the fiddling traditions of other parts of Ireland, in Shetland and in Norway.

Not that the older musicians around Feakle all play exactly the same Cs and Fs as one another. It is a matter of personal taste. And they might alter their favoured position a little, depending on whether the tune was moving upwards or down the scale. But in general they used just one position for their second finger, where a classically trained violinist would know two distinct positions (F and F#, C and C#).

Ambiguity is another hallmark of their fiddle playing. While their F in the lower octave is a neutral F made with the second finger on the D string, in the higher octave it is made with the first finger on the E string and will mostly be F sharp, or otherwise a slide up to and a little beyond F natural. For this reason, tunes often include both a lower F in the lower octave and a higher F on the higher one. Martin Rochford, for example, after playing a soulful F natural at the beginning of

Those who learned to play before instruments tuned in equal temperament entered their sound world have retained an older system of tonality, similar to that of *sean nós* ('old style') singing in Irish and the 'just tuning' of the uilleann pipes, which allows each note of the scale played on the chanter to ring sweetly against the low drones, but will always clash with instruments tuned in equal temperament.

'My Love is in America', continues by playing a note closer to the standard F sharp in the higher octave.

The musicians not only accept this ambiguity, but will exploit it by alternating between lower and higher Fs on the E string, as numerous fiddlers do when they play 'The Humours of Scariff', the area's most widely known tune. This is how it is notated in O'Neill's *1001*:

Recordings of this tune Jos Koning made around Feakle in 1975 reveal a variety of ways of playing the Fs in bars one and three (circled), elsewhere played as F naturals. Paddy Canny makes a slow slide onto the first F, to a point just higher than F natural, while in the third bar, his F is higher, almost to F sharp. Martin Rochford is inclined to do the same, although sometimes he plays both notes as neutral Fs. Mike Doyle, on the other hand, plays an almost F sharp throughout the tune, while Bill Malley plays a random selection of Fs, all somewhere between F natural and F sharp. The musicians' acceptance of ambiguous intonation also accommodates combinations of instruments, as when Bill Malley and Joe Bane play together. Their Fs may not match, but they and their audience do not mind.

Most of the fiddlers Koning recorded had re-emerged around 1960, after having left aside their instruments for twenty years or more. All had learned their music without exposure either to the accordion or to the piano and so still heard and played their music within the older tonality. At Lena Hanrahan's pub in Feakle, these older musicians were not invited to play with the accordionist at the big dance nights in the lounge bar Lena opened in the 1960s. Their tuning jarred and their playing was too soft and too slow. Besides, they did not know the accordion player's fashionable and technically challenging tunes. So they kept to their small gatherings in the front bar, where music with the lonesome touch was what sounded right to them and to their intimate circle.

This older tonality is at the heart of early-twentieth-century fiddling in north-east Clare, in East Galway and West Clare as well as in the fiddling traditions of other parts of Ireland, in Shetland and in Norway.

Tommie

Tommie. What inspiration he has given to Paddy. And what solace Paddy has found in their friendship, the visits exchanged, and the letters.

The kitchen clock measures out the afternoon. Paddy is in good humour: 'Dum-de-da-de-DUM' he lilts. Perhaps he'll play that tune when the young scholar turns on his tape recorder. Paddy asks Jos Koning whether they have their own language where he lives. Dutch, he's told, and is disappointed to learn that the Dutch play very little of their national music.

'When you go back you should try and bring it alive,' Paddy advises. 'Like here. It's only in the last twenty years we've had it back, the Irish music. The fleadh cheoil was what brought it alive. When I was younger, there wasn't much music around. I wish I'd had it more.'

Paddy's fiddle is tuned down half a semitone, the way he likes it, a mellower sound. He plays one tune after another while the Dutch boy captures them on his machine. Suddenly weary, Paddy asks Jos to play something, since he has his fiddle with him. Jos plays 'The Golden Castle', a hornpipe he learned from Martin Rochford, who has befriended the young man.

'No better boy! That's a lovely ... lovely ... lovely ... tone. That's very ... very ... very ... what I like. There's soul in it'.

Why do even the simplest words refuse him when he's speaking with a stranger?

'That's what I like, too. But sometimes I think that I put too much in,' Jos whispers modestly.

'Ah, no.'

'It would be no good for dancing, anyway!'

'Ah, well, I don't worry about the dancing part to it. I know you'd care for Tommie Potts. Oh, he's very ingenious, as far as the soul of the music goes. Pure genius!' Paddy says warmly. 'He's the only musician I ever met that has that special feel for the music.'

'I heard he was in hospital.' Jos has been in touch with Tommie's old friend, Breandán Breathnach, the Dublin piper with a passion for collecting tunes and writing about Irish music.

'Tommie! That's news to me. I'm very sorry to hear that. Oh God, I'm sorry.'

The clock ticks louder. Outside, the cows are complaining, for it's nearly milking time.

'My God, I'm very sorry to hear that,' Paddy says again, taking up the fiddle.

The tune that comes to him then is 'The Bunch of Keys', a reel Tommie has played here, in this house. Hunched beneath the icon of the Virgin who presides over the kitchen, Paddy plays intensely. More often than usual, he slides up to notes and the slides are slower and longer and louder, a kind of keening. The tune shifts restlessly away from the cheerful key of G into a sombre modality. He leaves gaps between the phrases, as Tommie does. After one of these abrupt silences, he inserts a long run of notes, which also conjures Tommie's interpretation of the tune.

Paddy plays a few disjointed phrases, searching around for another tune. He finds 'Garrett Barry's', an old jig, soulful and comforting. It is a tune Tommie likes to hear him play and one he likes to hear Tommie play. Once, Paddy recorded 'Garrett Barry's' with a broken chord spilling down the end of the tune, the way Tommie plays it. He fluffed the change to the next jig and the man in charge at the studio refused to let him have another go at it. That was fifteen years ago and tape was precious then.

When Jos has left, Paddy sits back down at the kitchen table. So tired these days, he can't understand it. The doctors can't understand it. His heart is racing; time is racing. Paddy climbs the stairs to pray for Tommie before going out to milk.

Tommie. What inspiration he has given to Paddy. And what solace Paddy has found in their friendship, the visits exchanged, and the letters. From that first night in Dublin, when Seán Reid drove them to Tommie's house, Paddy shaken by the ordeal of his radio debut, dazzled by the city lights and the maze of streets. The moment Tommie took up his fiddle Paddy's worries had dropped away. His music was a revelation. As much as the drama of Tommie's playing shocked and puzzled him, he was transported by the feelings—sorrow, tenderness, elation, anguish—that overflowed from the fiddle, while Tommie's heroically carved face remained still, his body bowed over his instrument, his whole being absorbed in creating music. Tommie played masterfully, his tone robust and his technique flawless, but he would make such strange deviations from a tune that Paddy wondered, could he ever make his way back to it? But he always did. It was as if he began speaking in tongues, only to return at last to the common language of Irish music.

Over the years, Paddy has been drawn back time and again to the Potts family house in Walkinstown and Tommie's sitting room. Secluded among his books and his watercolour paintings, Tommie would play for hours. He would speak earnestly about classical music, the way its melodies and harmonies give a language to emotion, and about his aim to create within the small forms of Irish dance music the same level of expressiveness. He said that he borrows bits from music that haunts him, but Paddy doesn't recognise any of that other music. To him, Tommie's fantastical extrapolations simply sound as if he has been

Tommie Potts, Dublin, 1979
(Ben Long)

possessed momentarily by some other music, so that the tune abruptly takes flight, soaring urgently like the lark or diving like the kestrel onto the deepest notes. Tommie plays as if in a trance, unaware of fingers and bow or the room around him and his friend listening. Sometimes, tears like those of a weeping Virgin appear on his impassive face. Then, it sounds as if Tommie's music escapes from some deep prison house of suffering.

When the two men are together, they might discuss Coleman's techniques and the way the settings from the American recordings differ from the playing of pipers like Willie Clancy and Johnny Doran, or they might talk about the character of different keys and their shared preference for the melancholy modes and the sombre truth to be found in D minor. Somehow, the subject of death will always arise and Tommie will tell, one more time, the story of the fireman, his colleague, who met his death by fire. The trauma of witnessing that death, many years ago now, haunts Tommie even on the sunniest days as he cycles the streets of Dublin, collecting rents for the Corporation. He never returned to his former employment. They will discuss death, Tommie and Paddy, and always with the wish that their own deaths might be peaceful and that they will see heaven. They say a prayer and play their music, and when it's time for Mass they go together.

For Paddy, the friendship has been liberating. He never reinvents tunes the way Tommie does and yet his music has expanded under Tommie's influence. As a lad, he had idolised Coleman, urging his fiddle to sing with Coleman's panache and inventiveness and imitating his every virtuosic caper. He pursued that perfection until it became a platform, then a runway, for his personal expression. Paddy understands that playing music is a refuge of the heart, a consolation when the lonesome feeling is with him. Knowing Tommie Potts has shown him that to mine the depths of music and self requires solitude and that to seek the soul of the music is a kind of devotion.

Facing page: 'The Bunch of Keys'
The pain Paddy feels at news of his friend's serious illness is expressed both in his choice of this tune—one that Tommie Potts also plays—and in his poignant exposition. While the tune is usually played in the key of G major, Paddy plays the first part in G minor (with F natural, B flat and E flat). In the second of the three parts, he changes to the F sharp of the melodic minor, an emotionally charged ambivalence that sharpens the melancholic mood. There are silences between phrases, as if it is painful even to play the tune—breaks in the tune that are also a hallmark of Potts's style. The small, stemless notes indicate where Paddy plays double stops, but emphasises the melody notes. Paddy's tempo and volume ebb and flow to a greater extent than usual and his emphatic slides onto long notes are more slowly stretched out. He echoes the way Tommie Potts plays 'The Bunch of Keys', not only in embellishing the tune throughout with finger triplets, but also in the long, mournful phrase, in bar 4 of Paddy's repetition of the tune (the one transcribed) and in the final, falling phrase. He plays neither of these phrases when he records the tune in a 1993 recording session in Minogue's hotel, Tulla.

'The Bunch of Keys'

Paddy Canny, 1975

The Bill and Joe Show

On Tulla's windy hill, the Boys National School sits just below the graveyard and its ancient monastic ruins. The night is cold, even for November, and the gas fire makes little impact inside the bare structure, abandoned along with segregated schooling and now used for meetings of the local Comhaltas branch. Andy MacNamara helps the radio crew from RTÉ set up their equipment. Andy drives his 'travelling shop' to householders in the outlying districts including Bill Malley in Magherabaun and Joe Bane in Glendree, who will be recording their music tonight.

The Long Note's young presenter is eager to introduce his listeners to the musicians, along with their music. Bill Malley, spokesman for the pair, sizes him up. With a sharp mind that brooks no nonsense—as a Fine Gael supporter in Fianna Fail country, he is used to being on the tough side of an argument—Bill is not going to give this lad anything he hasn't earned. The tape recorder is turned on and, after inquiring about their lessons from Pat Canny, the interviewer grows more confident.

'There's a very unusual style of playing around here, isn't there.'

'Do you think 'tis?' Bill responds.

'I do, anyway.'

'Good or bad?' Bill asks.

'Oh, it's a good one, sure. You were talking earlier about a reel called "The Beauty Spot". Was that one of Pat Canny's?'

'No, no. No, that wasn't. That wasn't.'

When Bill and Joe have played the reel, the young man turns again to Bill.

'When you were learning from Pat Canny, would he actually teach you how to hold the fiddle? Deliberately, way down from the chin?'

'Yes. That was the way it was done.'

'Why was that, do you think?'

Bill squints at him sceptically through the thick panes of his glasses.

'Well, that was the style. That was the way they learned theirself, them people that learned from old Paddy Mac.'

When the tunes are played and the interview over, the young presenter is keen to bring an end to his ordeal.

'Thank you, Bill and Joe, for your ...'

'Oh, Jaysus,' Bill and Joe reply in unison. 'Thank yourself for coming!'

While *The Long Note* has a national audience and respect for traditional musicians has grown, it is mainly older people from the mountain townlands who enjoy the old dance music. The men, Lena's regulars, file into her front bar every Sunday after Mass in Feakle. PJoe Hayes comes in to play and brings his son Martin. Bill and Joe were regulars for years. The small farmers know all the tunes and will ask for them by name. They might sing a song themselves or dance a set with one of the MacNamara twins, Mary and Anita. Andy brings his four children across from Tulla to listen and learn and play music with the older musicians. The few teenage boys in Feakle, though, wouldn't dream of joining the old men in Lena's and the girls shudder at the thought of being jigged up and down in a set with old men's breath in their faces, even if their parents would let them go into the pub. Their tastes run to pop or rock and country and western.

Bill Malley's style of playing is unmistakeable. His fiddle, with a crack held together with baling twine and Sellotape, is jammed against his ribs. There is a rough energy in his playing, his bow scratching and biting the strings, often two strings at a time. When he scoops onto the main beat, his fingers slide through as much as three semitones, his bow scraping another string for good measure, and always on an up-bow—whoomp!—where other fiddlers would take advantage of the down-bow's boost from gravity. Bill's music is never quite in tune—no wonder, when he dances the fiddle, and sometimes smokes his pipe, as he plays. But his music swings.

Bill and Joe began playing together at house dances in the early 1930s. Despite their age difference (Joe is nearly fifteen years younger), their partnership thrived until 1942, when Bill married and took over the family farm and put away his fiddle. He didn't take it out until after Ciarán Mac Mathúna's visits to Feakle around 1960. In his early days, Bill had played a dozen or so reels and twice as many jigs. Since he took up the fiddle again, he has learned dozens more reels. Some he got from Paddy Canny, who would write out tunes Bill had heard him play on the radio. Others came from records, for he was often in his neighbour's house, listening to their gramophone. Bill keeps just the essentials of what he hears, bringing out the plain tune with vigour and strength, the way he was taught. Like other local fiddlers, he uses his middle finger to make an all-purpose note on the fingerboard. He doesn't distinguish a C natural from a C sharp, for instance, but plays a note somewhere in between. This ambiguous intonation is exactly the sort of thing the classically trained musical experts at RTÉ deplore, but for the growing radio audience of traditional music enthusiasts it speaks of authenticity.

For local audiences who grew up in the house-dancing days, 'playing with heart' is the fundament on which their appreciation of music was built. Music with heart is not sentimental music. It can be direct and hearty, like Bill Malley's, or it can be gentle and plaintive, like Joe Bane's, which can bend listeners' heartstrings with its lonesome touch.

Joe Bane has been playing the whistle since he started lessons with Pat Canny in 1931 at the age of twelve. Joe lives with his brothers and a sister on their farm in Glendree. The land is poor, very wet at the bottom of the steeply sloping fields, and they farm in a very old-fashioned way. Joe is a big man, and stoops. In company, he will sit hunched over, as if hiding himself, and often apologises for his playing.

Bill Malley's style of playing is unmistakeable. His fiddle, with a crack held together by baling twine and Sellotape, is jammed against his ribs. There is a rough energy in his playing, his bow scratching and biting the strings, often two strings at a time.

At the same time, Joe always carries a whistle inside his jacket in case there might be music. He used to play the flute as well, after Paddy Canny brought one back from London nearly twenty years ago. When someone asks why he isn't playing it anymore, he could explain that it is broken and he can't afford a new one. Instead, he tells them, 'I'm like an old cow, I haven't any teeth'.

To listen to Joe Bane's playing is to be drawn into a peaceful sphere, without conflict or urgency. His playing is sweet and leisurely, rhythmic without being forceful. His tone is clear, except when he hums the tune into the whistle, which makes a buzzing sound that is not unlike the skylark's song. His rolls are sparse, but he uses grace notes and a tongued staccato to emphasise the beat. Andy Mac's kids and young Martin Hayes have learned Joe's versions of well-known tunes and others that no one else plays.

Although Paddy Canny has enjoyed many a night of music with Joe Bane, he finds it distressing that these young musicians are learning Joe's versions of tunes. According to Paddy, Joe didn't recall accurately the tunes he has picked up from the radio or at fleadhs and so the way he plays them is wrong. And yet, over a lifetime of playing and listening to the music around him, Joe has internalised its patterns and uses them to mend the holes in partly remembered tunes. In such ways, traditional music evolves and, sometimes, what the musician comes up with has a charm that was lacking before.

Facing page: 'The Flax in Bloom'
As Joe Bane explained to ethnomusicologist Jos Koning, he got this tune from Ayle fiddle player Vincent Griffin, but did not remember it fully. A bar-by-bar comparison of Vincent's setting with Joe Bane's shows the subtle ways in which gaps in Joe's memory are filled with new melodic material. The sweet charm of his music belies the sophistication of his understanding of conventional phrasing and the degree to which these can be varied according to his personal aesthetic and creativity, while still sounding right to the musically educated ear. Although Joe remembered almost all the tune as Vincent played it, he interpolates notes and phrases of his own in bars 3 and 8, where he contracts the melodic phrases, and also in bar 4, where he rises to the high A later than the standard setting. Accompanied by Joe's double-tapping boots and occasional buzzing into his instrument, the result is a slower, more lyrical and modest version of the tune.

'The Flax in Bloom'

The Elusive Fiddler

The hidden and the secret invite speculation and resentment. Many musicians in rural Ireland live as outsiders, even those as deeply embedded in local farming life as Paddy Canny. After all, they can be heard playing at odd hours, when normal people would be at work or in bed asleep. They go off without notice to the farthest end of the county or to who knows where. From inside the village or the townland, they seem to be bending the rules, getting away with things, as well as preferring the company of strangers to that of people like themselves.

In East Clare, as in other parts of Ireland, you will not have far to look to find a musician with a reputation as particular, or sensitive, or odd, or peculiar, or quare. Those of an introverted disposition are particularly well qualified. In times gone by, Blind Paddy Mac's star pupil Johnnie Allen developed a style of playing considered very sweet, but became very shy about playing, perhaps worried that other musicians would steal his tunes (which they did) or that people would not recognise the value of his art (although they did). Pat Moloney in Feakle was another of Paddy Mac's pupils who hid himself and his music. Vincent Griffin and many others would listen outside his house on the main street of Feakle until one incautious musician let out a shout of admiration and Pat's concerts ceased forever.

Other fiddlers who developed this sweet style of playing—a flowing style, with long phrases and an emphasis on tone and expression—behaved the same way, preferring to play for audiences whose rapt attention was a return on their emotional investment. Paddy Canny has taken this path, along with his friends, East Galway's Paddy Fahey and Martin Rochford in Ballynahinch, all three sweet fiddle players with a reputation for being anti-social in one way or another.

Since leaving the band, Paddy Canny has felt more exposed when he goes out to play. Solo performances have become a torture, concerts the worst. At the same time, he can't say no to anyone who asks for his music. That is the principle his father laid down, a sense of duty Pat Canny had inherited from his own father. More and more frequently, Paddy finds that, when the time comes, he can't go out. Audiences feel cheated, organisers embarrassed and angry. Soon, Paddy has a reputation he didn't have before.

Paddy gives excuses, usually related to the needs of his dairy herd, never anything personal. Besides, he has no idea what is wrong: why his heart races until he feels panicky or why his body burns up with heat, at night especially, giving him no rest. His weight goes down and his energy goes down and his mood goes down.

The doctors don't know the cause and the specialists don't know. And when Paddy becomes so sick that he ends up hospital in Ennis and later in Limerick, they can't say what is wrong with him. And so the problems persist.

Paddy can't think why he agreed to play at the concert with Seán McGuire. Even though he had not been playing for a long time, he felt an obligation to take part, for McGuire himself had requested it. Now he avoids passing the Auburn Lodge Hotel, the big new place on the Galway Road out of Ennis, with its thick carpets and mahogany furnishings. The night there was awful. He had been looking forward to hearing McGuire, for he has long admired his spectacular technique and powerful tone. Only a genius could make those gymnastic leaps up and down the fingerboard, or the astonishing variations in 'The Mason's Apron'. That night at the Auburn Lodge, Seán McGuire had introduced Paddy as his favourite fiddle player. And then he had played so badly he was disgusted with himself. How had he got so bad? Paddy knew the answer to that: he had stopped playing. He hadn't been well and he hadn't the heart for it.

By the time Paddy arrived home that night, he had resolved that he would get back to form on the fiddle. No matter how bad he felt, every day before the dinner he would take down his fiddle from where it hung on the kitchen wall, and play a tune or two. He resolved to make a solo recording and, more than once during the next few years, prepared a programme of tunes and they were recorded, but there was always some problem and nothing ever came of them. He let it go.

A new opportunity came when Ciarán Mac Mathúna wanted to record a concert group. It would bring together old friends: Paddy would be in it and Peter O'Loughlin on flute, Paddy O'Brien on accordion, Séamus Connolly, the young fiddler from Killaloe, and George Byrt on piano. Five of the best. They made the recording one evening in Ennis, after the cows were milked. Ciarán introduced them as the Inis Cealtra Quintet and played the recording afterwards on his shows. They kept the group going and the gate lodge at Kiltannon came alive with rehearsals. Soon, they were invited to play at concerts around Clare and Limerick and in the summer floorshows for tourists at Bunratty Castle. Paddy loved playing with this group. Then, one night, he felt so panicked before the show that he could not get into the car.

It happened again, when Tony McMahon asked Paddy to go on his TV show. They would film it in his own kitchen: no need to go to Dublin. Tony has produced groundbreaking series presenting traditional music to television audiences. He is the best there is. Paddy enjoys those shows and knows Tony from his short stint in the Tulla Céilí Band when he was just a kid.

'Jeemers,' Paddy told him. 'We'll do it.'

But when the van pulled up outside his house, Tony saw Paddy's face peer out, then vanish. He would not answer the door.

There are people in Tulla who feel hurt when Paddy passes them in the village street without greeting them. He will rush into the shop, head down between his hunched shoulders, pick up his few groceries, hand over the money with a 'Good girl!' at the counter and dash back to the car, without a glance at the traffic banked up behind. At the same time, people will always value his music. What a pity, they

The hidden and the secret invite speculation and resentment. Many musicians in rural Ireland live as outsiders, even those as deeply embedded in local farming life as Paddy Canny.

say, that he stopped playing music in his prime, because no one else has that feeling in his music.

Among friends, Peter O'Loughlin tells a story about an American who pulled up in his hire car outside Cannys'.

'Is this Paddy Canny's house?' he asks.

'It is,' says Paddy.

'Can I see him?'

'You've missed him,' says Paddy. 'He's just gone. I'm doing a few jobs for him. He'll be back in a few days.'

That is just one of Peter's stories, yet there is some truth in it. Each summer, more people come looking for Paddy, Americans on holiday and people from Dublin who have followed his music, all kinds of people. What do they want from him? If a stranger approaches the house, they might see him dashing away up the field. If Paddy is inside, he probably won't answer the door.

On the farm, Paddy has kept up with the changes in the dairy industry and with all the paperwork and regulations the European Economic Community has imposed. He has one of the biggest dairy herds in the district, nearly forty cows, to be milked twice a day for most of the year. He grows feed crops for them and makes sure they are in calf and dries them off over winter and helps them calve in the spring. It is work that he loves. He is good at it, and proud of the trailer loaded with milk cans he brings to the dairy in Tulla.

Paddy does his best not to let people down. His friend Jack Murphy, who played the fiddle for years in the Tulla Céilí Band, has invited Paddy around to play a few tunes for his father, who has suffered a stroke. Of course he will. The trouble then that young Jack goes to: buying a piano, getting it tuned and then finding someone to play it. The evening's music delights them all and Paddy goes home happy. But Paddy Canny has become known as an elusive fiddler, a man who can't be relied on. Paddy knows this and it only increases his distress, as he struggles with illness.

The Accident

Paddy's illness persists. His cows are all in calf, but he hasn't finished drying them off for the winter. It is a process he takes great care over: stopping their milking and managing the change in their diet, checking all the time against infection. Tonight he has taken a rare night out. It is a music session in Ennis, where he plays with old friends and some of the town's crop of energetic young musicians.

Paddy is late coming home and, though he has had no more than his usual half-pint, he is cautious on the road. And that is all he remembers. He comes to consciousness, aware of a barb of pain through his head. Trussed in bandages, he can see nothing, but knows by the antiseptic smell and the excruciating clang of metal instruments that he is in hospital. At first, he doesn't even know his own name. The doctor tells him his memory will be back to normal soon. He just won't remember the car crash. During his month in hospital the surgeon saves his eye, but he will never see out of it again.

Philomena comes in and brings the girls, Mary and Rita. He can tell by their voices that it must have been bad. Phil, who has a lifetime's knowledge of cattle, reassures him that the cows are well looked after. PJoe and Peggy are helping too, as Paddy and Philomena had helped when Peggy was ill some years ago: minding children, making meals, helping with work around the farm. The cold war between Philomena and Peggy has thawed somewhat and the Hayes family and the Cannys keep up their contact when Paddy gets out of the hospital. In the urgency of need there is generosity and a kind of reconciliation.

Three or four years later, the illness that has been tormenting Paddy is finally diagnosed. It has been so long—he more or less lost the 1970s to illness—and now he is told that the sudden exhaustion, the intense anxiety, the weight loss and the racing heart, the insomnia, the heat in his body and the weight on his mind; all are down to a small, butterfly-shaped gland in his neck, which is working overtime. Hyperthyroid. There are tablets for it.

The tablets work. Paddy's anxiety becomes less intense, although the years of illness have weakened his heart. He knows that his music has lost its fire and precision, which only compounds his reluctance to perform. The best he can do is to keep playing at home and with friends, cherishing the life he has been granted. Music, an obsession that became a devotion, is now his consolation.

The Hayeses and the Cannys drift apart. In the urgency of the situation, bridges were erected hastily, sincere and adequate to the immediate task. But there is no prospect of becoming close. Things have been said, boundaries crossed. Paddy

Paddy is late coming home and, though he has had no more than his usual half-pint, he is cautious on the road. And that is all he remembers. He comes to consciousness, aware of a barb of pain through his head.

cannot face his old friend now, any more than he could face a concert audience or any crowded place. If PJoe is to be at an event, or even his son Martin, Paddy will not go. And PJoe is just as scrupulous in avoiding Paddy. It is a miserable end to a deep and true friendship, one that had lit up both lives and enabled both to follow their desire to play music. Surely, neither could have imagined it would end like this, each of them resorting to silence.

Paddy Canny and
Peter O'Loughlin,
Miltown Malbay,
1997 (Tony Kearns)

The Two of Us Now

In the kitchen at Kiltannon, Peter O'Loughlin sits beside Paddy, flute on his knee, ready to join him in a few tunes and help out with the interview, if he is needed. Although the young man from the radio show is cheerful and animated, Paddy's anxious frame of mind soon emerges as he answers the usual questions.

The interviewer is keen to know what it was like, playing with the Tulla Céilí Band.

'It was great crack,' Paddy replies. 'For the while.'

The three men laugh. Peter supplies answers to questions about the band's engagements, mentioning their Saturday night céilís in Dublin.

Paddy interjects, 'That was tough.'

When his trip to New York comes up, Paddy recalls, 'I travelled to the States with Dr Bill Loughnane one time all right, then I was to go with the band again and I didn't make it with the band. I don't know what went wrong at all, but ...'

Paddy sighs. The disparaging voice inside him insists on being heard. Peter suggests they play a couple more reels and call it a day.

'I think I'm getting, getting a bit tense,' Paddy confides, softly.

'You won't get tense!' Peter cajoles. 'There is the two of us now, you know!'

They all laugh, tensely.

When he hears the interview on the wireless, Paddy cringes at the remarks he made about the band and America and is shaken that his aside to Peter was left in. It is a long time before Paddy gives another interview.

Homecoming

On her return to East Clare, Kathy sees how little it has changed. When she looks more closely, she notices how many houses are roofless ruins and how few are the large, new ones. Along the rollercoaster road down Magherabaun, she notices the hedges, once neatly cut, sprawling carelessly into the narrow lane.

'No better girl!' Paddy's bear hug nearly squeezes the breath out of her. Over his shoulder, Mrs Canny's smiling eyes. Phil. They go through the kitchen into the small sitting room with the comfy chairs. Before they sit down, Paddy puts his fiddle in her hands.

'You'll give us a tune, Kathy?'

She holds it at her shoulder and tries out a few notes, but the tune won't come. Between the cancer treatments and the arthritis, it has been too long since she played. She returns the fiddle with an apology.

'Ah, sure, you won't be able to play at all with those!' Paddy deflects her embarrassment to her shiny, red manicure.

After Phil's supper, Kathy sings for them, one of her mother's songs. It draws the three of them together, remembering the way people would sing with their eyes closed and everyone would listen. They talk of the days when Kathy crossed the fields to the Glendree School and brought her fiddle up to Pat Canny's for lessons. She is thrilled that Paddy, so accomplished and so famous, should credit her with teaching him his first tune, although she had done no such thing. He had listened and watched and learned it himself. They recall the winter evenings when they would practise their music together, the Canny boys and the McNamara girls, and the fun of dancing a set when Bill Malley would play for them. How they would go to platform dances on summer Sundays and to house parties where all the teenagers took their turn to dance and Paddy played his fiddle.

Kathy doesn't stay late. The illness, which she has not mentioned, drains her.

'We're old now, Paddy,' Kathy says, when he says there is no need to go. To Paddy, she looks young and polished in her brightly coloured clothes.

This trip home will not be repeated, for her life's final journey is approaching and she knows it. Forty-two years ago, she had made the crossing to America, despite her father's warnings. The voyage had terrified her, ten days and nights knowing that U-boats were hunting in wolf packs and might be lurking below at any—at every—moment. The horror on board when the ship they had been pacing vanished. Torpedoed. The *Samaria II* was a grand ship, built for holiday cruising, but it was slow and vulnerable. Kathy was not to know that her passage in 1940 was in fact the *Samaria*'s final voyage, the next aborted when the ship was hit by German air fire; nor that an apocalyptic bombing raid destroyed the docks from which she had departed, along with half the city of Liverpool.

In the Bronx, Kathy became Kay. In time, she married Hugh Quigley, a tailor from Donegal, who played the accordion and the piano. In a small town along the Hudson River in Orange County, New York State, they made a large and loving family. On special occasions Kathy and Hugh played Irish tunes and sang Irish songs, their children marvelling at the beautiful sound their mother could bring from the fiddle she had carried across the sea.

On her return to East Clare, Kathy sees how little it has changed. When she looks more closely, she notices how many houses are roofless ruins and how few are the large, new ones. Along the rollercoaster road down Magherabaun, she notices hedges, once neatly cut, sprawling carelessly into the narrow lane. She remembers them clipped, like a wall protecting her as she walked down to meet her friend Katy Shea.

What surprises Kathy is the sadness of returning to her old home and the shock of the absences, so potent after all this time. She hears echoes of her brother's frightful, consumptive cough and falters at the kitchen corner where she had held her mother and witnessed her passing. And now she has missed a reunion with her sister, who died only a few months ago: Lisbeth, whose oaten cakes Kathy had rationed to last until America.

When she meets her nephew Pat O'Connor at the farm in Magherabaun, almost the first thing Kathy says is 'Why don't you buy a fiddle for him?' indicating Pat's boy, Ivan. She is prescient, for Ivan O'Connor soon becomes a precocious fiddler and a brilliant musician. The family organises a night for their aunt at Lena's bar in Feakle. Paddy Canny and his friends play music and there is singing and dancing as Kathy stands at the head of a long receiving line.

Kathy McNamara
(USA Naturalization
Certificate)

An old school friend has something to tell her. Did she know that, every day after Kathy left for America, her father had visited this friend's house in Feakle, where they had a radio? Every day of her journey to America he had listened, morning and evening, to the BBC reports naming ships sunk, cities bombed and aircraft lost, until he was prepared to accept that no news was good news. Kathy never could have imagined such a thing. The Governor was a stern man whose scowl would brook no backchat. He intimidated children, with his hat pulled down over his eyes and his overbearing moustache. Now, Kathy pictures him by the fire, lilting a tune over and over as his four little girls dance. She remembers him whistling 'The Blackbird' while she practised the intricate steps and his pride when she won at the county Feis. How, for all he would 'eat' you, he had loved them. And how, only for Lisbeth staying at home, he would have lost them all.

Musical Friends

For twenty-five years, Paddy has been tied to the routines of dairy farming. He had hoped to expand his herd, but the bigger milk quota was so costly, the figures just didn't add up. So in the mid-1980s Paddy pulls in his horns and makes the switch to dry cattle. The steers look after themselves most of the time although, on a farm, there is always work to be done.

These days, Paddy has more time for playing music. From West Clare, Peter O'Loughlin is a regular visitor, and Paddy Murphy, 'the king of the concertina', as Peter calls him. From near Feakle, Michael Dinan might call in with the triangular fiddle he made himself. Pat McNamara—a chainsmoker, thin as a rake, and a professional on the piano accordion—comes so often, he is almost a part of the Canny household. Every few weeks, he swaps visits with Vincent Griffin, the fiddle player Paddy once mentored in his first attempt at an All-Ireland.

Paddy has many musical friends from around Clare and South Galway and likes to meet them on a quiet night of the week in places where the publican is sympathetic to musicians. For Paddy, who finds any crowded place oppressive, these small pubs are refuges—safe houses, where people won't hound him to give interviews or get up on a stage. Sometimes, he might take the back road to Joe Galligan's in Crusheen for an evening of music with his old friend, the reclusive Paddy Fahey.

Martin Rochford is always after him to go to The Blacksticks and sometimes he will, if Larry Gavin drives, because, besides knowing countless tunes on his accordion, Larry does not drink. Paddy Canny and Martin Rochford go back fifty years to when Paddy visited Ballynahinch for the potato harvest at Martin's neighbours, the O'Donoghues. That was around the time when Martin started learning to play the uilleann pipes. He loves the pipes' capacity for expression: the moaning squeezed from the bag, the strain of rising to a certain pitch, the hiccupping trebles and bubbling staccato, the regulators' fanfare of chords beating a rhythmic accompaniment, all grounded by the majestic drones. When either Johnny Doran or his brother Felix was camped in the area, Martin could think of nothing else, only the pipes: their soulful sound and the fluency of Johnny's variations and embellishments that sounded deceptively easy.

To find the soul of the instrument and the melody is Martin's quest on the fiddle, too. His playing is free and imaginative and in many ways similar to Paddy Canny's, with something of the sweet style of Johnnie Allen and Martin Nugent and Pat Moloney, all pupils of Paddy Mac—fiddlers who would bring out the emotional qualities they found in the music and who played to be listened to. His rhythm is

> Martin Rochford's distinctive sound is lyrical and yet wild, animated by emotional drama and at the same time haunted by an abstract, almost ghostly, quality, despite his bowing being often rough and his notes clumsily made.

Martin Rochford would write out tunes for his musical friends, indicating how different musicians played them. In later life, Parkinson's Disease caused his hands to shake, but his notation remained clear.

smooth, with little syncopation between the notes. Like Paddy, and like Johnny Doran, Martin alternates long sweeps of legato notes with bursts of staccato. Like Paddy, he emphasises a powerful phrase with an upwelling of volume and marks an important note by sliding onto it or adding a momentary drone on another string.

Martin frequently embellishes the tune with a long run of notes that sound the deep resonance of the fiddle's lowest string. His distinctive style is lyrical and yet wild, animated by emotional drama and at the same time haunted by an abstract, almost ghostly, quality, despite his bowing being often rough and his notes clumsily made. It is difficult for farmers like Martin and Paddy to bring out what they hear in the music, for their work is hard on the hands: building walls, digging drains, cutting hedges, handling animals and machinery.

Martin and Paddy remain firm friends, despite their very different natures. Paddy is a gentle man who does not swear—unless you count 'Jeemers'—and avoids conflict; his mantra in the face of hostility is to 'let 'em off'. Martin is the opposite. He has a hot head and a sharp tongue and while many are entertained by his wry humour, others dislike his cursing and cantankerous outbursts. He is never wrong, and when he falls out with someone he stays out.

Martin always has to be listened to, whether he is telling a story or playing a tune, sitting in Biddy O'Driscoll's kitchen at The Blacksticks, his great head of hair squashed beneath his cap. An attentive listener himself, he can recall and analyse any tune he hears. His notations, which he distributes to interested friends, are never simply copied from the music books in his collection. Thanks to lessons from Martin long ago, Paddy can interpret the little bits of paper Martin gives him and rarely consults O'Neill's big green book of tunes. At any time of year, the two friends might be found in the kitchen at Kiltannon, swapping opinions of new recordings and up-and-coming musicians. A whole evening might pass without them even playing a tune.

A Night in Kelly's

At nine on a Wednesday evening, the dimly lit lounge bar is empty except for the three men leaning on the counter, engrossed in a football match on the television. The room is bare and worn, brown vinyl covering the benches fixed to the rust-coloured walls. It could be any bar in Ireland, except that Kelly's in Carmody Street, Ennis, is a meeting place for musicians.

We order our drinks, myself and my good friend Máire O'Keeffe. It is sixteen years since I left the Connemara village I had landed in and returned to Australia. Now I am back in Ireland on holiday and Máire has organised this night with Paddy Canny, whom she knows well from Willie Clancy Week, where she calls on fiddle legends like himself to play for her classes.

Paddy is the first to join us. He has come from a funeral and is still wearing his grey suit and black cardigan, a tie hanging below his loosened collar. He shakes hands vigorously—his hands three times the size of mine—and insists on buying another round, although we have only taken a few sips from our drinks. Paddy is on the 7up.

Máire and I sit down beneath the dartboard, with Paddy between us. He is looking through Máire's gift, an album of photos of his brother Jack, together with a tape of the tribute she presented on Clare FM after Jack's recent death. Paddy recalls Jack's last trip home from Australia three years ago, in 1993. At more than eighty years of age, he had climbed Croagh Patrick in his bare feet and cycled all over the county to visit friends. Jack always was athletic. He had the build for it, rangy and strong, like his mother.

'How about a tune?' Máire suggests, and out come the three fiddles.

'What'll it be?' Paddy turns to me.

I play a few bars of a jig I learned from a cassette tape of Paddy's playing a friend had recorded years ago. Along with the prized *All-Ireland Champions* recording, it had been passed around among musicians in Australia who loved Paddy's music. The three fiddles are in perfect concordance, as if we have been playing together for years, which, in a way, we have, since both Máire and I are fans of Paddy's music. He plays the Paddy Fahey tune with gusto, with ripples and runs and subtle changes each time through the tune. The fingers on his huge hands are swollen. How does he manage to make those neat triplets? I look down at his polished shoes, tapping left and right, and in one of those joyous, synchronous moments we choose the same jig to proceed into.

We rhapsodise about Paddy Fahey, the beautiful tunes he composes, easily

> The three fiddles are in perfect concordance, as if we have been playing together for years, which, in a way, we have, since both Máire and I are fans of Paddy's music.

(l to r) Helen O'Shea, Paddy Canny, Máire O'Keeffe, Peter O'Loughlin, Mary Cotter and Eamon Cotter (David Spratt)

identified by their sweet and plaintive sound and unexpected dips into other keys. Máire and I play a pair of Fahey's reels, while Paddy watches my fingers.

'You've more Fahey tunes than I have!' says Paddy with a twinkle, his little eyes squeezed together, his ruddy cheeks puffed out above a wry smile. Paddy tells me he has played with Fahey many times. And Tommie Potts, he says, another great fiddle player. Do I know his music? Tommie commands great respect among fiddlers in these parts, Paddy tells me. I recall reading that, after Tommie had played his fiddle each night, he left behind a pool of tears.

'Oh, yes,' Paddy agrees. 'There was great feeling in his music. Sometimes he went too far, though, in his variations. I played with Tommie many times.'

'And when you played with him,' I ask, 'Did he fit in with you, did he play the usual versions of tunes or his own variations?'

'Oh, no,' Paddy says. 'He'd play it so it would fit in.'

Paddy's old friend Peter O'Loughlin has arrived. Peter can bring Paddy to a concert and play beside him and can persuade him to come out for a session with talented young musicians who have a deep appreciation of Paddy's music. Within their circle, Paddy can relax and be his most genial self. Peter peers down at us now from his great height, smirking to see Paddy sandwiched between two women. These days, Peter is on the fiddle. He seems used to taking charge and starts up 'Bunker Hill', shouting 'House!' to change into 'The Old Bush', although we all know to do this.

Eamon Cotter sweeps in with his wife Mary and his sister Geraldine, who has accompanied many musicians, including Paddy, on the piano. Tonight she has the fiddle with her.

'How're ye doing?' asks Eamon.

'Dragging away,' Paddy replies.

'We heard it outside,' says Geraldine.

'And was it good?' asks Paddy and everyone laughs.

His good humour is like a poker, stirring and brightening the still hesitant fire of our company. When drinks have been bought, introductions made and the instruments taken out and tuned, Peter asks if I know 'Lucy Campbell's' and we're into it. The sound of all the fiddles and the flute is strong and full. Away from the forceful dynamic of the Shaskeen Céilí Band he plays in, Eamon brings out the mellow voice of his wooden flute. It is a very old instrument, he tells me, a Hawke, and has great subtlety. The flutes he makes himself are louder, for people don't value the softer sort of flute now. They want to be heard and to hear themselves in sessions, above all the other instruments.

A few sets later, I play Paddy a few bars of a tune Jack Canny used to play, 'Lena Madden's'. He hasn't played it in donkey's years, he says, but it comes to him with more fluency, and more notes, than Jack ever played. This tune only came back to him recently, I tell Paddy.

'Oh, it did,' says Paddy. 'When he was a boy he'd hear a tune my father would be teaching us and he'd get it all mixed up. I'd have to show him how it went and, do you know, there was eight years between us!' He turns to Máire. 'It's true, isn't it, when you were out in Australia and you were giving the workshops, Jack would be sitting there?'

'Paddy's brother,' Máire explains to the Cotters' amazement. 'I'd be giving fiddle workshops and there is Jack Canny, sitting up at the front!'

I tell Paddy how much the musicians in Australia appreciated Jack, how his enthusiasm for the music had inspired us, how his choppy bowing was our rhythm section and how, in his quiet way, Jack had helped so many of us, turning up with his toolbox or a concrete mixer when a job needed doing. I tell Paddy that his funeral had been packed out with people who loved Jack. Paddy nods his head, thoughtfully. Finally, he looks at me sideways, speaking confidentially. 'But he never could play. He never could play the fiddle.'

There is something in that. Before he gave up driving at night, Jack would often get lost in the maze of Canberra's streets on his way home from a party. It was the same with tunes. He never managed to internalise the common patterns and would often skip notes and continue a few beats ahead until he'd look up, confused, before plunging in again. Jack's fiddle had lain in its case for decades before some Canberra musicians got wind that Paddy Canny's brother was living nearby. It hadn't taken much persuading for Jack to take out the fiddle again, but it was a long road back. The talk turns to Jack's prowess as a cyclist, but we're all flagging. We gather ourselves together and head out through the back door and into the lane, for the blinds have long been drawn and the front door locked.

'Lena Madden's'

Paddy Canny, 1976

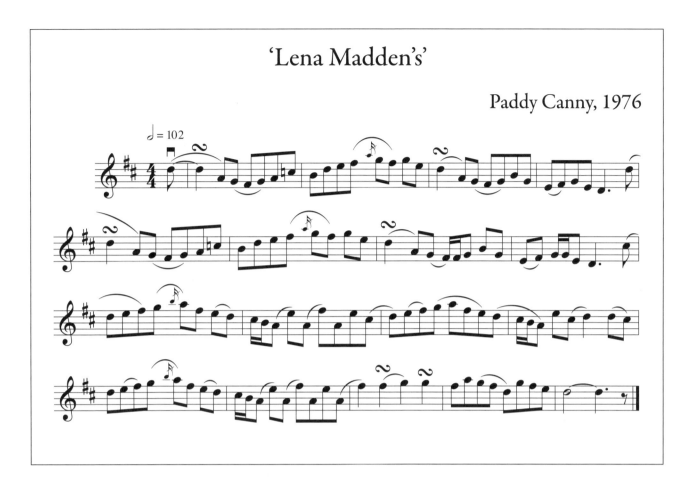

'Lena Madden's'

This transcription is made from Breandán Breathnach's 1976 recording, made in Kelly's bar, Ennis, at a time when Paddy was in poor health. Before he begins the tune, he can be heard telling Breathnach, 'I don't know whether I'll be able to get through it'. He plays the tune four times. When Jack Canny resumed fiddle playing after a break of fifty years, he played 'Lena Madden's' with almost exactly the same bowing Paddy used in this recording, which suggests that the brothers also learned how to bow a tune when they learned the melody. Lena (Helena) Madden was a local girl from the parish of Feakle, one of Pat Canny's pupils and a nice fiddle player, according to Jack. She would play for dance parties at her house when relations came home on holiday from America. This was one of the tunes Lena played.

A Living Legend

A young woman
hurrying down High
Street veers sharply
under the archway
beside the barber's
shop and follows the
sound of the fiddle
up the narrow
staircase to Galway
Violins to discover
who is playing this
haunting music.

Just another rainy Saturday in Galway. At the heart of the city, it seems half the county is swarming the shopping streets. The new season's university students are emerging, bearing their hangovers like medals. Tourists peer at Ó Máille's window display: Connemara woollens so authentic, they might have been there for fifty years. A busker has taken the lucrative corner at the health food shop, his guitar case filling with coins, and rain. It is not a scene where you would expect to find Paddy Canny.

A young woman hurrying down High Street veers sharply under the archway beside the barber's shop and follows the sound of the fiddle up the narrow staircase to Galway Violins. She hasn't the price of a set of strings, but can stretch to some resin. Any excuse to discover who is playing this haunting music. Kevin Sykes's workshop is tiny, a magical cave where violins hang like stalactites, resonating in sympathy with the fiddling. Nóirín Ní Ghrádaigh is thrilled when Kevin introduces her to Paddy Canny.

Nóirín's admiration for Paddy's music tumbles out. She tells him about her Dad, who was in America with Joe Cooley and back home had played *All-Ireland Champions* all the time and loved Paddy's music, as she does. Paddy's face lights up. He plays another tune for her. Nóirín is amazed at how small the fiddle looks in his hands. She reminds Paddy then of her letter, six weeks ago now, inviting him to make a recording for Cló-Iar Chonnachta. It is her job at the company to locate legends of traditional music and offer to see them through the recording process. Nóirín has already produced an album for the Clare concertina player, Chris Droney. By the time she skips down the stairs again, Nóirín has Paddy's phone number in her pocket and a hunch that Paddy will go ahead with the recording, for he seems to have warmed to her. And why would he not: a beautiful young woman who adores his music and wants to bring it forth into the world.

Kevin Sykes sees Paddy in his shop only when it is too wet for farm work. Kevin always offers him a fiddle to try out, often one of those he has made himself. While he fetches the strings Paddy always buys—Jargar's, long-lasting steel strings that give a strong, clear sound—Kevin assures him that Nóirín will see him right and that the record company has a reputation for producing the purest of traditional music.

1996 has been a difficult year for Paddy. His family have been urging him to make a solo recording, something substantial to leave behind. Peter O'Loughlin was dead against the idea.

'You're past your prime, Paddy, same as myself,' he said. 'You've left it too late. Let it go.'

And Paddy was inclined to agree. But, apart from a couple of tracks that came out in 1960, no solo recording has been released. In the end, Paddy did put down a few tracks at a studio in Ennis to see how it might go. There was a fellow backing him there and he was good. Paddy needs any accompaniment to be light. He has suffered before at the hands of thumping piano players. And his hearing is not so good now; he has that ringing in his ears, tinnitus. In the quiet of the recording studio, it comes on louder than ever. Eugene Kelly had an electric piano and could get the volume just right.

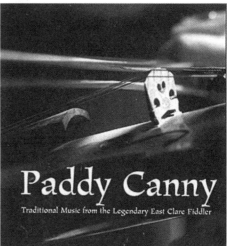

Last year, Paddy recorded more sets at a studio Eugene recommended in Galway. Paddy was keen to try a guitar backing on some of the tunes and Eugene, who plays guitar in his own band, was happy to oblige. Ever since hearing the guitar on Hugh Gillespie's records long ago, he had liked the idea. They chanced it with one of Gillespie's tunes, 'Dick Cosgroves', paired with 'Seán sa Cheo', starting on D, the way Bobby Casey plays it. It went well. But the recording sessions were often a case of two steps forward and one back. Paddy would surprise Eugene, wanting to go over tunes they had finished at the previous session. He could be so hard on himself.

Now Paddy has someone who will move the project forward again. Over winter, Nóirín Ní Ghrádaigh is a regular visitor at Kiltannon. The two fiddlers sit for hours on end in the cosy sitting room, sometimes playing together, sometimes Paddy playing for Nóirín, pausing only when Phil brings in tea and sandwiches.

In the spring, Paddy is ready to go back into the studio. He is confident and well prepared, and Kevin Sykes has lent him a fiddle he has made himself. Paddy is keen to get the project finished. They are in a different studio, but the technician, Pat Neary, is the same. Eugene is gentle and encouraging and Nóirín assures him he can take all the time he needs. Paddy doesn't like to go over material again and again, as he had before, for he knows how much it is costing the company. Even so, he repeats tracks a good few times, looking over his shoulder at the finish to see if it has gone down well.

Working out which tunes to include is like working out the seating at a wedding. Your budget will stretch only to thirty people. Who can you bear to leave out? Who will you put together? Paddy's selection brings together old favourites: tunes he has played with friends and tunes he has learned from them, tunes they had composed themselves and his own composition, 'The Caves of Kiltannon'. He has ended up with a lot of jigs. He has always liked playing jigs, the beautiful balance in them that you can savour at a steady pace. Pat Canny always started his pupils on jigs like 'Old Man Dillon's' and 'The Campbells are Comin''. Paddy doesn't reach back that far, except for 'Sporting Nell', one of his first reels. Many other tunes Paddy has selected arrived in Glendree on 78 rpm records from America. Over the decades since then, he has played them so often, he might have composed them

Philomena Canny, Martin Hayes, Paddy Canny at Áras an Uachtaráin, Dublin, 1997 (Steven de Paoire)

himself, the way they are phrased and embellished according to his own way of hearing them.

The music Paddy has recorded is a distillation of seventy years of playing. He no longer has youth's vigour and resolve, which emerged in the birdlike clarity of his sound and his ambitious technical display. Years of absorption in this music, exploring its depths and playing with its surfaces, living with it through times of hardship and grievous loss, have transformed it. Where his aim as a young man had been to play the best music possible, like the recorded music he listened to obsessively, now Paddy's life has grown into his music. Like his hands, it bears the damage of hard labour. Like his face, it has weathered and worn. Like his outlook, it is both generous and anxious.

When they put the tracks in order, Paddy wants the album to finish with a set of tunes from his days of living and breathing Michael Coleman's music. 'The Boys of the Lough' and 'The Old Blackthorn' are also tunes he used to play with his friend, Joe Cooley. Before the album is pressed, Pat Neary gives him various mixes to listen to. He chooses the one with a bit of echo on it.

How easy it had been to make the *All-Ireland Champions* LP. It was simply a day's work and the chance to play their favourite tunes together. Now there are interviews and publicity and reviews and Paddy has Nóirín and the record company organising all that. People seem to like the CD. The family like it and that's the most important thing. It is the best he can do.

Reviews come in from around the Irish music world. They agree that this fiddle-playing farmer is a master of the tradition and a living legend.

'The Old Blackthorn'

Paddy Canny, 1997

'The Old Blackthorn'

Preceded by 'The Boys of the Lough', this is the final tune on Paddy Canny's solo recording. Paddy plays it fast, although, typically, his tempo varies slightly. The two tunes share a key and a rhythmic pattern and the initial melodic phrases are mirror images. Where the first tune follows Michael Coleman's recording, this one follows The Flanagan Brothers, the setting Joe Cooley played so sweetly. Paddy's expressive legato contrasts with almost-staccato passages and a 'bow bounce' (marked with an ✕), when he lifts his bow right off the string after an accented note and slaps it down again with a percussive splay of descending notes to begin the next phrase. Paddy started using his bow in this way in the 1980s, perhaps influenced by his friend Paddy Fahey's similar bow action.

Gradam (n.): esteem; mark of honour; respect

So overjoyed and overwhelmed at receiving his Lifetime Achievement Award, he could do nothing only beam with gratitude and delight. Playing beside him on the stage that night was his friend, the banjo player Kieran Hanrahan.

There is a hush in Pepper's lounge bar, where you would expect the clatter of dinners coming out from the kitchen, even in these quieter months after the clamour of Feakle's music festival and the summer tourists. The room is lit with lamps and candles, the flagged floors and rustic décor suggesting the welcome of a country cottage. The audience of local people obediently put down their drinks and turn their chairs towards the centre of the room. The crew from TG4's *Geantraí* programme adjust the lights and test the musicians' microphones. 'Geantraí' may refer to the kind of music that brings laughter and delight, but making the programme is a serious undertaking.

But nowhere near as serious as TG4's annual *Gradam Ceoil* awards. Two years ago, thousands packed out the Cork Opera House and among those honoured was Paddy Canny. So overjoyed and overwhelmed at receiving his Lifetime Achievement Award, he could do nothing only beam with gratitude and delight. Playing beside him on the stage that night was his friend, the banjo player Kieran Hanrahan.

Tonight, Kieran is at Paddy's side once more. While only Paddy Canny is truly a local hero, and the focus of this television recording, the audience in Pepper's also claim Kieran as their own, even though he is from Ennis. In the 1980s, they might not have listened to his electrifying trad band, Stockton's Wing, but everyone here knows his Saturday night radio show *Céilí House*.

Paddy is as comfortable as it is possible to be with a crowd of locals attuned to every note he plays and the television people issuing directions and the camera almost in his face. The musicians lift their instruments and set off into a pair of jigs, 'Banish Misfortune' and 'The Pipe on the Hob'. These tunes are as comfortable as old shoes, as familiar as old friends. Paddy conjures them with loving attention, his body swaying slightly. As they move into the third part of 'Banish Misfortune', he smiles to himself and on the repeat does the little turn-around that is his alone. Kieran is with him all the way, nimbly tipping out the trebles and rolls, tight at every corner. The tunes are tightly matched, too—same key, the second parts almost identical. Paddy swivels his good eye to meet Kieran's and they finish together.

Between the sets of tunes, there is a chance for the audience to take another mouthful of drink. The producer calls for silence—that also means 'don't move'—before the musicians get the go-ahead to start into some reels. The brightest spot

Paddy Canny and Kieran Hanrahan, 2001 (Eamon Ward)

in the room is Paddy's face, his features strong and handsome, although time has ploughed deep creases. His back is hunched over so that his fiddle is settled lower now, above his heart, but his playing is fluent, his bowing arm strong, his wrist firm.

Behind Paddy, Micho 'the Kerr' McMahon sits stiffly inside his Sunday jacket, his head wagging with the music. He takes out a cigarette and lights it, but by the time the tune changes from 'The Concert Reel' into 'Rakish Paddy'—passionate music that strikes the flags and rises again bright and clear—Micho's cigarette is out, his mouth a taut line. Like everyone else in the room, his feet are rooted to the floor, toes tapping silently inside his shoes.

Micho is the same age as Paddy and lives alone on his farm in Magherabaun. All his enjoyment is in music and dancing. There is not a Thursday night when he doesn't come dancing through the door of Lena's bar—Shortt's, now—lifting everyone's mood. If the music is good, he will draw up the nearest woman to dance a few steps. Music, for Micho, is movement. But he would not miss tonight's recording for anything and, once the TV people are finished, Micho is in the thick of it, his cigarette alight and a new drink in his hand, jigging on the spot without spilling a drop. He'll be the last to leave.

Kieran Hanrahan has always been aware of Paddy's greatness. As a young child, he had listened to the *All-Ireland Champions* record and heard him on Ciarán Mac Mathúna's radio programmes. After Kieran began winning his own All-Irelands on the tenor banjo, he would hear Paddy at fleadhs, and once listened to him play all night in a quiet session of music at Brogan's bar in Ennis. Somewhere along the way, Paddy and Kieran fell in together, despite nearly forty years' difference in their ages.

Paddy is comfortable in Kieran's company and there is a depth of musical understanding between them. The banjo's precise intonation, its clarity cutting through Paddy's deafness, Kieran's solid rhythm and his alacrity in matching Paddy's interpretations and changing to the next tune as if he can read Paddy's mind—all build a platform from which Paddy's playing can expand freely. As Paddy moves deeper into old age, Kieran has become his regular companion at the few public performances he gives.

Kieran's visits to Kiltannon have developed into a ritual of music and friendship. Greeting him at the kitchen door, Paddy will reach out to shake his hand heartily.

'No better boy!'

They move through the kitchen and into the sitting room, chatting for a few minutes before fiddle and banjo come out. The tunes fly past until they have been playing for nearly an hour. Philomena gets up from her chair then and disappears into the kitchen. Before long, she brings in the tray with tea and sandwiches and sweet cake.

It is getting late in the night when Kieran leaves, for there is no end to the music they might play together. After the tunes, there is more chat at the back door. Kieran doesn't want to keep him from his bed, but Paddy assures him, he's fine.

'I thank the great God for my health, and He with me every day.'

Kieran goes out to his car, stopping to marvel at the splendour of stars that shine so brightly in quiet, country places. And hears the fiddle striking up again inside.

> Kieran goes out to his car, stopping to marvel at the splendour of stars that shine so brightly in quiet, country places. And hears the fiddle striking up again inside.

Facing page: **'Banish Misfortune'**
These two D mixolydian tunes, popular in County Clare, have almost the same melody, especially in the second part: a pigeon pair, each with its own character.

'Banish Misfortune'

Paddy Canny, 2003

'The Pipe on the Hob'

The Death has Occurred ...

The death has occurred of Paddy (Fiddler) CANNY
Kiltannon, Tulla, Clare
Reposing at O'Halloran's Funeral Home, Tulla this Monday evening from 6pm
with removal at 8pm to St. Peter and Paul's Church, Tulla. Funeral Mass to-
morrow, Tuesday, at 11am. Burial afterwards in the local cemetery.
Date of Death: Saturday 28th June 2008

(Kevin Costello)

The Other Paddy Canny

He didn't mind being called 'the Other Paddy Canny'. As a boy, he had been proud to sit next to his older cousin at the movies in Feakle and, when he was big enough, proud to tag along with him to dances and hold his fiddle while he smoked a fill of his pipe before going inside to play. Their two houses were within shouting distance, the same build of stone cottage along the same narrow avenue, the same land full of rocks and rushes. When the Other Paddy's sisters went to America, he had stayed to work the farm with his father. When his father died, he had stayed on with his mother, working the land in the old way, watching his cousins leave for better farms. And when his mother died, the Other Paddy Canny stayed on to live out his days on a small farm of bad land.

During his year of mourning, the radio was full of talk about the backwardness of small farmers. In his father's time, these same farmers had been the ideal citizens of Ireland; now they were holding back progress. It was no surprise when the letter arrived from the Farm Modernisation Scheme advising him that, his farm being unviable, it was time to retire. At fifty-four years of age, Paddy was not ready to be pensioned off. He decided he would go out to Buffalo in New York State, where his sisters had emigrated so long ago. The neighbours thought it unwise to be emigrating at such an age, but they didn't say it to him directly. So he closed the door of the cottage behind him and spent his last week in Ireland at Kiltannon, following his cousin around the farm, silent in his sorrow and uncertainty. At Shannon Airport, the Canny family watched him disappear into Departures. A lonesome sight.

Paddy's flight arrived late and he missed his connection to Buffalo. For a day and a night, he sat in the John F. Kennedy Airport, alone and frightened, with everything he owned inside his suitcase and in the breast pocket of his black suit. Forcing himself to stay awake for fear of being mugged or missing his plane, he was exhausted when at last he arrived in his sisters' America.

Where, against the odds, Paddy thrived. A neighbour on holiday from Glendree called on him, but was told he had gone to Florida for the winter. Florida for the winter! People at home could scarcely believe such prosperity could have found him. This was not the extent of his good fortune, either, for Paddy had married a kind woman who loved him so much that, when he died, she made her own lonely journey to Ireland. From Shannon Airport, a taxi took her to the overgrown avenue at Curraun and the old home place, where she scattered the Other Paddy Canny's ashes on the hillside that looks down the valley of Cloonnagro.

**Letter to Mary Canny after her father's death in 2008,
from his cousin Paddy Canny**

Well Mary, I am very sorry to hear of your Dad. He was so nice of a person. Always we worked together for a lot of years; it was a pleasure to work with him. We used to start off and walk to Feakle to see the old movies there that used be there, with an old engine running the film, with all the old-time westerns on them. We worked in the garden, the bog and the quarry together, we went down to Glendree for a long time to the dances that used to be at Michael Moloney's. I used to carry the fiddle and he would fill his pipe and take a good smoke on the way. He had a lot of friends, Mary. Everybody liked him. His music will never be forgotten. He was so good at it and made so many people laugh and happy. Everyone wanted him to play at their party: it was no good if Paddy Canny was not there. I sure will never forget him, Mary and Peter. He will be always on my mind as long as I *live* as I will say, RIP Pat.

From your neighbour, cousin and friend,
Paddy Canny
in South Carolina

Time Line

1824	John Canny (Paddy's grandfather) born
c. 1875	Catherine (Kate) McNamara (Paddy's mother) born
1867	Pat Canny (Paddy's father) born
1907	Bill Malley born
1909	Paddy Grogan born
1912	Pat Canny marries Kate McNamara
1912	Jack Canny (Paddy's brother) born
1915	Bill Loughnane born
1916	Mickie Canny (Paddy's brother) born
	Martin Rochford born
1919	War of Independence begins 21 January
	Paddy Canny born 9 September
	Joe Bane born
1921	PJoe Hayes born
c.1926	Philomena Hayes born
1926	2RN starts broadcasting
1928	Paddy O'Donoghue born
1929	Peter O'Loughlin born
1930	Vincent Griffin born
1933	Athlone radio transmitter opened
1934	Peggy McMahon born
1935	Jim Brody born
c.1936	Jack Canny emigrates to England
1940	Pat Canny dies
1945	Mickie Canny marries
1946	Tulla Céilí Band formed as St Patrick's Band, Tulla
1947	Band wins at Féile Luimnigh
1948	First Tulla Céilí Band radio broadcast
	Paddy successfully auditions for solo broadcasts
	Paddy meets Tommie Potts
1949	Paddy's first radio broadcast
1952	First Fleadh Cheoil na hÉireann, Monaghan
1953	Paddy wins All-Ireland senior fiddle, Athlone
1955	Ciarán Mac Mathúna's first recordings with Outside Broadcasting Unit
	Paddy moves to Kiltannon
1956	Paddy's trip to New York with Dr Bill Loughnane
	Tulla Céilí Band makes five 78 rpm recordings
1957	Tulla Céilí Band wins All-Ireland title
1958	Tulla Céilí Band USA tour, records first LP
	Paddy's recording in Minogue's hotel
1958–64	Tulla Céilí Band annual tours to Britain
1959	Paddy records 78s for Gael Linn
	All-Ireland Champions—Violin recording
1961	Paddy Canny marries Philomena Hayes
	PJoe Hayes marries Peggy McMahon
1962	Jack Canny emigrates to Australia
	Martin Hayes born to PJoe and Peggy
	Ciarán Mac Mathúna records at Hayeses
1963	PJoe's and Phil's parents die
	Paddy's mother dies
	Mary Canny born to Paddy and Philomena
1966	Tulla Céilí Band on RTÉ's *Club Céilí*
	Paddy leaves Tulla Céilí Band
1971	Iniscealtra Quintet radio recordings
c.1977	Paddy's car accident
1996	Jack Canny dies
2001	Paddy receives lifetime *Gradam* award, TG4
2004	Philomena Hayes Canny dies 3 April
2008	Paddy Canny dies 28 June

Glossary

From the Irish

An madra rua	the fox
Bearna bhaoil	gap of danger, breach (in battle)
Beart	bundle
Bóithrín, boreen	country lane
Draíocht	enchantment
Garda, gardaí	guard/s, police
Grá	love
Meitheal	work party
Sceallóg, skeelog	slice
Sleán	turf-spade
Spailpín	seasonal farm labourer

From Irish politics and warfare

Black and Tans	RIC auxiliary force recruited from Britain from 1920, feared for their lawless ferocity
Dáil Éireann	lower house of the Irish parliament
Fianna Fáil ('Soldiers of Destiny')	Irish Republican party formed by de Valera in 1926, following a split within Sinn Féin
Fine Gael ('Irish Family/Race')	originally the pro-Treaty political party
Flying Columns	guerrilla bands
IRA, Irish Republican Army	the 'old IRA', formed 1917, mainly Irish Volunteers
Irish Volunteers	nationalist militia formed 1913
RIC, Royal Irish Constabulary	police force in Ireland until 1922
Sinn Féin ('Ourselves')	Irish Republican party founded 1905
Taoiseach	prime minister
Treaty	Anglo-Irish Treaty 1921, which brought the War of Independence to an end, acceding only the counties of the now-Irish Republic and marking the start of the Irish Civil War and a continuing division in Irish politics

Other expressions

Bob	one shilling
Gaelic League, Conradh na Gaeilge	founded 1893, this nationalist organisation promoting the Irish language and arts became increasingly politicised in the early 20th century
Crack (often gaelicised as craic)	banter, fun
Drink	alcoholic beverages
Gaelic Athletics League, GAA	established 1884, this nationalist organisation promoted Irish sports, especially hurling and athletics as well as music and dancing
Gael Linn	nationalist organisation founded 1953, promoting the Irish language and arts, from 1956 produced recordings of sean-nós singing and traditional music
Haggard	field next to farmyard where crops were stacked before threshing; kitchen garden
Mass rocks	following the Penal Law of 1695, which restricted Catholic worship, people worshipped secretly in isolated places, the Mass rocks used as altars
Meat tea	high tea, featuring meat along with salad or vegetables
Penal times	period from the early 17th century until 1829 in which various laws victimised Catholics and dissenting Protestants in religious, political and civil life, notably in land ownership
Radio Éireann	founded in 1926 as 2RN, the Irish national broadcaster adopted this name in 1938
Raidió Teilifís Éireann (RTÉ)	Radio Éireann adopted this name in 1966 with the launching of its television service

Small farmers	while generally referring to farmers of land less than 30 acres, the 'small' relates more to the farm's economic output		most commonly in two repeated 8-measure sections, used for solo dances and the last figure of the set
Strong farmers	have larger, more productive farms, use modern agricultural methods aimed at increasing economic output	Jig	fast dance tune in triple time (two groups of three quavers per measure) most commonly in two repeated 8-measure sections
TG4	Irish-language free-to-air television network established in 1996, which broadcasts its annual traditional music awards (Gradam Ceoil)	Modes	musical scales including the dorian and mixolydian common in Irish traditional music, which carry more nuanced emotional 'flavours' than the ionian (major) and aeolian (minor) common in Western art music
The room	the (parents') bedroom in a rural cottage		
Townland	civil division of land typically covering 40–200 hectares	Oireachtas	the major feiseanna (the same word used for the two Houses of the Irish parliament)
Travellers	marginalised itinerant community with their own culture, traditionally working as tinsmiths, horse traders and musicians	Polka	lively dance with four quavers to the measure, often played for the last figure of the set
Tram	made by gathering together several haycocks	Press and draw	style of accordion playing like that of Joe Cooley in which consecutive notes are played by reversing the direction of the bellows action, as on the older melodeon, compared to the modern chromatic style like that of Paddy O'Brien, where consecutive notes may be made within one press or draw, giving a smoother sound

Use of surnames

The prefix 'O' is often dropped in informal use. Both forms are interchangeable, as in the following.

O'Donoghue = Donoghue; O'Malley = Malley; O'Connor = Connor, Connors

Terms used in Irish traditional music and dance

Around the House, House	figure in which all couples dance anti-clockwise around the set, each couple progressing by turning clockwise	Reel	a running flow of eight quavers to the measure, most commonly in two repeated 8-measure sections, punctuated by longer notes according to the tune's specific pattern of phrases
Comhaltas Ceoiltóirí Éireann (CCÉ)	Irish Musicians' Association, established 1951 to promote Irish traditional music, song, dance and language	Session	informal gathering of musicians, often in a pub
Feis, pl. feiseanna	festival comprising competitions in Irish dancing, music and language arts organised by the Gaelic League	Set dances	'the sets', originally French quadrille sets of the upper classes, by the late 19th century had become popular among rural farming communities, having adapted to Irish music, rhythms and dance steps, and comprising four couples dancing five or six figures
Fleadh cheoil	festival of Irish traditional music organised by Comhaltas Ceoiltóirí Éireann		
Fling	often played for the last figure of the set, the fling has the structure and rhythm of a hornpipe but is faster	Step dance	a precise, technical dance regulated by the Gaelic League and subsequently other dance organisations
Hornpipe	its 8-quaver measures slower and more syncopated ('dotted') than the reel and	Showbands	Irish dance bands popular from the 1950s to the 1970s, featuring brass and performing covers of pop and country and western songs

Sources

Photographs and images

Cover Photo by Peter Conway. Courtesy Tamiment Library, New York University.

ix Photo by Nutan, with kind permission.

xii Photographer unknown. Courtesy Tamiment Library, New York University.

5 Map by Markmaking, with kind permission Mark Carter.

15, 37, 73
  Courtesy Old Photos of East Clare Facebook group.

39 Photo by Dean McNicholl, © Canberra Times/ ACM.

45 Image courtesy Mary Canny.

52, 128 Photos by Peter Laban, with kind permission. Courtesy Irish Traditional Music Archive (ITMA).

54 Photo by David Lyons, Alamy Stock Photo.

78, 91, 103
  Photographer unknown. Courtesy ITMA.

81 Photo by Mal Whyte. Courtesy ITMA.

83 Photographer unknown. Courtesy Tulla Comhaltas.

96 Photographer unknown. Courtesy Seán Quinn and ITMA.

110 Photographer unknown. Courtesy Séamus Connolly.

115 Photographer unknown. Courtesy Na Píobairí Uilleann.

135 Drawing with kind permission of the artist, Ben Long. Image courtesy ITMA.

147 Photo by Tony Kearns, with kind permission. Courtesy ITMA.

149 Courtesy Kathy Quigley.

151 Image courtesy Mary MacNamara.

153 Photo by David Spratt, with kind permission.

158 Photo by Steven de Paoire, with kind permission. Courtesy ITMA.

161 Photo by Eamon Ward. Courtesy Glór, Ennis.

164 Photo by Kevin Costello, with kind permission.

166 Image courtesy Mary Canny.

Other illustrations either the author's photographs or out of copyright.

Recorded music

The musical sources for this book comprise both commercial and archival recordings, including those made by Ciarán Mac Mathúna in the 1950s and 1960s and retrieved from the RTÉ Archives and the Irish Traditional Music Archive. These include Paddy Canny's first solo recording, made in 1955, containing three exquisite items: the reels 'Sporting Nell' and 'Ballinasloe Fair', jigs 'The Luck Penny' and 'Coppers and Brass', and 'The Cuckoo Hornpipe'. Séamus Connolly, the great fiddle player and friend of Paddy Canny, has remixed and gifted to the Burns Library at Boston College what may be the best recording of Paddy, made in Tulla in 1958. Sadly, that recording has not been released commercially. Another recording, made during Paddy's trip to New York in 1956, is another gift from Séamus Connolly to the Burns Library. Over the years, various cassette copies of informal recordings have also found their way to me via the musicians' grapevine: recordings made by Paddy's guests and visitors, including his brother Jack, and at pub sessions from the 1970s to the 2000s, including the evening of music described in 'A Night in Kelly's'.

Commercial recordings

Canny, Paddy, with P. J. Hayes, Peadar O'Loughlin and Bridie Lafferty, *All-Ireland Champions—Violin*. First issued 1959 in New York (Dublin Records) and Dublin (Shamrock Souvenir), with several reissues.

Canny, Paddy, *Paddy Canny: Traditional Music from the Legendary East Clare Fiddler* (Cló Iar-Chonnachta CICD 129, 1997).

Compilations featuring Paddy Canny

Friends of Note (Ennis: Cois na hAbhna, 2019). Archival recordings of Peter O' Loughlin, Paddy Canny, Paddy Murphy and Geraldine Cotter, made in the 1970s and 1980s.

Milestone at the Garden (Cambridge, Mass.: Rounder Records CD 1123, 1996).

Past Masters of Irish Fiddle Music (UK: Topic TSCD065, 2001).

Seoltaí Séidte Setting Sail: Ceolta Éireann 1957–1961 (Dublin: Gael Linn CEFCD 184, 2004).

Recordings of other musicians

Coleman, Michael, *Michael Coleman 1891–1945* (Dublin: Gael Linn Viva Voce CEFCD 161, 1992).

Cooley, Joe, *Cooley* (Dublin: Gael Linn CEFCD 044, 1975).

Potts, Tommie, *Tommie Potts: Traditional Fiddle Music from Dublin* (Dublin: Claddagh Records CC13CD RTÉ, 2012, recorded 1971).

Potts, Tommy, *The Liffey Banks: Traditional Irish Music Played by Tommy Potts* (Dublin: Claddagh Records, 1972, reissued CC13CD, 2015).

Resources accessible at the Irish Traditional Music Archive, Dublin

The main recordings of Paddy Canny and some other East Clare musicians were made by Ciarán MacMathuna, RTÉ Field Recording, in 1955, 1958, 1962 and 1964.

The Breandán Breathnach Collection includes recordings of Martin Rochford with Mikey Donoghue, with Martin Woods, and with Paddy Canny.

Resources accessible at the Clare Library's Local Studies Centre, Ennis

The Jos Koning Collection, field recordings of East Clare musicians including Paddy Canny, Bill Malley, Joe Bane, Paddy Grogan, Bill Loughnane, Martin Rochford, Paddy Loughnane, Mikey Donoghue, Mike Doyle, Matty Ryan, Vincent Griffin, Jack Keane, 1975.

Sources of transcriptions

Transcriptions were made from the following recordings, often based on the second time through a tune, in order to represent a typical use of bowing and ornamentation.

p. 25   Paddy Canny, 'The Britches', recorded Kieran Hanrahan for RTÉ radio's *Céilí House*, 1999.

p. 31   Jack Canny, 'Sandy's Reel', 1994, recorded Helen O'Shea, Melbourne, private collection.

p. 35   Bill Malley, 'Ballinasloe Fair', recorded Tim Moloney, Glendree, 1970s, private collection. Michael Coleman, 'Ballinasloe Fair' (following 'Lord McDonald's') (New York: Columbia, 1927), remastered and re-issued on *Michael Coleman 1891–1945* (Dublin: Gael Linn Viva Voce CEFCD 161, 1992).

p. 41   Jack Canny, 'O'Malley's', recorded Jennifer Gall (Canberra: National Library of Australia, Oral History and Folklore Collection TRC 2734/1, 1991).

p. 51   Paddy Fahey, 'Paddy Fahey's', recorded Breandán Breathnach, Ballinasloe (Irish Traditional Music Archive [ITMA]: Breathnach Collection 1157-ITMA-REEL, 1992). Martin Rochford, same Paddy Fahey tune, recorded Tim Moloney, Feakle, 1970s, private collection.

p. 57   Rooney Moroney, 'The Mills are Grinding', recorded Dr Bill Loughnane, Feakle, *c.* 1960, private collection. Played to the author by Jim Brody (1935–2020), flute player and onetime neighbour of Rooney's. Ballinakill Traditional Dance Players, 'The Mills are Grinding' (London: Parlophone E3949, 1931), accessible at http://www.juneberry78s.com/sounds/ListenToIrishDance.htm.

p. 61   Paddy Canny, 'Ballinasloe Fair' (following 'Sporting Nell'), recorded Ciarán Mac Mathúna, Crusheen for RTÉ's Mobile Recording Unit, 1955. (RTÉ Archives: AA01350, also ITMA: 1289-ITMA-REEL). On a better known recording, with piano accompaniment, a 78 rpm for Gael Linn, 1959, where he plays Coleman's set, beginning with 'Lord McDonald's', is available on *Seoltaí Séidte*, details above. Other recordings of Paddy Canny playing 'Ballinasloe Fair' accessible at ITMA: 340-RTE-WAV, 1958, and 320-RTE-WAV, 1962).

p. 64   Paddy Canny, 'The Great Big Roaming Ass', Feakle, private collection, *c.* 1970.

p. 70   'Goodbye, Johnny Dear' transcribed from the author's memory.

p. 75   Michael Coleman, 'Murray's Fancy' (New York: Vocalion 14201, 1921), available in Gael Linn collection, details above.

p. 86   Paddy Canny, 'Rogha Ghearóid De Barra' ('Garrett Barry's') and 'Bruacha Loch Gabhna' ('The Banks of Lough Gowna'), 78 rpm recording (Dublin: Gael Linn, 1959). Reissued on *Seoltaí Séidte*, and *Milestone at the Garden*, details above.

p. 98   Paddy Canny, 'Paddy Kelly's' and other excerpts from a concert in the house of Louis Quinn in New York, 1956 (Boston: John J. Burns Library, Boston College, Séamus Connolly Papers, Box 30, Folder 17).

p. 107 Paddy Canny, 'The Caves of Kiltannon', 1997, *Paddy Canny: Traditional Music from the Legendary East Clare Fiddler*, details above.

p. 113 Paddy Canny, 'The Cuckoo', recorded Johnny Byrnes, Tulla, 1958. (Boston: John J. Burns Library, Boston College, Séamus Connolly Papers Box 29, Folder 7).

Ciarán Mac Mathúna also recorded Paddy Canny playing 'The Cuckoo' in Crusheen, 1955, accessible RTÉ Archives AA01350 and ITMA: 1289-ITMA-REEL, and in Clonea, Waterford, 1957, ITMA

1150-RTE-WAV.

p. 119 Paddy Canny 'Rolling in the Barrel' and 'In the Tap Room', recorded Gary Brown, Kiltannon, 1984, private collection.

p. 125 Paddy Canny, 'Trim the Velvet', 1962, recorded Ciarán Mac Mathúna, accessible RTÉ Archives AA013495 and ITMA: 320-RTE-WAV.

p. 130 P. J. Hayes, 'Kathleen Collins', *Tulla Céilí Band, 40th Anniversary, 1946–1986* (Galway: GTD Studios GDT HCD014, 1986). Kathleen Collins, *Traditional Music of Ireland* (New York: Shanachie, 1976, reissued 1995, Shanachie 34010). Paddy Canny, 'Sergeant Early's Dream', *Paddy Canny: Traditional Music from the Legendary East Clare Fiddler,* details above.

p. 137 Paddy Canny, 'The Bunch of Keys', recorded Jos Koning, Kiltannon, 1975, accessible on Koning's fieldwork tape JK019B at Clare Library's Local Studies Centre, Ennis. Tommie Potts plays 'The Bunch of Keys' on *The Liffey Banks*, and a different setting on *Tommie Potts: Traditional Fiddle Music from Dublin*, details above.

p. 141 Joe Bane, 'The Flax in Bloom', recorded Jos Koning JK013A, 1975, accessible at Clare Library's Local Studies Centre, Ennis. Vincent Griffin, 'The Flax in Bloom', recorded Jack Canny, 1993, private collection.

p. 155 Paddy Canny, 'Lena Madden's', recorded Breandán Breathnach, Kelly's bar, Ennis, 1976 (ITMA: 1209-ITMA-REEL). Jack Canny, 'Lena Madden's', recorded Jennifer Gall (Canberra: National Library of Australia, Oral History archive TRC 2734/1, 1991).

p. 159 Paddy Canny, 'The Old Blackthorn Stick', *Paddy Canny: Traditional Music from the Legendary East Clare Fiddler*, details above. Michael Coleman, 'The Real Blackthorn Stick' (1924) reissued on the Gael Linn collection, details above. Flanagan Brothers, 'The Auld Blackthorn Stick' in 1927, (New York: Columbia 33195-F, 1927), reissued on *Past Masters of Irish Fiddle Music*, details above. Joe Cooley, 'An Bata Draighin (The Blackthorn)', *Cooley,* details above.

p.163 Paddy Canny with Kieran Hanrahan (banjo), 'Banish Misfortune' and 'The Pipe on the Hob', recorded RTÉ, *Geantraí* , Pepper's bar, Feakle, 2003, accessible at https://www.youtube.com/watch?v=wDJK_GeLyGU.

Videos

The Fleadh Down in Ennis 1956, Chapter 10 (Ennis: Cois na hAbhna, 2006), www.fleadhnua.com.

Hayes, Martin, 'Drawing from the Well' series, ITMA, 2020.

O'Keeffe, Máire, interviews with Paddy O'Donoghue, John Minogue, Jack Murphy and Peter O'Loughlin, *Paddy Canny Tribute*, Willie Clancy Summer School, ITMA, 2003.

Author's interviews

Given the scarcity of primary written records—a single diary entry; a birth record; a handful of newspaper advertisements, a letter, reviews and obituaries—oral sources were crucially important. Interviews were conducted under the guidelines of the University of Melbourne's Ethics Committee for the project 'Listening to East Clare Music' and supplemented by informal conversations. Valued informants included Harry Bradshaw, Jim Brody, Paula Carroll, Séamus Connolly, Joe Fitzgerald, Paddy Fitzgerald, Amy Garvey, Larry Gavin, Vincent Griffin, Kieran Hanrahan, Helen Hayes, Martin Hayes, Pat Hayes, Peggy Hayes, Kitty Leyden, Mary MacNamara, Pakie Malley, Michael Moroney, Nóirín Ní Ghrádaigh, Ivan O'Connor, Pat O'Connor (builder), Brid O'Donoghue, Toby O'Meara, Joe Pearl, Sean Quinn, and Kevin Sykes. I am particularly indebted to Mary Canny (Mrs Coughlan), who gave many hours of her time to tell me about her father's life and family history, showing me photographs and memorabilia and driving me to visit the family house in Glendree.

These interviews have been supplemented by correspondence with Kathy Quigley and Hugh Quigley (Kathy McNamara's children), Séamus Connolly, Mary MacNamara, and Larry Gavin, among others.

Other interviews

Interviews broadcast on RTÉ may be accessible on application to RTÉ Archives, Dublin.

Browne, Peter, interview with Paddy O'Donoghue, RTÉ, 2008.

Browne, Peter, interview with Bill Malley and Joe Bane, RTÉ, 1977.

Browne, Peter, interview with Paddy Canny, RTÉ, 2007.

Carroll, Paula, interview with Peggy Hayes and Martin Hayes, 2005, private collection.

Gall, Jennifer, interview with Jack Canny, National Library of Australia, Oral History and Folklore Collection, TRC 2734/1, 1991.

Hanrahan, Kieran, interview with Paddy Canny, RTÉ, n.d.

Hill, Noel, interview with Martin Rochford, RTÉ, 1981.

King, Philip, interview with Paddy Canny and Peter O'Loughlin, RTÉ, 1984.

Koning, Jos, interviews with Paddy Canny, Mikey Donoghue, Vincent Griffin, Paddy Grogan, P. J. Hayes, Bill Malley, Mikey O'Donoghue (Ennis: Clare Library's Local Studies Centre, 1975).

Lawler, Brian, interview with P. J. Hayes, ITMA: 254229, 1999.

Meek, Bill, interview with Bill Malley and Joe Bane, RTÉ, 1975.

O Dulaing, Donncha, interview with Paddy Canny and Vincent Griffin, RTÉ, 1980s.

Ó Suilleabháin, Mícheál, interview with Paddy Canny, RTÉ, 2003.

O'Shea, Helen, interviews with Jack Canny, 1990s, private collection.

Small, Jackie, interview with P. J. Hayes, ITMA: 234-ITMA-MP3, 1992–3

Small, Jackie, interview with Joe Bane, ITMA: 235-ITMA-DAT.

Selected written sources

The many secondary sources consulted include books and articles about Ireland's political and economic history at each stage of Paddy Canny's life, from the War of Independence into which he was born to the Economic War of the 1930s, the rise and long incumbency of the nationalist Fianna Fáil government, the endemic poverty on unproductive farms in the western counties and massive emigration from them. Other sources include local histories and memoirs from Co. Clare and the Irish Folklore Commission's vast repository of oral history and folklore recorded by schoolchildren in the late 1930s, in addition to online newspaper archives and genealogy sites and the collection of *Clare Champion*s in the Clare Library's Local Studies Centre. Here also are located Jos Koning's kindly donated publications, dissertations and field recordings from his research around Feakle in 1975 and 1976. The Clare Library's online resources in history, geneaology and music proved invaluable, while Fintan Vallely's *Companion to Irish Traditional Music* always remained close at hand. The following is a selection of resources considered most useful, and most accessible to readers.

Irish culture and history

Bell, Jonathan and Mervyn Watson, *A History of Irish Farming 1750–1950* (Dublin: Four Courts, 2008).

Brown, Terence, *Ireland: A social and cultural history 1922–2002* (London: Harper Perennial, 2004).

Connell, K. H., *Irish Peasant Society: Four historical essays* (Oxford: Clarendon Press, 1968).

Daly, Mary E., *The Slow Failure: Population decline and independent Ireland, 1920–1973* (Madison, Wis: University of Wisconsin Press, 2006).

Drudy, P. J. (ed.), *Ireland: Land, politics and people* (Cambridge University Press, 1982).

Foster, Roy, *Modern Ireland 1600–1972* (London: Penguin, 1989).

Lee, J. J., *Ireland 1945–1985: Politics and Society* (Cambridge University Press, 1989).

Meenan, James, *The Irish Economy Since 1922* (Cork: Mercier Press, 1970).

Neville, Grace 'Rites de Passage: Rituals of separation in Irish oral tradition', in Charles Fanning (ed.), *New Perspectives on the Irish Diaspora* (Carbondale and Edwardsville: Southern Illinois University Press, 2000).

O'Carroll, Íde B., *Models for Movers: Irish women's emigration to America* (Cork: Attic, 2015 [1990])

Ó Gráda, Cormac, *A Rocky Road: The Irish economy since the 1920s* (Manchester University Press, 1997).

O'Neill, Timothy, *Life and Tradition in Rural Ireland* (London: Dent, 1977).

Robinson, Lennox, 'The Priest's Housekeeper', in *I Sometimes Think* (Dublin: Talbot Press, 1956).

Wills, Clair, *The Best are Leaving: Emigration and post-war Irish culture* (New York: Cambridge University Press, 2015).

History and folklore of County Clare

Arensberg, Conrad M., and Solon T. Kimball, *Family and Community in Ireland* (Ennis: CLASP, 2001).

East Clare Development Association, 'Family Life in East Clare' and 'Pastimes and Entertainment', http://homepage.tinet.ie/~ecda/index1.htm.

Fitzpatrick, David, *Politics and Irish Life 1913–1921: Provincial experience of war and revolution* (Dublin: Gill & Macmillan, 1977).

Frost, James, *The History and Topography of the County of Clare*, Clare Library online.

Ireland, Bureau of Military History, 1913–1921, *Witness Statements*, Clare Library online.

Leonard, Nora T. Goonane 'The Roadmen and the Wren Dance', *Sliabh Aughty*, vol. 2, 1990.

Lillis, Kieran, *Kieran Lillis Remembers: Stories of life in rural Ireland from the 'twenties to the present day* (Kilmihil, Co; Clare, 1994).

Mac Conmara, Tomás, *The Time of the Tans: An oral history of the War of Independence in County Clare* (Cork: Mercier Press, 2019).

Mac Conmara, Tomás, *The Scariff Martyrs: War, murder and memory in East Clare* (Cork: Mercier Press, 2021).

McGuire, James and James Quinn (eds), 'Sir Robert John

Kane' and 'Robert Romney Kane', in *Dictionary of Irish Biography* (Cambridge University Press, 2009).

McNamara, Pakie, 'Marriage customs in East Clare', *Sliabh Aughty*, vol. 5, 1994.

Northern Standard, 2004, 'The Travelling Thresherman', http://www.irishidentity.com/extras/wayoflife/stories/thresherman.htm.

Nugent, Pat 'The historical geography of the Sliabh Aughty', keynote talk, 2006, http://www.aughty.org/heritage.htm.

O'Gorman, Michael, 'The Fair Day in Scariff'. *Sliabh Aughty,* vol. 8, 1998.

O'Gorman, Tony, 'Mowing, Threshing and "Meitheal"', 2010, http://irishbeo.com/Irish_Beo/Stories__Rural_Life/Entries/2010/7/14_Mowing%2C_Threshing_%26_Meitheal.htm.

Ó Murchadha, Ciarán (ed.) *County Clare Studies* (Ennis: The Clare Archaeological and Historical Society, 2000).

Ó Ruairc, Padraig Óg (ed.), *The Men Will Talk To Me: Clare Interviews by Ernie O'Malley* (Cork: Mercier Press, 2016).

Schools Folklore Collection, 1937–8, https://www.duchas.ie.

Sheedy, Kieran, (ed). *The Clare Anthology* (Ennis: CLASP, 1999).

Sheedy, Kieran, Feakle (Feakle GAA Hurling Club, 1990).

Irish traditional music and dance

Anick, Peter (1996) 'P.J. Hayes: Fifty Years with the Tulla Céilí Band', *Fiddler Magazine*, September 1999, http://www.fiddle.com/Articles.page?Index=8&ArticleID=17724.

Austin, Valerie A. (1993) 'The Céilí and the Public Dance Halls Act, 1935'. *Éire–Ireland*, vol. 28, no 3.

Bradshaw, Harry, booklet accompanying CDs, *Michael Coleman 1891–1945*. (Dublin: Gael Linn Viva Voce, 1998).

Breathnach, Breandán *Folk Music and Dances of Ireland* (Dublin and Cork: Mercier Press, 1971).

Brennan, Helen, *The Story of Irish Dance* (Dingle, Co. Kerry: Brandon, 1999).

Canny, Paddy, 'My Memories of House Dances', *The Humours of Tulla* (Tulla: Comhaltas Ceoltóirí Éireann, 2007).

Childress, Micah, 'Examine the Contents: Clowning and songsters in American Circuses, 1850–1900', *Popular Entertainment Studies*, vol. 1, no. 2, 2010.

Cotter, Geraldine, 'Institutional and social teaching, learning and performing of Irish traditional music in Ennis, County Clare 1961–1980', PhD thesis, Irish

World Academy of Music and Dance, University of Limerick, 2013, http://hdl.handle.net/10344/5817.

Gedutis, Susan, *See You at the Hall: Boston's Golden Era of Irish Music and Dance*. (Boston: Northeastern University Press, 2004).

Hall, Reg, 'Heydays Are Short Lived: Change in music-making practice in rural Ireland, 1850–1950', in Fintan Vallely et al. (eds), *Crosbhealach an Cheoil: The Crossroads Conference 1996: Tradition and change in Irish traditional music* (Dublin: Whinstone Music, 1999).

Hall, Reg, liner notes to CD, *Round the House and Mind the Dresser: Irish country house dance music* (London: Topic, 2001).

Hayes, Martin, *Shared Notes: A musical journey* (Dublin: Transworld Ireland, 2021).

Hayes, Martin and Don Meade, liner notes to CD, *An Historic Recording of Irish Traditional Music from County Clare and East Galway* (Newton, NJ: Shanachie, 2001).

Hitchner, Earle, 'Remembering P. J. Hayes', *Treoir*, vol. 33, no. 2, 2001.

Hopper, Russell (2007) 'Critical Regionalism and the East Clare Fiddle Style of Paddy Canny'. MA thesis, Irish World Academy of Music and Dance, University of Limerick, www.scribd.com/doc/4983054.

Hughes, Harry and Muiris Ó Rochain, 'Talking with Martin Rochford', *Dal gCais* 4, 1978.

Hughes, Harry and Eamon McGivney, 'Playing it Solid and Straight: A talk with Peadar O'Loughlin', *Dal gCais* 11, 1993.

Keane, Chris *The Tulla Céilí Band* (Shannon: McNamara Printers, 1998).

Koning, Jos, 'Irish Traditional Dance Music: A sociological study of its structure, development and functions in the past and at present', Doktoraal skriptie (Master of Arts), Department of Anthropology, University of Amsterdam, 1976. All Koning's work on East Clare music is accessible at the Clare Library's Local Studies Centre, Ennis.

Koning, Jos, 'An Anthropological Approach to Development and Change in Irish Traditional Dance-Music', Doktoraal skriptie (Master of Arts), Department of Anthropology, University of Amsterdam, 1977.

Koning, Jos, '"That old plaintive touch": On the relation between tonality in Irish traditional dance-music and the left hand technique of fiddlers in east Co. Clare, Ireland', *Studia Instrumentorum Musicae Popularis*, vol. 6, 1978.

Koning, Jos, 'The fieldworker as performer: Fieldwork objectives and social roles in County Clare, Ireland', *Ethnomusicology,* vol. 24, no. 3, 1980.

Lyth, D., *Bowing Styles in Irish Fiddle Playing Vol. 1.* (Dublin: Comhaltas Ceoltóirí Éireann, 1981).

Mac Conmara, Padraig and Packie McNamara, 'The Life and Times of Johnny Patterson: "The Rambler from Clare"', *Sliabh Aughty,* vol. 3, n.d.

MacMahon, Tony, *Potts*, pamphlet (Dublin: Paul O'Connor, 2014).

Miller, Rebecca, 'Irish Traditional and Popular Music in New York City: Identity and social change, 1930–1975', in Ronald H. Bayor and Timothy J. Meagher (eds), *The New York Irish* (Baltimore and London: The Johns Hopkins University Press, 1996).

Moore, Christy, 'The Scariff Martyrs', https://www. christymoore.com/lyrics/the-scariff-martyrs.

Myers, Kevin, 'The rebirth of Irish music is Ciaran Mac Mathuna's legacy', *Irish Independent*, 15 December 2009.

O'Neill, Francis, *The Dance Music of Ireland: 1001 gems* (Dublin: Waltons, 1965 [1907]).

O'Neill, Francis, *Irish Folk Music: A fascinating hobby* (Chicago: Regan Printing House, 1910).

O'Connor, Barbara, *The Irish Dancing: Cultural politics and identities, 1900–2000* (Cork University Press, 2013).

Ó hAllmurháin, Gearóid, *Flowing Tides: History and memory in an Irish soundscape* (Oxford University Press, 2016).

O'Shea, Helen, *The Making of Irish Traditional Music* (Cork University Press, 2008).

O'Shea, Helen, '(Re) Working Fieldwork: Jos Koning in East Clare', *Éire-Ireland*, vol. 54, nos. 1 and 2, 2019.

Ó Súilleabháin, Mícheál, 'The Litany of the Saints: Musical quotations and influences in the Music of Tommie Potts', *Inbhear, Journal of Irish Music and Dance*, vol. 1, no. 1, 2010, www.inbhear.ie.

Piggott, Charlie, 'Paddy Canny', in Fintan Vallely and Charlie Piggott, *Blooming Meadows: The world of Irish traditional musicians* (Dublin: Town House and Country House, 1998).

Pine, Richard, *Music and Broadcasting in Ireland* (Dublin: Four Courts Press, 2005).

Potts, Tommie, sleeve notes to LP, *The Liffey Banks: Traditional Irish music played by Tommy Potts* (Dublin: Claddagh Records, 1971, reissued CC13CD, 2015).

Smyth, Jim (1993) 'Dancing, depravity and all that Jazz: The Public Dance Halls Act of 1935, *History Ireland*, vol. 1, no. 2.

Taylor, Barry, *Music in a Breeze of Wind* (Danganella, Co. Clare, 2013).

Taylor, Barry, 'The Tulla Céilí Band', *Dal gCais* 9, 1988; also Clare Library online.

Tubridy, Michael, liner notes to CD, *Elizabeth Crotty: Concertina music from West Clare* (Dublin: RTÉ, 1999, 2004).

Vallely, Fintan (ed.), *Companion to Irish Traditional Music*, second edn (Cork University Press, 2011).

Acknowledgments

Writing this book about Paddy Canny's life and music has been a labour of love and a journey that has taken many years. I have not been alone. Along the way, I have benefited from the help of professionals, from the many people who have generously offered their memories, hospitality and thoughts, and from those who have nurtured the project and the writer in other ways.

Four people in particular have provided the fundamental support without which the project could not have proceeded. My beloved partner in life, David Spratt, whose constant loving care has extended from household chores and moral support to the gift of his professional skills in book design and typesetting. No thanks will ever be enough.

Paddy Canny's daughter Mary (Mrs Coughlan) welcomed me into her home and spoke with me over numerous interviews, giving me invaluable information and insight about her father and his family. I will always be grateful for her trust and generosity.

My dear friend Mary MacNamara has also provided crucial support to this project, not only through her hospitality and moral support on so many occasions, but in sharing musical resources and her deep understanding of the music and musicians of East Clare.

Séamus Connolly has been the godfather (in a good way!) to this project right from the beginning, advising and encouraging, discussing and informing. I am as grateful to his friendship and support as I am to the wonderful archive of music recordings he has deposited at Boston College, allowing me access to a whole new dimension of Paddy Canny's music.

Librarians and archivists are the guardian angels in a researcher's life, guiding them to the resources that illuminate the writer's path. Peter O'Beirne, Librarian at the Clare Library's Local Studies Centre, this is you: thank you. And many thanks to Elizabeth Sweeney, Irish Music Librarian at the John J. Burns Library, Boston College, for helping me to access recordings of Paddy Canny in the Séamus Connolly collection and the librarians at the University of Melbourne's Archives and Special Collections Reading Room for setting up a secure computer to listen to them. Also in the USA,

I thank archivists at the Carnegie Hall Archives and New York University's Tamiment Library and Hugh Quigley and Kathy Quigley, for information about their mother, Kathy McNamara, Seán Quinn, for his recollections of Paddy Canny's New York session. I also thank Billy Loughnane for his search for information about his father the late Dr Bill Loughnane's trip to New York with Paddy Canny.

I am most grateful to the archivists at the Irish Film Archive, the National Folklore Centre, the RTÉ Archives and the Irish Traditional Music Archive—Treasa Harkin in particular, for her invaluable help in sourcing images—as well as Na Píobairí Uilleann's Terry Moylan and Emmett Gill, Breda McNamara at Tulla Comhaltas's Cnoc na Gaoithe, and Frank Whelan at Cois na hAbhna, Ennis, for helping me access videos, books and recordings of Paddy Canny and other musicians. I also thank Cló Iar Connachta for sending me reviews of Paddy Canny's solo album.

Researchers have to sleep sometimes and I am very grateful to my friends Mary MacNamara and Kevin Costello in Tulla, Pauline Flynn and Conor O'Reilly in West Wicklow and Tadhg Foley and Maureen O'Connor in Galway, who have kept me well fed and cosy on many a research outing. A big thank you also to Marie Heaney for her generous support.

Jos Koning, who has generously donated his research materials from 1975 to the Clare Library Local Studies Centre, is among many who have offered intellectual support, critiques, and opportunities to present work in progress. These also include Verona Burgess, Geraldine Cotter, Emily Cullen, Aileen Dillane, Máire O'Keeffe, Graeme Smith, Ros Smith, Fintan Vallely and my colleagues in the Faculty of Fine Arts and Music at the University of Melbourne, in the Melbourne Irish Studies Seminar, and at the University of Galway's Irish Studies Centre (Louis de Paor, Meabh Ni Fhuartain, Verena Commins) and Moore Institute for Research in the Humanities and Social Studies, where I held a Visiting Fellowship.

While I read and listened and researched in books and archives, it also took a vast number of interviews and informal conversations to build a picture of farming and musical life in north-east Clare during Paddy Canny's lifetime. In addition to the many informants whom I have listed as sources, whose memories and insights are the foundations on which this book has been built, I would like to thank Paula Carroll for the muddy walk over Ballycroum, Nóirín Ní Ghrádaigh for her vivid account of working with Paddy Canny on his solo album, Joyce Obolewicz for showing me around the old Canny home, Larry Gavin, the late Jim Brody and the late Vincent Griffin for our many conversations, and Paddy and Joe Fitzgerald for their memories of growing up in Corrignoe, East Clare.

My sincere thanks to Ben Long, Nutan, Peter Laban, Tony Kearns, Steven de Paoire, Kevin Costello and David Spratt for allowing me to reproduce their images, to Mark Carter for creating the map of north-east Clare, and to Neil Conning for his masterly proofreading..

Lastly, my warmest appreciation to Antony Farrell and his team at The Lilliput Press for bringing forth *No Better Boy* into the world of readers.

Index of Names

Allen, Johnnie 30, 58, 142, 150
Andrews, Eamonn 117
Bane, Joe 64, 123, 133, 138–41
Bohan, Mrs 62
Breathnach, Breandán 134, 155
Breen, Paddy 90
Brennan, Michael 14, 15, 20
Brody, Jim 44–5, 64
Brody, Liz 9
Burke, Joe 129
Byrne, John, Tulla cinema 108
Byrnes, Johnny, Galway music lover 109–10, 112
Byrnes, John, London dance hall entrepreneur 115
Byrt, George 124, 129, 143
Canny, Catherine (Kate) McNamara 10–12, 19, 21–2, 24, 28, 65, 72, 73, 104, 127, 152
Canny, Eileen 104
Canny, John (Jack) viii, 3, 19, 21, 22, 27, 31, 39–41, 47, 59, 63, 71, 72, 121, 152, 154–5
Canny, John, grandfather 6, 8
Canny, Mary 145, 165, 156
Canny, Michael (Mickie) viii, 3, 19, 21, 22, 23, 26, 27, 39, 41, 65, 71, 72–3, 85, 90, 91, 104, 105, 121
Canny, Michael, Ballyglass 27, 72, 104
Canny, Michael, Glendree 6
Canny, Paddy ('Other') 165–6
Canny, Pat viii, x, 6–9, 21, 22, 23–4, 26, 27, 28–9, 32, 33, 36, 40, 58, 59, 62, 65, 66, 72, 73, 88, 90, 91, 92, 118, 138, 142, 148, 156, 157
Canny, Patrick 6
Canny, Philomena, see also Hayes, Philomena 106, 121–2, 127, 145, 148, 157, 162, 165
Canny, Rita 145, 165
Carthy, Kate (Sis) 29
Carthy (also McCarthy), Michael (Sandy) 29, 31

Casey, Bobby 115, 116, 157
Clancy, Willie 52, *78*, 81, 83, 86, 109, 116, 136
Clune, Bridget 104
Clune, John 104
Coleman, Michael 32–5, 37, 42, 58–61, 66, 74–6, 92, 94, 97, 98, 99, 100, 109, 110–11, 112, 124, 136, 158–9
Collins, Kathleen 129
Commins, Maureen Tubridy 77–8
Conlan, Fireman Barney 33
Connolly, Mick 109
Connolly, Séamus 109, 112, 143
Connors, see O'Connor
Cooleen, Mickey 56
Cooley, Ben 56
Cooley, Joe 2, 79, 81, 82, 83, 88, 93, 97–8, 101, 103, 104, 116, 156, 158, 159
Cooley, Séamus 98, 103
Cotter, Eamon 153, 154
Cotter, Geraldine 154
Cotter, Mary 153, 154
Crehan, Junior 90, 92, 106, 126
Crotty, Elizabeth 90–1, 126
De Valera, Éamon 14, 19
Delaney, Tommy 84–5
Dinan, Michael 150
Donahue, Bridget 68
Donnellan, Francie *78*
Donnellan, Mike 14–15, 26, 127
Donoghue, see O'Donoghue
Doohan, Hughdie 90
Doran, Felix 150
Doran, Johnny 50, 52, 109, 136, 150–1
Doyle, Michael (Mike) 49, 133
Droney, Chris 156
Early, Bridget (Biddy) viii, 49
Early, James 129
Egan, Michael 16–18
Ennis, Séamus 124
Fahey, Paddy 50–1, 98, 106, 142,

150, 152–3, 159
Fitzgerald, Joe 17–18
Fitzgerald, Joe, Knockjames 106
Fitzgerald, Paddy, Knockjames 106
Flanagan Brothers 33, 159
Fuller, Bill 1, 94
Galligan, Joe 150
Gavin, Larry 150
Gildea, Martin 16–18
Gillespie, Hugh 33, 74, 157
Griffin, Patrick 15
Griffin, Vincent 140–1, 142, 150
Grogan, Paddy 42–3
Hanrahan, Kieran 160–62
Hanrahan, Lena 64, 133, 149, 161
Hartneady, fiddler 9
Hayes, Delia 74
Hayes, Liam 122, 123, 127
Hayes, Margaret (Maggie) Hogan 36, 37, 124, 127
Hayes, Martin (Quillan) 36–7, 127
Hayes, Martin 139–40, 146
Hayes, Mary 37
Hayes, Paddy 9
Hayes, Patrick Joseph (PJoe or P. J.) x, 36–8, 47–8, 74, 77–8, 80, 88–9, 93, 101, 103, 109, 110, 114–5, 117–8, 120–4, 127–130, 139, 145–6
Hayes, Peggy McMahon 114, 120–3, 127, 145
Hayes, Philomena, see also Canny, Philomena 37
Hennessey, Mrs, also 'The B' Moroney 32, 37–8, 42–3, 60, 74
Houlihan, Patrick (Pak) 29
Humphrey, Mr, Feakle cinema 108
Hunt, Peter 117
Kane, Robert Romney 5
Keane, Jack 88, 103
Kelly, Eugene 157
Kelly, John 85
Kelly, Paddy 98–99, 106
Kelly, Tadhg 13

Killoran, Paddy 2, 33, 42, 97, 99, 100
Koning, Jos 132–5, 140
Lafferty, Bridie 117–18
Lane, Eileen 84
Leydon, Jimmy 123
Long, Jimmy 49
Loughnane, Dr Bill 2, 94–6, 99, 103, 115, 147
Loughnane, Paddy 34
Mac Mathúna, Ciarán 61, 84, 90–1, 102, 110, 123–124, 126, 139, 143, 161
MacNamara, Andy 138, 140
MacNamara, Anita 139, 140
MacNamara, Mary 139, 140
Madden, Helena (Lena) 155
Malley (also O'Malley), Bill 29, 34–5, 39, 41, 85, 87, 133, 138–9, 148
McCall, Nora 104
McCarthy, Jim 108
McCarthy, Mikey 108
McCourtney, Harry 117
McElvaney, Paddy 84, 85
McGann, Andy 2, 100, 110
McGuire, Seán 84, 87, 92, 143
McKenna, John 33
McMahon, Michael (Brud) 15–18
McMahon, Micho ('the Kerr') 161
McMahon, Paddy 95
McMahon, Peggy, see Hayes, Peggy
McMahon, Tony 143
McNamara, Catherine (Kate), see Canny, Catherine
McNamara, Della 67
McNamara, Elizabeth (Lisbeth) 67, 149
McNamara, Ellen (Ellie), later Moran, Ellie 11–12, 94–5, 104
McNamara, Hannah 11–12, 94–5, 104
McNamara, Joe 103
McNamara, John ('the Governor') 66–7, 149
McNamara, Kathleen (Kathy), later Quigley, Kay 23, 47, 148–9
McNamara, Michael 10, 12, 28
McNamara, Minda 67
McNamara, Nora 10
McNamara, Paddy ('Blind Paddy Mac') x, 8–9, 24, 30, 33, 36, 49, 58, 103, 138, 142, 150

McNamara, Pat 150
McNamara, Tommy 9, 36
McNulty, Bert 78–80
Merriman, Brian viii–ix
Minogue, John 79, 82, 109, 111
Moloney, Billy 53–6
Moloney, Denis 91
Moloney, Eddie 120
Moloney, Michael 166
Moloney, Pat, East Galway composer 106, 120
Moloney, Patrick (Pat), fiddler 9, 142, 151
Molony family, Kiltannon 105
Moore, Christy 17
Moran, Ellie (see McNamara, Ellen)
Moroney, Mick (Rooney) 56–8
Morrison, James 33, 66, 74
Mullins, Sonny 115
Murphy, Bridget 85
Murphy, Dennis 90
Murphy, Jack, fiddle player 78, 144
Murphy, Jack, flute player 78
Murphy, Jack, Paddy Canny's uncle 85
Murphy, Paddy 150
Neary, Pat 157–8
Ní Ghrádaigh, Nóirín 156–7, 158
Nugent, Martin 30, 59, 60, 150
Nugent, Ted 123
Ó hAinreacháin (also O'Hanrahan), Fachtna 82
O'Beirne, James (Lad) 2, 97, 110
O'Brien, Eileen Seery 97
O'Brien, Paddy 2, 88, 93, 97, 98–9, 103, 104, 106, 116, 118, 132, 143
O'Connor, also Connors
O'Connor, Ciarán 77
O'Connor, Danny 77–9
O'Connor, Frank ix
O'Connor, Ivan 149
O'Connor, Master, school teacher 62, 92
O'Connor, Pat, builder 149
O'Donoghue, also Donoghue
O'Donoghue, Bridget 50
O'Donoghue, Jim 77–80
O'Donoghue, Mary 50
O'Donoghue, Michael (Mikey) 9, 42, 49–50
O'Donoghue, Paddy 42–3, 49–50, 78, 80, 85, 109

O'Donoghue, Tommy 50
O'Driscoll, Biddy 151
O'Halloran, Pat 105
O'Hanrahan, Fachtna, see Ó hAinreacháin
O'Higgins, Frank 33, 87
O'Keeffe, Máire 152–4
O'Loughlin, Peter (Peadar) 109, 110, 111–12, 117–8, 120, 124, 143, 144, 147, 150, 153–4, 156–7
O'Malley, see Malley
O'Neill, Cpt Francis 30, 58, 99, 129, 133, 151
O'Neill, Jim 99, 117–8
O'Neill, John 99
O'Shea, Helen 152–4
Patterson, Johnny 49, 68–70
Patterson, Selena 68–70
Peacock, Joseph 4
Pickering, Johnny 90
Potts, Tommie xi, 85, 86, 109, 134–6, 153
Preston, Michael 90, 103
Quigley, Hugh 149
Quigley, Kay, see McNamara, Kathy
Quinn, Carmel 1
Quinn, Louis 96–98, 110
Quinn, Mary 96
Quinn, Seán 96, 98
Reavy, Ed 96, 100, 120
Redican, Larry 2, 100
Reid, John (Seán) 52, 77, 78, 80–3, 84, 88–9, 90–91, 93, 103, 104, 109–11, 115, 117, 126, 135
Reynolds, Paddy 100
Rochford, Martin 49–52, 77, 109, 131–3, 134, 142, 150–1
Rodgers, Alphie 15–18
Rooney, see Moloney, Mick
Rowsome, Leo 87, 109
Ryan, Martin (Mattie) 123
Ryan, Seán 92–3, 106, 120
Seery, Eileen 97
Shaughnessy, Jack 103, 115
Shea, Katy (Baby) 67, 149
Sweeney, Paddy 33
Sykes, Kevin 156–7
Tubridy, Michael 90
Tubridy, Teresa 77–9, 80
Tully, Michael 40
Tuohy, Michael 9
Whyte, Aggie 78, 80, 92, 118, 120